# THE DEVIL'S DISCIPLE

# THE DEVIL'S DISCIPLE

## Ben Jonson's Debt to Machiavelli

by

Daniel C. Boughner

**PHILOSOPHICAL LIBRARY**

*New York*

# TO ROSALIND

# CONTENTS

# Preface

For assistance in gathering materials for this book, I am indebted to the Folger Shakespeare Library, the Huntington Library, the Newberry Library, the American Philosophical Association and the Modern Language Association, all of which provided necessary grants. I am also deeply grateful for a Guggenheim Fellowship and a Fulbright Research Scholarship to Italy. Materials for Chapter 5, "The Tyrant's Arts in *Sejanus*," have already appeared in *Studies in English Literature*, I (1961), 81-100. Finally, I want to express my gratitude to Dean Harry G. Albaum of Brooklyn College and Dean Mina Rees of the City University of New York, who believe in scholarship.

Brooklyn College, 1968

Daniel C. Boughner

# Chapter 1

## MACHIAVELLI'S *ANDRIA*: THE ARGUMENT AND STRUCTURE OF COMEDY

The brilliance and wealth of meaning in Machiavelli's political and historical writings have diverted attention from his comedies. Conscious himself of this side of his creative mind, he described his talents in a letter to Francesco Guicciardini as inspiring him to history, tragedy, and comedy.[1] His contemporaries, in fact, esteemed him as a playwright, ranking him above Terence and even the legendary Menander; and they flattered him by plagiarism and imitation:[2] their high opinion is our cue for a long overdue critical analysis of his dramatic works. In the first place, he wrote with a clearly defined theory of comedy in mind. It aided him to discern in his experiments with Terence and Plautus, the existence of a dramatic structure that cuts across the formal division into five acts. This discovery inspired the creative revolution by which the humorous farce *Casina* by Plautus became a romantic comedy, *Clizia;* and the same intuition impelled him to take the great stride forward in his original masterpiece, *La Mandragola.* It served later playwrights as a prototype capable of infinite refinements and variations. This

11

might flower in the perfection of Ben Jonson's satiric or genial pieces or in the illimitably rich golden comedy of Shakespeare.

Moreover, the Florentine Secretary left behind him three very important statements about his dramatic practices. Two of these he prefixed to his original comedies, and thus he invented the critical prologue in which the author does something never met in classical literature: he analyzes and discusses his own art, a device seized and fully exploited by the playwrights of the *commedia erudita* and by Ben Jonson. The first of these statements, *The Dialogue on Our Language,*[3] enlightens our understanding of Machiavelli's aesthetic principles only partially though the part is important, style. The treatise, a reply to Dante's *On the Vulgar Tongue,* is a defense of the living language of Florence against the condemnation of the great poet. The lucid and concise exposition breaks with characteristic dramatic vividness into an imaginary conversation. The two writers analyze words and phrases in *The Divine Comedy* so as to show that it is not written in the idiom of the court (as Dante had claimed) but in a language that is entirely Florentine. Dante at last concedes that he was wrong and Machiavelli right.

The latter then applies this analysis of spoken dialogue to comedy. He endorses the definition ascribed by Aelius Donatus to Cicero that the aim of comedy is to set up a mirror of daily life.[4] Nevertheless, he adds that it does this with a certain elegance [5] and with expressions that arouse laughter. Thus men who come to enjoy the spectacle savor afterwards the useful lesson that lies beneath. The personages that comedy presents, therefore, can hardly be dignified; for there can be no seriousness [6] in a cheating servant, a ridiculous pantaloon, a love-crazed

12

youth, a flattering harlot or a gluttonous parasite. Machiavelli, thus, demands in persons and in language alike that decorum which neo-classical art prized and which required that there be a congruity between the characters and their speech as well as the ordinary events portrayed. When one represents such things in a comic way,[7] one must use words calculated to produce comic results. If the expressions are not one's native expressions, and also widely understood, they do not and can not produce such results.

Machiavelli then claims for the Tuscan dialect a unique capacity for arousing laughter. For proof he invites us to consider a comedy written by one of the Ariostos of Ferrara.[8] Here you find a pleasing arrangement of episodes[9] and a refined and well-ordered style, a complication[10] plotted well[11] and resolved better. But you also find the comedy devoid of the wit and pungency[12] which the genre demands. He offers examples of this linguistic failure in Ariosto[13] and sums up that here and in many other places you see how great was his difficulty in maintaining decorum in borrowed language.

Machiavelli's play *Clizia* is an adaptation of *Casina* by Plautus. The latter's prologue, full of horseplay and jesting, is a give-away narrative summary that establishes the spirit of humorous irony. The Italian changes this altogether by substituting a critical essay.[14] First, he asserts that the same men, enduring the same reversals,[15] recur over and over in our world, so that 100 years later people would do the same things we do now. For instance, in the noble and most ancient city of Greece, Athens, a gentleman with one son brought up a girl (who had come into his house by chance) most respectably till her seventeenth year. Then all at once he and his son both fell in

13

love with her. This rivalry led to several adventures and strange happenings. These surmounted, the son took her for his wife and lived happily with her ever after. What do you say to the fact, Machiavelli asks, that the same reversal occurred a few years ago in Florence? Our author, desirous of dramatizing such a turn-about, chose Florence for the setting since he felt the spectators would enjoy it more than Athens. And though the story is true, the author (to avoid trouble) has changed real names to fictitious.

Next, he introduces his characters before the play begins, so that the audience may recognize them easily during the performance. They are, in order of presentation, Nicomaco the amorous dotard, his son and rival Cleandro, the latter's friend Palamede, the servant Pirro and the bailiff Eustachio (also rivals for the girl), Nicomaco's wife Sofronia and her maid Doria, and their neighbors Damone and his wife Sostrata. The author then kindles expectation by noting that still another personage, since he has not yet arrived from Naples, is not presentable. The play is entitled *Clizia* from the name of the girl they are fighting over; but Machiavelli, despite the substantial part given to the son and lover, declines to bring her forward because Sofronia, who has reared her, does not think it decent for her to leave the house. The law of decorum, therefore, serves the author to rationalize the absence of his heroine from the stage.

Then he turns from these stimulating implications to an exposition of the purpose of comedy. He assures us, with sly solemnity, that as far as he can tell his play contains no indecency. If the audience find any, he will only say in vindication that comedies happen to exist for the pleasure as well as the profit of the spectators. Certainly it is

14

profitable for any man (especially a young man) to learn about an old man's avarice, a lover's madness, a servant's tricks, a sponger's gluttony, a pauper's misery, a rich man's ambition, a harlot's flatteries—and the faithlessness of all men. Of such examples comedies are full, and they can represent them all with the greatest propriety.[16]

Finally, Machiavelli reverts to a theme conspicuous in *The Dialogue on Our Language,* the aim of entertaining the spectators. If the author wants to please them, he must excite their laughter. This he cannot do by sustaining a serious and solemn discourse; for the words that make people laugh are either silly, or insulting, or erotic. Comedies full of these three kinds of expressions are full of laughter; those without them have no fun. The present author, Machiavelli asserts in conclusion, wants to please and sometimes make the audience laugh. Drily lamenting the omission from his *dramatis personae* of foolish characters as well as of abusive turns of expression, he says that he has perforce fallen back on lovers and the unforeseen events that love inspires.

By emphasizing the universal sameness of humanity and its experience in all civilized places and in all epochs of history, Machiavelli has implied the existence of universal laws in art as in life. The fable of a father's impeding the smooth course of true love by becoming the rival of his son for the love of a girl, whether in ancient Athens or in modern Florence, obeys exactly the same principles of development. The term "reversal," [17] used twice within half a paragraph, suggests that the writer had the intuition of a structure which differentiates his own *Clizia* even from its obvious source, *Casina.* Consequently, he intuitively assigns to the young lover an extensive role (which Plautus had eliminated) because comedy demands it since

15

his very presence as well as his trials arouse interest. To this end, the confidences entrusted to his close friend and his several strategically placed soliloquies match the emphasis on the careful nurture of the beloved girl. By shifting the center of interest from the infatuated graybeard (where Plautus put it) and sharing it between father and son in a love rivalry, Machiavelli converts the sequence of events from ironic farce to romantic comedy. This while obeying vastly different aesthetic laws, nevertheless does not altogether sacrifice the satire.

A humanistic salute to Horace, the favorable repetition of his dogma that the aim of comedy is to profit and delight, does not obscure two significant modifications of the conventional statement. First, the profit (which comes from seeing certain personages enact their parts) derives from the application to present life of lessons from the past; for men and their vicissitudes are always alike: especially notable is the perfidy of humanity, an obsession in our author. He climaxes his argument by singling out for full treatment the comedy of love's uncertainties. Second, the pleasure of the spectators comes from laughter. The style necessary for this purpose employs the speech of silly, malicious and amorous personages. A cleverly impudent apology, expressed in the language of neoclassical convention, masks without concealing the author's feeling that lovers are the central characters and the unexpected tribulations which their love creates the basic plot. In effect, he urges the primacy of romantic comedy.

The prologue of *La Mandragola* reinforces these impressions. It is an address to the spectators promising an episode which, though it might have happened in Pisa or Rome, occurred in Florence and which will inspire hearty laughter. Machiavelli gives a detailed description of the scene, a street—the Avenue of Love—dominated by the church of Fra Timoteo, with separate dwellings for the lawyer Nicia and the young man Callimaco: the concentration of the setting shows the author's awareness of the claims of neoclassical unity. The equally remarkable concentration on a limitation of the basic plot to the love affair and its happy outcome emphasizes the author's steady perception of the demands of romantic comedy. He assures the audience that he will dramatize the struggle of the girl, a clever person, and the final success of her lover as the heart of his play. Again he prepares the auditors for the character of the persons, singling out for particular mention a doltish lawyer, a languishing lover, a wicked friar and a scheming parasite. The cast summons up an expectation of satire in the enactment, but the author repeatedly stresses his intention of delighting as well as entertaining.[18]

In short, Machiavelli's critical essays are remarkable for the exposition of certain definite principles of dramaturgy. First, comedy portrays the actions of ordinary people in everyday life for the enjoyment of the spectators. It therefore rejects dignified personages, as decorum requires, in favor of those which provide amusement. These are the absurd (like the lustful graybeard) the scurrilous (like the gluttonous sponger or the enticing whore), but above all love-obsessed youth. Second, the words used by these personages must have the elegance, the wit and the pungency of the language spoken in Florence. Third, the episodes must fall naturally into the articulated structure of a good plot, marked by a complication that creates suspense and by a fitting resolution. In other words, our author gropes toward a comic imitation of the peripety commended by Aristotle in tragedy.

This analysis explains sufficiently why Machiavelli chose not only the *Andria* of Terence for the study of comediography but also the *Casina* of Plautus afterwards. The former had won the praise of ancients and moderns alike. Aelius Donatus applauded its skillful construction.[19] Giraldi Cinthio found pleasure in the variety that enriched the complicated action: delighted by the double plot, he showed how this produced a differentiation of character— two dotards of opposite temperament, two servants of different habits, and two lovers of diverse personality.[20] Performances during the playwright's formative years took place in the palace of the Medici and in the Signoria.[21] Thus circumstances combined to thrust the play upon his attention.

Terence's *Andria* deals with the domestic troubles of ordinary people; at the center of these is the rough course of true love within the hearts of two young men. The style possesses refinement and a witty concision that results in a profusion of gnomes. The author scattered these pearls of wisdom with a prodigal indifference to the humanist's strong sense of decorum. A famous example is the retort of the cunning servus, "Davos sum, non Oedipus." [22] This is just such a howler as distressed Ben Jonson (as Drummond reported) when he condemned Guarini for making the shepherds in *Il Pastor Fido* talk like himself.[23] To the neoclassical mind the fault of Terence was graver since Davos was a slave. Machiavelli's tact inspires a rendering that is close and yet unexceptionable: "Io son Davo, non profeta." [24] Such exercises trained him in the hard economy of style that is one of his most characteristic literary virtues.

Some passages show the translator feeling his way toward a command of stylistic originality. For example, the bland remark by Mysis, "Nilne esse proprium quoiquam!" (716): Nothing indeed is really our own, becomes "Veramente e' non ci è boccone del netto" (684) and foreshadows the colloquial proverbialism of the original plays. A still more triumphant Cinquecento touch improves "adducti qui illam hine civem dicant: viceris" (892): you have suborned someone who will say she is a citizen: you will prevail; this becomes "E, chi dice ch' ella è cittadana ateniense, abbi nome di Vinciguerra" (692). This happy inspiration echoes Dante and points forward to the boasting liar on the Renaissance stage.[25] Even more arresting is the enrichment of the sapless mutter by Davos as to Simo's intentions: "qua de re?" (184): what about? This becomes "Che vuole questo zugo?" (656); the quibble of "ass" and "phallus" fills the chaste emptiness of Terence with a Plautine naughtiness of phrase, a linguistic resource developed in *Clizia* and masterfully exploited in *La Mandragola*.

A felicitous and seminal touch occurs early in *Andria*, where Machiavelli goes beyond the original to suggest the clash between poet-son and merchant-father that dramatizes a fundamental conflict in life and theatre. The sententious freedman Sosia butters up the heavy father Simo, anxious about his son, by declaring, "namque in hoc tempore/obsequium amicos, veritas odium parit" (67-68): for nowadays subservience makes friends and truthfulness animosity. Machiavelli charges this with a Renaissance paronomasia: "perchè in questo tempo chi sa ire a' versi acquista amici; e chi dice il vero acquista odio" (652). Just a few lines before Simo had used "studium" (56) in the sense of exertion and had then specified one such in "ad philosophes" (57): in philosophical lectures. Machiavelli, by condensing the two in "allo Studio" (652),

19

presents the Italian Panfilo as a poet and a scholar, unlike the Latin Pamphilus. This foreshadows the quarrel between age and youth in the persons of the business man and the artist.

If the expressive pungency of style is so important, we are tempted to ask, what was the attraction of Terence over Plautus? The answer is clear: his preference for romantic comedy and his superior dramatic structure. Machiavelli's *Dialogue of Our Language* scatters a number of wise saws culled from Horace's *Ars Poetica*. The latter's brief mention of the parts of a play prescribes neither more nor less than five acts. Terence and Machiavelli follow this division, and Aelius Donatus organizes his commentary on the plays of Terence act by act. In addition, Donatus puts a constant emphasis on the *four* parts of a Terentian drama. He says that a comedy is divided into four parts; these he terms *prologue, protasis, epitasis* and *catastrophe*. The *prologue* is the first speech or utterance of words preceding the actual unfolding of the plot, sometimes presenting matter extraneous to the argument either on behalf of the poet, of the play itself or of the actors. There are four different kinds: the commendatory, in which the playwright or the fable is praised; the reportorial, which presents the answer to the slander of a rival or thanks to the spectators; the expository, which explains the argument of the play; and the mixed, which comprises all these within itself.[26] The *protasis* is the first act of the tale in which part of the narrative is unfolded and part concealed for the purpose of maintaining the interest of the audience.[27] The *epitasis* is the complication of the plot by the elegance of which the parts are joined together. Here the author portrays the increase and development of the turmoil and the whole knot of the error.[28]

The *catastrophe* is the resolution of the plot or the conversion of events into a happy ending.[29] In short, Donatus sensed the presence in Terence of a paradigm for
comic form consisting of the mutually dependent phases
of the plot and running in an articulated sequence beneath the mechanical division into five acts. This significant general analysis paves the way for an examination of
the individual plays.

The next question is, Why in particular did Machiavelli
choose the *Andria?* The answer appears to be that Donatus singles out this play for praise of its structure. He
notes that the reportorial prologue is separable from the
comedy itself, and Machiavelli (following the implied
suggestion) eliminates this undramatic preface altogether. Donatus then explains the effectiveness, in the
opening dialogue, of using characters implicated in the
action to reveal the dramatic situation, a procedure that
enabled Terence to get the story under way skillfully.[30]
In this play, the commentator admiringly states, the *protasis* is brisk, the *epitasis* full of confusion, the *catastrophe*
almost tragic; yet unexpectedly, out of all the turmoil, it
comes to a serene end.[31] Donatus describes the unforeseen twist of the plot at the end of the *epitasis* as the
consequence of the appearance of a personage introduced
to precipitate the *catastrophe.*[32] Later critics like J. C.
Scaliger and Ben Jonson called such a figure more appropriately a *catastatic* [33] personage. The surprises and the
reversal from tragic fear to laughter show a refinement
of art achieved only after the discovery that the inner
structure of comedy demands a happy ending all the more
effective for its unexpectedness.[34]

The setting of *Andria* is Athens. The long *protasis* runs
through Act II, scene one (to 1. 337), and thus presents

21

the exposition of the unhappiness of Charinus as well as that of Pamphilus, two young men in love. Mistaken identity, as Donatus observes, is the basic misunderstanding that sets the plot in motion. From it, misapprehensions and fears multiply and produce that fine confusion in which the chief characters work at cross purposes.[35] Their ignorance as to who Glycerium ("Sweetie") is (except that she is the girl from Andros of the play's title) persists till the advent of the *catastatic* personage at the very end of Act IV clears up the puzzle. In the first lines of Act I, the *senex* Simo tells his freedman Sosia of his wish that his son Pamphilus should marry Philumena, daughter of his friend Chremes. Sosia appears only for the purpose of this explanation and is thus a protatic character, a technical discovery by Terence whose usefulness even Ibsen did not disdain in the Berta of *Hedda Gabler*. But the grief of Glycerium over the death of her sister Chrysis, a courtesan from Andros, and the efforts of Pamphilus to solace her reveal the secret of their love to his father. On the latter her modesty and beauty as well as her devotion to the dead girl make a good impression, but not on Chremes, who refuses to marry Philumena to the youth.

A step toward the *epitasis* comes when Simo decides to test his son's feelings by pretending that the marriage will take place and that, if Pamphilus agrees, he will persuade the girl's father. Davos, the unscrupulous *servus* of Simo, comments on his dilemma, whether to obey the father or help the son. Though he fears for Pamphilus's life if he deserts him, he fears for his own skin if he doesn't. Donatus points out that in this hesitation as to where duty lies, Terence inspires uncertainty in the audience and therefore suspense about things to come.[36] Another step forward in the plot comes when Davos discloses that Glycerium—wife, mistress, or whatever she is—is pregnant with Pamphilus's child and that the lovers will acknowledge it as legitimate. A most important step, since it reaches far ahead in the plot, occurs as they invent a wild tale (as Davos calls it) to the effect that the girl was actually born in Attica, shipwrecked on the coast of Andros, and reared by the father of the dead Chrysis. Donatus observes that the recurrent allusions to Glycerium's charm, her chastity, her wholehearted devotion to her lover and her belief that she is Athenian (and therefore marriageable) keep alive the spectators' curiosity about her identity and prepare subtly for the recognition scene.[37]

At scene five of Act I the hero appears, groaning aloud as the midwife is fetched for Glycerium. Simo and Chremes are so eager for his marriage to Philumena that he suspects she is a monster they are palming off on him. He swears passionately that as the dying Chrysis, anxious about Glycerium's chastity and wealth, joined his hands with hers, so he would remain true to his trust. Terence sets up a contrast between the riches willed to the girl by the Andrian, which constitute a solid, practical motive for a dispute between Pamphilus and the relatives of Chrysis,[38] and Simo's pleasure in her looks and deportment, which is sentimental and evanescent. Meanwhile, a fine elaboration brings into the action the faithful lover of Philumena, Charinus. His presence (as Donatus, with a commendable intuition of the essence of comedy, says) is necessary to contrive a happy ending for her, otherwise to be left scorned and spouseless when Pamphilus marries his true love.[39] Charinus fears that his friend loves Philumena as the old men want him to, and he appeals to him not to ruin his happiness and marry the wrong girl. Pamphilus assures him that he is more eager to avoid the marriage than Charinus to contract it. Here the *protasis* ends.

The *epitasis* opens at Act II, scene two (1.338), with the appearance of Davos, trusted counselor (as Pamphilus thinks), to tell the youths of his suspicion that Simo has some trickery in mind and to advise Pamphilus to obey his father and agree to marry Chremes' daughter. He firmly believes that the latter will not give her to him. Overhearing the report that Pamphilus intends to acknowledge Glycerium's child and then the suffering of the girl in labor pains, Simo suspects a cheat to scare off Chremes. He therefore threatens Davos. One plan wrecked, the *servus* thinks up another to prove his good faith, the display of the pretended baby before the house. Simo retorts by deciding to celebrate the nuptials the same day. To Chremes he declares that Pamphilus and Glycerium having quarreled, now is the time to reclaim the youth with a respectable wife; and Chremes departs to get Philumena ready. Now Davos finds events moving too fast for his cunning. Pamphilus denounces him, and Charinus denounces both for buying the happiness of Pamphilus at the cost of his own misery. This is the point where Simo and Pamphilus, Chremes and Charinus, and Davos have reached the universal mistrust that inspires the famous praise from Donatus for the fine confusion contrived by Terence.[40]

Again Davos cudgels his brain and promises to each youth his beloved girl. How? He does not say. He instructs the servant Mysis to place Glycerium's baby on Simo's doorstep, but hastily abandons this plan on seeing Chremes. He tricks Mysis into playing with him a comedy of errors in which the *senex*, having made all preparations for the wedding, sees the baby and learns who the parents

24

are. Davos repeats for him to hear the wild tale that he had sneered at before, Glycerium's claim to be Attic. This tricky slave is laughable not in the manner of the *servus* of Plautus, but precisely because all his schemes fail. These have dramatic effectiveness: since they do not remove, but exaggerate the problems of Pamphilus, they intensify suspense. Even with a sure-fire comic resource like this fertile rascal, Terence keeps the primary interest steadily and unwaveringly on the plot. At this crisis the *epitasis* comes to a close.

By the end of Act IV, scene four, the cross-purposes of fathers, lovers and servants (as Donatus observes) [41] create such danger for Pamphilus and Charinus alike that the knot of the plot, its bewildering complication of action, is impossible to untie. In order to resolve it and so to bring the comedy to a happy ending, Terence uses the advent (at Act IV, scene five, 1. 796) of an already prepared yet totally unexpected character. By this device he introduces a counterturn or *catastasis*, which precipitates the *catastrophe* and makes necessary a fifth act. Crito, cousin of the dead Chrysis, comes to Athens from Andros. Lured by a claim to her reputed wealth and then fearing that Glycerium, as Chrysis' alleged sister, will be named her heir, he at first confounds the already confused relations among the personages and increases the perturbation that Donatus had judged as skillfully contrived. [42]

The play may now move to the *catastrophe*. In Act V Chremes recognizes in Crito an old friend, who reveals that Glycerium is indeed Athenian: more, she is the daughter of Chremes. Shipwrecked on a voyage with her uncle off Andros long ago, she had been rescued and reared as the sister of Chrysis. Pamphilus, thus, can at once obey his father by marrying the daughter of Chremes

25

and keep his true love. Charinus and Philumena share in the happy conclusion. This Terence has provided by means, as Donatus terms him, of a personage invented for the sake of the catastrophe. All give every indication of living happily ever after as the Cantor leads the applause.

Terence can no more be censured for his methods than for writing comedy rather than tragedy in the first place. It remained for Victorian and modern character criticism to object to the felicitous appearance of Crito as depending on "coincidence in its crudest form." [43] Such an approach is an abdication of true criticism. By confusing agent and object, it obtrudes material fact upon dramatic fiction. In a comedy, the happy ending is the only important object and coincidence a mere device. The playwright turns to it precisely because its long arm is always capable of sweeping away obstacles and smoothing the course of true love.

In Terence's *Andria* Machiavelli found a paradigm for comedy that has the advantage of the comments of Donatus. Such a structure undergirds the five acts and therefore unifies and strengthens the mechanical division with the articulated ebb and flow of a dramatic movement that leaps across these separations. They may, thus, be primarily a grammarian's or a printer's convention. The paradigm in the *Andria* consists of four parts. First there is a *protasis*, rather long in this play because of the complication produced by two sets of lovers, which by extension beyond the opening act moves the action forward without pause and yet closely links I and II. Second comes an *epitasis* that runs from Act II, scene two, through Act IV, scene four, to a climax of uncertainty. Third is the counterturn, placed by the author in IV, 5, taking the form in this play of the advent of a new character who can untie

26

the plot's seemingly indissoluble knot. He is awkwardly described by Donatus as a personage invented for the sake of the *catastrophe*. This is the fourth part, which transforms all things into happiness for all persons by reason of the counterturn. Reconciliation and forgiveness, climaxed by the double wedding, mark the joyous end.

Donatus, in other words, showed by his awareness of the presence of the four-part structure that he had made the crucial discovery, the perception of Terence's technique. But he tried to minimize it,[44] and hence his effort to define the third part is fumbling and incomplete. Ultimately it received a more adequate description in the *Poetics* (1561) of J. C. Scaliger, who had before him the practical applications of Machiavelli and Bernardo Dovizi da Bibbiena.[45] This work is an important supplement to Donatus for three reasons. First, he saw how to clarify the analysis of that commentator by observation of what such dramatists of the Cinquecento had done by applying the lessons of Terence to their structures. Second, he clearly defined all four major parts of a comedy, whereas Donatus had wavered between the Horatian division into five acts and the perception of the paradigm that lay beneath this, with the result that he made a confused exposition. Third, he supplied the Renaissance playwrights, groping for mastery of the essential organization of episodes, with a rational statement of sound practice.

Arguing in favor of a flexibility diminished by mechanical division, Scaliger rejects the three-part theory of some critics (who detached the prologue and accepted the other parts described by Donatus [46]) and agrees that the number of parts is four. Although he concedes that the major sections are generally called acts, he observes that there are ways in which the actual parts do not coincide with this division. The fifth act may not be limited to the catastrophe, and the protasis may not end with the first act. In *The Braggart Warrior*, for example, it extends into the second act. Scaliger therefore finds greater discrimination in his own analysis.[47] He points to the confusion about the prologue: it is separate from the comedy proper unless worked into the *protasis* as in the *Andria*.[48] In his fairly complete exposition, known to students of English drama through its use by Ben Jonson and John Dryden, the Italian humanist concentrates on what he regards as the four integral parts without which a play cannot exist. In the *protasis* the principal subject of the story is set forth and narrated without disclosure of the outcome. In this way it is more lively, always keeping the audience in suspense as to the end; whereas if it is revealed, the play becomes dull. Nevertheless, you must develop the entire plot out of this subject, and so brief and rapid should it be that it rather excites the mind than satisfies it. The next part, the *epitasis*, is the section in which the turmoil of events is either stirred up or intensified.

Scaliger terms the third part the *catastasis*, that situation or phase of the plot in which it is thrown into confusion by the tempest to which fortune has led it. He insists that despite the failure of some critics to recognize this part, it is indispensable. Finally the *catastrophe* is the conversion of all troubles of the plot into unexpected calm.[49] This analysis, thus, clarified and rationalized the terminology of Donatus. It gives the authority of the author's great name to an emphasis on the counterturn, the new twist in the action, toward the end of Act IV or at the beginning of V. Terence invented this, and Machiavelli revived it. Dryden, paraphrasing the *Poetics* with beautiful lucidity, exalts Scaliger by ascribing his exposition to

Aristotle.[50] Earlier, Ben Jonson not only disposed his plots in the four parts outlined by him, but also adopted his terminology to describe this practice.[51]

In summary, we may say that Machiavelli, politician and historian, embarked on a career of playwriting with a clearly defined theory of comedy in mind. In his critical essays, two of them cast in the original form of aesthetic prologues, he analyzed style and the kind of pleasure inspired by comedy, together with the kind of personages calculated to provide it. He found it excited especially by the misfortunes of young people in love, organized in a carefully articulated structure having complication, suspense, and a comic peripety at the end. In short, he advanced the claims of romantic comedy.[52] These considerations explain why he turned to Terence rather than Plautus when he decided to play the sedulous ape of translator of a play. From a literal adherence to the Latin text, he departs occasionally in the direction of the more expressive pungency that anticipates the style of his mature comedies. In the *Andria* he found, above all, the pattern of a four-part drama on which Donatus, even when at times he obscurely analyzed it, fixed his attention. He revived this dramatic structure and bequeathed it to the Renaissance theatre. Machiavelli was the first to perceive its usefulness for heightening the agitations into which romantic love plunges the youthful protagonists and then for converting these into a happy issue. He set playwrights on the road they were to follow for over a century by making a basic reinterpretation of the argument and structure of comedy.

## Chapter 2

## *CLIZIA*: FROM FARCE TO ROMANTIC COMEDY

Was Machiavelli on the right track? He tested its validity by a remarkable experiment, the transformation of the riotous farce *Casina* by Plautus into a romantic comedy, *Clizia* (1506). There had been nothing like it on the European stage since Terence, and from this time modern comedy follows Machiavelli. That the play is an adaptation of Plautus [1] is at first glance less surprising than the choice of *Andria* for a first venture in drama, for it possesses an expressive pungency of language. Yet so masterly is the adjustment of action, idiom and persons to Florence that *Clizia* has strong claims also to originality. Above all, it is a triumphant vindication of the discoveries made by Terence in argument and structure.

The plot of *Casina* [2] consists in a series of confusions resulting from calculated lies and impersonations. It begins with an expository Prologue; the scene is Athens. Lysidamus, perhaps the most lecherous pantaloon in Roman comedy [3]—no mean eminence!—lusts to deflower a foundling, Casina, brought up like a daughter by his wife Cleostrata. To enjoy this satisfaction he has arranged a marriage between the girl and his bailiff, the slave Olympio. The old

30

man's nameless son, who like Casina never appears, seeks her for another slave, his valet Chalinus. This, as the Prologue brutally says, has the convenience for the son of tethering his mistress in his own stall: no one ever mentions a marriage between him and Casina. Cleostrata discovers her husband's scheme and comes to the aid of her son; Lysidamus on finding him a rival ships him abroad. Hence, the Prologue warns the audience not to expect to see the hero of the play during its performance. In his absence the canny mother carries on the intrigue for him. The Prologue promises a recognition scene in which Casina will turn out to be the freeborn daughter of an Athenian and therefore marriageable. By suppressing the dramatic rivalry of father and son and by contemptuously banishing the lover from the play, Plautus concentrates the attention on a satiric portrayal of the amorous pantaloon in a swift-moving farce. To this the recognition scene and the marriage of true lovers are irrelevant. The play's central action, therefore, is the hilarious discomfiture of the lecherous dotard, knowledge of which the audience shares with his persecutors in the spirit of comic irony.

On his first appearance Lysidamus delivers a skipping soliloquy on love, as a sneaking whoremonger understands that emotion: What spice love gives to life! What bloom the love of Casina gives him! Suddenly aware that Cleostrata has overheard, he diverts her suspicion by flattery till his perfume betrays him. To choose which slave is to be Casina's husband, they draw lots; and Lysidamus reveals his own farcical impatience to his worst enemy by begging his wife not to oppose *his* marriage with the girl. The lot favors Olympio, and so Lysidamus prepares joyously for a night with the bride at the house of his obliging friend Alcesimus. Cleostrata and Chalinus obstruct him with one laughable frustration after another; he merely pants the more lustfully. They invent a frightening tale of Casina's madness, how she looked for the old man to kill him, and with her sword drove the entire household into hiding. They disguise Chalinus as the bride. Then Olympio cheats his master by locking him out of the bedroom. But instead of caresses the supposed bride gives the slave kicks and batters his face in a naughty humiliation as he discovers the other's male sex. He only hopes Lysidamus will get the same welcome. So he does as Plautus again stages the humiliation, the audience laughing at the repeated action by reason of its ironic intensification. Thus the desperate schemes to indulge in a little convenient adultery redound in cringing disgrace. Cleostrata finally brings his sufferings to an end because (she says) she hates to make this long play longer. Plautus condescends to add a curt Epilogue of seven lines summarizing the recognition scene: Casina is the daughter of Alcesimus and therefore may marry the son, only now given a name, Euthynicus. This cavalier indifference to romance and to the structure of comedy throws the emphasis conspicuously on the farce of the amorous pantaloon.

In *Clizia* [4] Machiavelli incorporates the events so casually mentioned by Plautus's Prologue and Epilogue in the text of his play. He then imposes on the materials of *Casina* the technique invented by Terence and explained by Donatus in his analysis of *Andria*.[5] The Florentine brings the young lover onstage, giving him a sympathetic prominence in the action, and he develops the dramatic rivalry of father and son. He maintains a double focus on satire and on romance throughout *Clizia*, so that the audience is now perturbed by the anxieties of the lover and then amused by the follies of the pantaloon. By dramatizing the perfunctory Epilogue of Plautus, Machiavelli exploits the hazards of true love running smooth at last. This new purpose enables him to diversify the irony of *Casina* with the pleasure of surprise and joyful satisfaction. He takes suggestions from Plautus, adds his own inventions and fits both into the four-part structure he rediscovered in *Andria*. He introduces the counterturn in the action named *catastasis* by Scaliger [6] and takes some advantage of the inherent flexibility of this design. By this means he inspires in the audience a state of pleasant confusion until recognition and reconciliation precipitate the *catastrophe* of young love's happiness in wedlock. Paradoxically, therefore, Machiavelli's debt to Terence in *Clizia* is just as great as his theft of details from Plautus.

The long *protasis* begins with the appearance of the young lover Cleandro and his friend Palamede (I. 1), to whom he explains the rivalry with his father for Clizia. Here Machiavelli adopts the practice of Terence, whose *Andria* presents such a protatic character in Sosia. The youth's parents keep a sharp eye on the girl, and because she has no dowry his father Nicomaco discourages him, being (unlike Lysidamus) a bit of a miser. While the latter schemes to wed her to the servant Pirro (the Olympio of *Casina*), he and his mother Sofronia have their own candidate in the foreman Eustachio (Chalinus). Since Nicomaco is bent on marrying her to Pirro this very night, Cleandro has made a countermove by ordering Eustachio to return at once to Florence. Significantly, therefore, Machiavelli assigns the initiative in the action to the lover. Moreover, the contrast between his moody sentiment and the gaiety of his friend accomplishes an effective heightening of his emotions. Cleandro laments that Fortune has led him up a blind alley. In a delicate reliance on the other's trust, he sketches the natural growth of his love for the orphan reared by his parents. But Nicomaco's infatuation and his trick to possess her have created an immediate crisis.

Alone, Cleandro (I. 2) voices the conflict within him between yearning and despair. This is the first of a series of soliloquies placed at strategic climaxes to focus primary attention on the romantic action. Machiavelli has removed the first monologue from the mouth of Lysidamus and converted it into the utterance of a lover's hopelessness. By expressing the similarity of the soldier who dies in a ditch to the lover who dies in dejection, the Florentine enriches Plautus with the erotic fancies of Ovid.[7] Cleandro fears he will meet that dismal end. Nevertheless, he tries to be alert to opportunity and trusts in unforeseen events. Eustachio arrives (I. 3), and the youth orders him to improve his appearance lest Clizia reject him as a pig. Again he sounds a note of delicate refinement. Thus Machiavelli has devoted the whole first act to a hero who arouses interest by the profound turmoil of first love and its uncertain course.

Those critics go badly astray, therefore, who narrow the scope of the play to the satire of Nicomaco.[8] This view ignores the fundamental problem, the adjustment of the argument to the laws of comedy observed by Terence but irrelevant to Plautus. Cleandro stands almost outside the wordy quarrel between father and mother, yet his conspicuous presence in the action from first to last signifies that the play, unlike its Latin source, will deal primarily with young love frustrated by the opposition of both parents equally until the *catastrophe* removes it.[9] Machiavelli's change within the family makes of Sofronia a secondary blocking character; in Plautus Cleostrata actively

34

assisted her son. As Cleandro's rival, Nicomaco remains the primary blocking character. Thus the author tests the comic usefulness of two such personages in prolonging suspense and adding intensity to romance. A happy ending requires the assent of mother no less than father, and to gain this Machiavelli introduces a character who precipitates the *catastrophe*. Act I, however, presents and analyzes the hero's situation, his feelings, his plans and especially his devotion.

The *protasis* continues without dramatic pause into Act II for the presentation of the antagonist, the father. In the seventy-year-old Nicomaco, infatuated by a girl of seventeen, the author delineates the half-pathetic, half-absurd spectacle of former citizen sobriety suppressed by a senile obsession. The highly individual Wellerism of his language also proclaims his independence from Lysidamus and displays the salt of the truly comic style. In a soliloquy (II. 1) that structurally corresponds to the introduction of the *senex* in *Casina*, he grumbles humorously about the afflictions of old age; but even so, he is capable of breaking a lance with Clizia. When Pirro (II. 2) brings the news that Eustachio has come to Florence, he promises with comic grimness to give her to the boy in spite of all they can do.

The *protasis* maintains an unbroken flow of events in II. 3 with the introduction of the wife. The corresponding scene in *Casina*, where Cleostrata bullies her perfumed dandy of a husband, undergoes a complete transformation. Sofronia's first words emphasize her determination to protect Clizia from son, servants and husband. Nicomaco sneers at her going to mass during the carnival; the author postpones the wholly Florentine explanation for her communion till II. 4. No shrew like Cleostrata, she replies with the quiet reproach of a wise spouse. Without equivocation she comes to the point. Let's not delude ourselves, she argues; we have in our house a very good and beautiful girl. We've taken the trouble to rear her, and we're not going to throw her away. Once everyone praised us and now all will condemn us if we give her to that stupid guzzler. Sofronia combines her solicitude for Clizia with a defense of Nicomaco's reputation.

He remains, however, an old man grown silly in his confidence in the well-rehearsed fiction centering on Pirro. The latter, he boasts, has youth, good looks and devotion to Clizia, a superficial judgment that subverts the values of the honest burgher. True, he's got no money, but Nicomaco will not desert him. Sofronia laughs at the fiction screening the real situation, and sharply reminds him that bribery of Pirro is robbery of his son—a suggestion of her strong maternal conscience [10] and an unhappy commentary on his decline.

When she senses that his bluster is about to explode in quarreling, she turns the conversation from his adultery to the objections to Pirro, championing Eustachio as a better husband. But Nicomaco counters by asserting that he has no manners and lives with his cattle; if they gave her to him, she'd die of grief. With Pirro, she retorts, she'd die of hunger! Then the husband flaunts his domestic authority: Haven't I made clear what I intend to do for him? Sofronia utters blunter reproaches. Haven't I made you see what you're throwing away? Nicomaco, look what you've spent on that girl and the trouble I've taken to rear her! I want to know what's to become of her. Otherwise I'll gossip so wickedly and get into so many scandals that you won't be able to hold up your head. She dares to remove the screen and discuss the real situation. Angrily he retaliates by promising to hold the wedding that same evening. And she comments enigmatically, Either he'll get her or he won't. The hint of laconic irony fixes the attention of the audience again on Cleandro's counter-intrigue.

By speeding up the action with the imminent consummation of the marriage and the suggestion of obstacles, Machiavelli sets the action forward in the *epitasis*. Its commencement in the middle of II. 3 shows the flexibility of the structure imposed on the materials. Nicomaco sneers furiously at his wife's enigmatic prophecy, panting, Maybe you think I am blind to your tricks, eh? I knew mothers loved their sons, but I did not believe they helped them in their vices. She still refuses to sacrifice the girl. He is the first to give way, jesting in a bitter pun that she is rightly named Sofronia: she is as full of wind as a bellows.[11] Is there any way out of this mess so that people won't think we're crazy? Crazy, no; she replies; but wicked, yes. He proposes that they consult Father Timothy, their confessor, who has (he asserts) become a little saint since he performed the miracle of making the sterile Madonna Lucrezia pregnant. She exclaims, A priest make a woman pregnant! A real miracle would be the insemination of Lucrezia by a nun! [12]

Sofronia's soliloquy in II. 4 is another conspicuous development of *Clizia* that has no counterpart in *Casina*. In it she defines the contrast between Nicomaco a year ago and now. Then he was dignified, industrious and respected, hearing mass and spending his time decently in the transaction of business or honorable discussion. Sometimes he withdrew to his study to examine his contracts and balance his accounts. He gave his son advice, and with some example ancient or modern he taught him how to live. The Ave Maria always found him home. But since

37

his infatuation, Sofronia sighs, he neglects his business, and his affairs languish. He's always shouting, without knowing why; he goes in and out of the house a thousand times a day, not knowing what he's doing. He never comes to his meals on time, and if you speak to him he ignores you or answers distractedly. The servants laugh at him, and his son has lost all respect for him. What I fear is that this poor family will break up. Therefore she goes to mass to beg God's help. Her going to church, which Nicomaco derided in II. 3, is thoroughly Florentine.

The absurd claimants (II. 5) provide a farcical pause. The tell-tale perfume of Lysidamus is now part of the barbering urged on Eustachio by Cleandro (I. 3), who in consequence (Pirro says) reeks not of sheep but of civet. With you, the foreman retorts, Clizia would either be a whore or end in the poorhouse; how much better for Nicomaco to drown her in his well!

Act III, continuing the *epitasis,* begins with an invention by Machiavelli, a confrontation of the actual rivals. The father scolds the son (III. 1) for hanging around the house. Why doesn't he get out like other youths during the carnival and look at the masks or play football? Cleandro meets the attack with filial deviousness, slyly saying he remained behind to lend his father a hand. Aha! Nicomaco jeers, look what he's up to. Well, I have no need of you. Thus the undeclared opponents fence, each unwilling to leave the other with Clizia.

Cleandro adjusts the mask of an obedient Italian son and so tries to conceal his emotions. Though skeptical, Nicomaco cannot suppress his grievance against Sofronia, declaring that she is crazy and will destroy the family; the best thing Cleandro can do is to stop her. Sorely taxed, the son obliquely defends his mother: Either she's crazy or somebody else is. Suspicious, Nicomaco nevertheless turns to the matter that obsesses him, asking what Cleandro thinks about the troubles with Clizia. The latter breathes, Now we've got to the point! But he is noncommittal. Nicomaco persists: Don't you think your mother has got hold of a hot potato [13] in not marrying her to Pirro? The father charges the son with taking the mother's side; surely he knows that she favors Eustachio. The youth's stubbornness in denial makes the other's temper rise. He accuses Cleandro of trying to ruin the marriage by ordering the foreman to come to Florence. As for you and him, he threatens, I'll throw you both in the Stinche prison; [14] I'll repudiate Sofronia and give her dowry back; for I intend to be master in my own house. This wedding is going to take place tonight, and if there's no other way out I'll set fire to the house! No one can teach grandmother to suck eggs. [15]

Cleandro's soliloquy (III. 2) is, of course, Machiavelli's addition and shifts the primary focus again upon the lover. The profound misery caused by Nicomaco's tirade ravages him. A lover of a beautiful girl, he tells himself, has many rivals to cause him agonies. But I never yet heard of anyone whose rival is his own father. Instead of comfort, I find in him the source of my unhappiness. And if my mother seems to help, she does it not to encourage me but to frustrate her husband. I can't tell her my feelings or she'll think I've made the same arrangement with Eustachio as my father did with Pirro. Then her conscience would make her let things take their course and not bother any more about them. I'd be completely ruined, and in my grief I'd want to die. He sees that he must outwit the guile of this blocking character by ingenious deceptions.

39

He takes advantage of her affectionate greeting (III. 3) to pretend to be a close confederate. He reports Nicomaco's threats, and the latter's demand that she consent to the marriage or he'll have nothing more to do with her. He parries the vigilant matron's quizzing. He confesses that he loves Clizia, but like a sister; and it would cut him to the heart if she fell into Pirro's hands. His mother is sarcastic: I'll tell you this, if I thought that by snatching her from Nicomaco I'd put her in your hands, I'd not meddle. But Eustachio loves her. As for you, your own wife—for we're soon going to find you one—will make you forget Clizia. Behind filial submission he dissembles his alarm. Meanwhile, he begs her, do everything to forestall the wedding. She might find her parents, who if they were of good family would not be grateful for your giving her to a servant or a peasant. The argument moves Sofronia: she has thought the same thing, but this old man's infatuation frightened her. Here Machiavelli has aroused suspense by the first hint of a resolution, and the audience enjoys the possibility of a new twist in the action that stimulates a pleasant uncertainty.

III. 4 combines materials from two scenes of *Casina*. Nicomaco mocks Sofronia by his flattery, but she rejects his caresses, calling him crocked.[16] While he damns the scoundrel who gave him perfume, she wags her tongue much like a Cleostrata. But in a more original passage she reproaches him for his decline during the past year. A fine example for your son! Don't tell me all my sins in one breath, he grumbles; keep some for tomorrow. He reasserts his authority by demanding that a wife do as the husband wishes. So she should do, Sofronia agrees, in honorable matters. Isn't marriage honorable? Again she agrees, Yes, if it is a good marriage. Then each openly threatens to force the other's candidate to give up the girl. Nicomaco sums up, In short, we're now competing against one another.

In III. 5 and 6 Machiavelli harmonizes materials from Plautus with the portrayal of a Florentine household. The most striking change is the suppression of the son's claim to Casina as advanced by Cleostrata.[17] The effect is to give prominence to the two sorry candidates and so to render uncertainty more exquisite. In *Clizia*, moreover, the son, not the mother, sends their claimant to his master for cross-examination (III. 5). With delicious irony, each dissuasion urged on the foreman by Nicomaco is a compelling argument against a senile infatuation. Undaunted by the latter's warning that he'd lose his job and both he and Clizia would end up as beggars, Eustachio boasts that in this city a man with a beautiful wife need never be poor.

Pirro joins Nicomaco in III. 6, and his impudence also shows the loss of discipline in the household. He pertly points out that in doing as his master wishes he has made enemies of the wife, the son and all the servants. Machiavelli converts Lysidamus's pompous identification of himself as Jupiter [18] into a purely Italian fatuity. What, Nicomaco replies, does that matter to you? Love Christ and make the sign of the horns at the saints.[19] The pantaloon now mentions a plan to get around Sofronia: they will cast lots for Clizia. This is the device of Plautus, used for a sudden twist in the action that again increases uncertainty. But the silly trust in a beneficent deity is a Florentine touch.[20] What if luck fails? Nicomaco assures him that God, in whom he rests his hope, will not permit

41

that. The adapter invents a sardonic murmur for Pirro: Oh you infatuated pantaloon! You would have God lend you a hand in your wickedness!

In III. 7, Sofronia hears the proposal. Her readiness to accept it dismays Eustachio, but she organizes the lottery with suspicious efficiency. The triumphant Nicomaco, like an ass, thinks they are in perfect agreement. This masterly refinement of the bride-bartering moves the action toward the *catastasis*, for the dotard's ill-timed confidence arouses the expectation of comic surprise lurking behind the domestic harmony that Sofronia has faked by her apparent submission.

The lottery ready, Machiavelli substitutes for the single drawing by Cleostrata in Plautus two pouches with two names each, one having Clizia's name on a slip and a blank, and one having slips with the names of Pirro and Eustachio. Thus Nicomaco's hope dies and revives. He mutters a prayer to the holy guardians of matrimony. Seizing the first slip drawn, he groans, Eustachio! Alas! I'm ruined! The second slip is blank, and he recovers, shouting to Pirro, We've won! Sofronia accepts the result with ominous quiet. She diverts suspicion by arguing that there ought to be a nuptial mass, and he jeers, There will be, a phallic mass! [21] Other jubilant puns express his sense of triumph. She pretends to temporize and even to lose her temper. As he departs in joy to prepare Clizia for the news, Sofronia waits anxiously for Cleandro: perhaps he has thought of some plan. Thus the son again comes into prominence as Act III closes. Meanwhile, the *canzona* at the end of the act prepares for a counterstroke. It warns against offending a woman; prayers and tears will not move her, and spite and jealousy will give her more than mortal strength.

42

As the *epitasis* moves into Act IV, scene 1 (Machiavelli's invention), by centering attention on the hero, brings the play again within the laws of romantic comedy. When the foreman reports the lottery, Cleandro feels only stupefaction. How could his mother possibly be so blind? The old man's victory seems almost conspiratorial. He condemns her bitterly for trusting to chance a matter so vital to everybody. Since Eustachio is a trusted confidant, the scene has the force of a soliloquy in which the lover removes the mask of filial obedience and pours out his disappointment and bitterness. Everything has turned out just as Nicomaco wished! He blames Fortune in an eloquent complaint that subverts the celebrated passage in *The Prince*.[22] Feature by feature, he renounces the dear memory of the girl he loves. Are you not ashamed, he asks the goddess, to destine her delicate face to that stinking mouth, her tender flesh to those shaking hands and embraced by wrinkled, smelly limbs? With this one blow she has robbed him of mistress and patrimony. He experiences the outrage of a cast-off son, a painful anxiety that complicates the action in proportion as the audience sympathizes with the unhappy lover. Eustachio tries to comfort him by saying that Sofronia went into the house with a false smile on her face, and he bets that the old guy won't pluck that sweet pear.

When Nicomaco and Pirro enter (IV. 2) Cleandro eavesdrops, his presence on the stage being another departure from Plautus. Machiavelli keeps attention on the central conflict, the rivalry of father and son. In his merry insolence the pantaloon conjures up an ironically improbable vision of felicity.[23] The summit of happiness will come as he takes Clizia in his arms and caresses her. A moment of almost Catullan rapture settles incongruously

43

on him: Oh sweet night, will you ever come? (The crazy dotard! Cleandro mutters.) Thus the author puts in his mouth a satiric transposition of the *serena*,[24] a prosaic yet still lyric reduction of that beautiful stanza to comic irony. The context makes the scene aesthetically exciting. If one listens to the lyric emotion, as Cleandro does, he feels the power of the victorious opponent. But if one listens to the satiric overtones, as the audience will do also, he laughs at the senile absurdity. The comments of Pirro point up this ambiguity, and the amorous pantaloon in company with a cynical youth form a contrast resembling Captain Fright-All's brag with the depreciation of his page in the *commedia dell' arte*.[25] Then Nicomaco outlines the trick of the substitute groom (which follows *Casina*), and it is Cleandro's turn to feel a grim felicity in knowing his rival's every move.

One detail invented by Machiavelli is a more farcical commentary on senile delusion than the brilliant exaggerations of Plautus. This is Nicomaco's solemn effort to anticipate every demand on his physical resources. First he will swallow a pinch of the wonder drug, satyrion.[26] Pirro snickers at the ironic name. Missing the satiric thrust, the old man gravely praises its virtue as potent enough to rejuvenate a nonagenarian, to say nothing of a mere seventy-year-old like himself. After that he will eat nourishing things like boiled onions, beans and spices, with finally a fat roast pigeon so rare it still bleeds. Pirro warns him of indigestion, and a laughable pause intervenes as an old man's gluttony distracts Nicomaco from lust.

IV. 3 follows III. 1 of *Casina* in general outline. Plautus made the neighbor Alcesimus pour amused contempt on Lysidamus, whereas Machiavelli stresses the successful appeal by Nicomaco to friendship. Other slight but sig-

nificant changes keep alive the curiosity of the audience.
Nicomaco refers vaguely to the matter he has told
Damone. The latter agrees to let him use his house and
to send his wife Sostrata to Sofronia. The lover struts
jauntily to the druggist's to buy something; the audience,
knowing it is satyrion, enjoys the ironic anticipation.

In IV. 4 Machiavelli uses III. 2 of *Casina*, but changes
the emphasis. To Damone, Sofronia sneers at Nicomaco's
joust with Clizia, a sardonic repetition of the pantaloon's
sexual brags.[27] She upbraids the neighbor as a pillar of
the community who has lent his house for a shameless
deed. Nonplussed like Alcesimus, Damone petulantly deplores his assistance to an infatuated, bleareyed, slobber-
ing and toothless dotard. He wraps his cloak about his
face and slinks away. Sofronia turns swiftly to the gulling
of her old man.[28]

Thinking himself alone (IV. 5) Nicomaco is complacent about his drug and also the fragrant ointment which
arouses dormant physical powers. Stupified by a sudden
noise (IV. 6), he sees the maid Doria stagger from the
house. In scene 7 (which corresponds to *Casina*, III. 5)
she tells of Clizia's mania and of the dagger she seized to
murder Nicomaco and Pirro. The old man, aware of his
years, groans about this misfortune. The author portrays
an infatuated dotard at the moment when he begins to
suspect that his felicity is only a dream. Yet lust drives
him on though his reason resents the high cost of adultery, in disgrace, in misery and in fright. The contrast
between anticipation and reality vexes the adulterer into
sighing for slippered ease, and a comfortable wife. Here
the *epitasis* ends.

The structural function of IV. 8 is to impose the Terentian *catastasis* on materials from Plautus.[29] This compli-

cates the action by adding to the trickery of Nicomaco a still uncertain hope as to the fate of the young lover. Doria breathlessly gasps out a soliloquy broken by pent-up laughter. What fun they are having at the expense of the old guy! What an entertainment to see the afflictions of this house! The dotard and Pirro are shaking with fright in the kitchen; in the bedroom they are dressing the servant Siro in Clizia's garments, and they will send him to the husband in place of the girl. This information seems at first glance a dead giveaway of the trick so carefully reserved by the injured wife. But it is a stroke of excellent comic procedure to conceal and yet lay the basis for the actual twist in the plot. The slight but outrageous possibility of bedding an old man with a young escapes Doria, but not the attentive spectator. Moreover, the desires of Cleandro remain obstructed unless Nicomaco ceases altogether to be the primary blocking character, a peripety not at present foreseen.

In IV. 9 Doria assures him that Clizia, calmed, has promised to do what he wants. He recovers his old eagerness. Sofronia and Sostrata (scene 10) lead the weeping bride forward. Nicomaco (scene 11) only faintly senses why she is so tall; it must be her slippers. Damone finds her attractive and envies Nicomaco for his felicity. This rouses the braggart sexual warrior, who boasts that he feels as strong as, as—a sword. Sofronia (scene 12) speeds him on: There in Damone's house he will meet his match; this "lady" of his will soon have a plump belly pierced by an erect spout, like pitchers from Impruneta.[30] The smirking jest emphasizes the *catastasis* in IV. 8. Such an ambiguous sally leaves the spectators at the end of Act IV eager to know Nicomaco's fate and yet still uncertain about Cleandro.[31]

The last act of *Casina* is only 163 lines long, and the text is full of hopeless *lacunae*. Machiavelli in his Act V takes brilliant advantage of the opportunity to maintain the satiric farce and then precipitate a *catastrophe* appropriate to romantic comedy. At break of day (V. 1) Doria reports a night devoted to laughter. The playwright again employs a convention from the lyric repertory, the account of the lovers' night being a satirical transposition of the *alba* or dawn-song. The maid tells how they said, Now he is entering the bedroom; now he lies beside the bride; then he begins the battle, and meets vigorous opposition. Instead of the twice-staged humiliation of *Casina*, Machiavelli concentrates on the discomfiture of the pantaloon. Furthermore, he makes this action an essential step toward the resolution.

Nicomaco's account (V. 2) follows the repetitious hilarity of the Latin only in part, arousing not scorn but amused pity. For Machiavelli removes the chief blocking character from the path of true love by a comic catharsis. In *Casina*, on the other hand, the once-frustrated Lysidamus is ready to resume a lecher's career at the first chance. The scene opens with ironic laughter when the envious Damone inquires about Nicomaco's energy during the night. His folly purged, the old man reaches out to renew normal human ties. Appealing for help, he wails that he does not know where to hide the great shame he has incurred. Never can he face his wife, his son or the servants. He has sought his own dishonor, and his wife helped him to find it; he's ruined now.

With agonized reluctance, he stammers out the scandalous story, then weeps. His humiliation is far more abject than Sofronia foresaw. He describes Clizia's hugging the mattress, face down, so tightly that all the levers in the cathedral's repair shop could not turn her over. Tired out, he dozed, and then sprang into shocked wakefulness at the assault of something hard and pointed. Scared by the memory of Clizia's dagger, he jumped from the bed. There he saw, not the girl, but Siro stretched out naked and jeering at him with obscene gestures,[32] enjoying the sodomite degradation of his master. The infamous jest reduces Damone to roars of laughter, but Nicomaco desperately begs him for advice. His friend counsels him to put everything in Sofronia's hands and to do whatever she wants with Clizia, and her husband.

The spectator remains uncertain and tends to expect, like Doria when she reports to Sofronia, a renewal of the sport. For Plautus baited Lysidamus with two, not one shrew (11. 969-90). Machiavelli, however, keeps the emphasis on Nicomaco's lapse from and restoration to respectability. The wife (V. 3), instead of blocking the husband's way as he sneaks by, seeks him out with some compassion. She has the psychological penetration to understand her victim's feelings even as she rubs wholesome salt in his wounds. You seem unhappy, she remarks. Please don't torment me, he asks. You torment *me*, she replies; when you ought to comfort me I have to console you; when you ought to manage things I have to do it. Look at the way I've had to take charge! [33] He bitterly accuses her of making him a laughing-stock.

Firm and reasonable, Sofronia insists he face facts. Aren't you ashamed, she demands, to bring up a young girl as a member of your own family, and then throw her away on a wicked servant because he would let you sleep with her? I confess I planned all the tricks, for there was no other way of making you feel shame for your follies. If you will be the Nicomaco you were a year ago, we'll all look up to you and forget this affair. The husband who responds to this unanswerable reproof is the husband of old, again trusting his wife and no longer the rival to his son. He is now a father sympathetic with Cleandro's devotion to Clizia. Now when he assumes domestic authority, he finds that the good wife submits to his judgment. He decides that a girl of unknown parentage is not a suitable match for their son, but he will annul the marriage with Pirro and wait till they know more about her.

The young lover becomes the center of the action at the end of the play, as at the beginning and the middle. In V. 4 Cleandro's first words are a disrespectful sneer at the old man. But Sofronia describes his poor father's humiliation; he has given her the authority to arrange things as she wishes. Eustachio welcomes the new order, for he thinks he will win Clizia. Cleandro quickly retorts that she is not a morsel for *him*. Sofronia silences both: neither Eustachio nor Pirro will get her, nor Cleandro either. At least, he begs, bring her back to the house so that I may enjoy the sight of her. She promises nothing, and he sulks in discontent. He pours out his anguished disappointment (V. 5) in renewed complaint against Fortune's malice. First he fought against his father's passion; now he fights against his mother's ambition. He cannot forget her: from the time Clizia came into their house, he has never known any pleasure but thinking of her. This soliloquy maintains the uncertainty as to the lover's fate, placed as it is strategically just before the resolution.

The *catastrophe* occurs in a recognition scene (V. 6) that transforms his gloom to joy. Damone bears the happy tidings that Clizia's father Ramondo has come in search of his long-lost daughter. In this scene, unfortunately merely reported because of the absence of the heroine from the stage, Machiavelli removes the secondary blocking character. The orphan in the household now gets an identity and is, since her father is rich, an unexceptionable match. Cleandro is delirious with pleasure and calls his parents to hear the good news. Ramondo agrees (V. 7) to marry Clizia to the youth, with Nicomaco's consent. The now upright father gives immediate approval of the troth. Machiavelli, by insisting on the double joy of reconciliation within the family and of happiness for the young lovers, signalizes the triumph of romantic comedy over Plautine farce and the rightness of the quadripartite structure of Terence.

# Chapter 3

## *LA MANDRAGOLA:* THE HEROINE EMERGES

Machiavelli's campaign to embody his critical principles in actual comedies had thus far been only partially successful since it exhibited one glaring deficiency, the absence of the heroine. She makes her triumphant appearance in his third play, *La Mandragola: The Potion* (1518), in which the two young lovers share the same prominence. In the scenes that bring them vividly before the audience, the author undertakes a compassionate exploration of their feelings, their hopes, their fears and their enchanting raptures. United at last, each surprises the other with singleminded devotion. In the action that leads to this happy resolution, the playwright manipulates the Terentian structure with consummate skill, audaciously prolonging the *epitasis* and postponing the *catastasis* to the extreme limit of flexibility. The uncertainties that continue into Act V heighten a suspense which nothing but a union of the lovers can relieve. In this denouement Machiavelli has taken a giant stride toward romantic comedy.

The Prologue promises the audience a new peripety [1] that will make them split their sides with laughter. The author then whets curiosity about this reversal as he establishes the humor of his main characters: Judge Nicia Calfucci is both learned and slowwitted;[2] Callimaco Guadagni is a gallant youth; and the young girl he loves, though clever, falls into his power by a trick that will delight the ladies. The author prepares at the very beginning, therefore, to give equal emphasis to the satire of the blocking character and to the romance of the lovers. By the presence of the heroine onstage, the author has solved the centuries-old problem that defeated Plautus and Terence.[3] Dramatic necessity imposes a restraint by dictating the circumstances in which she appears: she *must* be a wife. There they are, the Prologue continues, his men and women: an unhappy lover, a stupid lawyer, a wicked friar and a crafty parasite. Calling attention particularly to the comic reversal, Machiavelli is confident of the effectiveness of the structure he praised in his criticism.[4]

The author expertly conceals the machinery of the *protasis* in Act I, scene 1. The salient facts come from the lips of the hero, who gives relief to his frustrations, like all lovers, by talking about them. The assimilation to the comedy of themes from the political treatises has the artistic effect of creating an atmosphere of intrigue. Callimaco's man Siro alerts the audience to this aspect by paraphrasing chapter 22 of *The Prince* on the reliability of attendants, whose duty is to serve their masters with fidelity.[5] The lover heightens it by his charge that Fortune,[6] disturbing his happy bachelor's life in Paris, had aroused in him the uncontrollable desire for Judge Nicia's beautiful wife Lucrezia. The chaste name is significantly harmonious with the gaiety of the whole work. Calculating the strength of this fortress of chastity, Callimaco has, with hopeful guile, pitched his camp beside the headquarters of the enemy and prudently made ready his amorous siege. He symbolizes his campaign by the image of war, in which he comprehends the deviousness of nego-tiation and intrigue.

Lucrezia's defenses are discouraging. Her own virtue and her indifference to the gregarious pleasures of other wives are formidable obstacles; the servants stand in such awe of her that bribery is useless. Two things give him hope, the stupidity of Nicia, the silliest fool in Florence, and his deep longing for children. To exploit these possi-bilities he has enlisted the parasite Ligurio. Siro's warning against such spongers draws from his master a maxim from *The Discourses:* when you act through another, you must trust him to serve you faithfully.[7] Ligurio's opening move is to persuade Nicia to take his wife to a watering-place. There her lover will be, and he would soon be friends with them. With fear and expectation, Callimaco now watches the parasite approach the judge.

The man of laws (I. 2) is extremely reluctant to leave Florence and abandon his home base.[8] Besides, the physi-cians who prescribe the cure can't agree on a resort: to my sharp eyes—ahem!—they seem so many quacks. At Li-gurio's sneer at his unwillingness to get out of sight of the cathedral, Nicia protests fatuously that as a youth he strayed far from home, even to Pisa and Leghorn. Why, he wandered almost to the borders of—Tuscany! But he will do anything, so badly does he desire a son. Thus Machiavelli establishes the humor of the blocking character.

Ligurio's recapitulation (I. 3) of the drolleries of the lawyer maintains the satiric mood. Here's the biggest fool alive, yet how good Fortune has been to him! He is rich and has a beautiful wife who is gentle, well-bred and fit to rule a kingdom. Well, at least his stupidity gives the lover

53

hope. That fellow, he asserts as Callimaco joins him, says he will do anything. But he warns the lover against the hazards of a resort. He succeeds only in releasing a flood of passionate language. Better die than live like this! If he could eat, sleep, converse or enjoy anything, he would be patient. But this scheme is his only hope; even if he has to perish he will use every expedient, however brutal, violent or vicious. Ligurio quiets him by renewing his promise of aid.

Nicia's reliance on Ligurio to find a physician suggests the first step in a conspiracy taking form in his mind. Let the lover pretend to be a doctor who has practiced in Paris; his educated manner will defeat the judge's simplicity, especially any flourish of Latin; they can thus get him to a watering-place. Then a more promising expedient occurs to the parasite. But it is risky, and Callimaco must trust him absolutely. The hopeful lover agrees to follow his lead. On this tantalizing note the first Act ends. In the swift and masterly *protasis* Machiavelli, by dangling two threads of the action into the *epitasis*, links the two tightly and keeps the spectator eager to know what precisely Ligurio's conspiracy will be and what Lucrezia will be like.

The unusually long *epitasis* begins (II. 1) with the parasite's scheme fully matured. He plays on Nicia's gullibility by seeing in Callimaco God's fulfillment of the judge's desire, but warns him against his inevitable return to Paris. Throughout the play the always imminent departure of the remarkable physician leads the husband ever deeper into the snare. Now in obedience to comic law he displays his humor in absurd pretentiousness. He will test the knowledge of the doctor: no one is going to pull the wool over his eyes,[9] and if he doesn't like it he can drop his drawers.[10]

Nicia greets Callimaco (II. 2) in baby-talk Latin and is answered in kind. This so inflates his self-conceit that he swears by the Gospels he likes him well. He effusively confides his dearest wish, to have a son, and asks about a watering-place that would aid his wife toward pregnancy. The bogus doctor beguiles him by ascribing the sterility to his wife and then mouths a Latin formula that emphasizes impartially male as well as female barrenness. This ironic erudition arouses admiration. But Callimaco warns that there is no remedy if Nicia is himself impotent. Laughing, he brags that in all Florence no man is more virile. The physician refers vaguely to some remedy, and Nicia hopes for something more convenient than baths.

Ligurio breaks in as a stroke of genius smites him. Indeed there is; the doctor is too modest. Isn't there a certain potion that always results in pregnancy? With mock reluctance the Parisian concedes that there is. But he does not deal with strangers lest they take him for a quack. Nicia snatches the bait: he will believe anything the young doctor says. Ligurio, with expert duplicity, first calls for urinalysis. Thus he cunningly guards the beginning of the conspiracy from the danger of too confident improvisation. Nicia expresses an almost lyrical trust in Callimaco, greater (he says) than the reliance of the cavalry on their swords.[11]

Self-deception assists the plot. Left alone with Siro (II. 3) the judge asks whether the king of France esteems his patron. The alert boy has only to reply laconically, Very much. The other sighs, for in his growing trust there is a fear of his departure. This town, he comments sourly, is full of tightwads[12] who ignore merit; so if Callimaco stayed nobody would look up to him. Me, I've strained my guts just to learn *hic, haec, hoc,*[13] and if I had to live on that I'd be in a fine mess. If you haven't got some standing

55

in this place even the dogs won't bark at you! He leaves to get a specimen from Lucrezia.

Returning with it (II. 5), the lawyer reproaches his wife (who remains offstage) for her sterility, but this time things will be done *his* way. No sons! If he'd known that beforehand, he'd have married a peasant. He complains about the trouble his foolish wife just gave him. Here she's always longed for children even more than he, yet when he wants her to do something about it she gives him nothing but evasions.

Ligurio warns Callimaco (II. 6) that Nicia's gullibility will be matched by the stubbornness of his wife. But they will not lack stratagems, a matter left in suspense at this point. The physician now examines the specimen and tosses off a Latin tag. The learned words prompt a slangy compliment from Nicia: By Brother Puccio's pussy,[14] this man gets sharper every second! With an inward laugh Callimaco suggests that the wife is not, at night, adequately covered, and because of this the urine is cloudy. The ass is deaf to the salacious quip. Why, he retorts, she sleeps under a heavy blanket. But—now he thinks he sees the cause—she kneels four hours saying her prayers before she comes to bed; she's a fool to suffer cold. Callimaco presses his advantage. Now judge, trust me and I'll show you a sure cure. I'll pay you 200 ducats if a year from today your wife does not hold her son in her arms. The significant pronoun is part of Callimaco's private joke. The solemnity of a cash vow moves the husband to protest that he believes in the doctor more than in his confessor.

The method of the conspirators, so hilarious in its simplicity, introduces to the *epitasis* a dramatic surprise. The surest way to impregnate a woman, the physician explains, is to give her a mandrake potion. I've found that it always works, and except for it the queen of France would be barren and also countless princesses of that realm. He murmurs pious thanks—to Fortune, who favors the judge since all ingredients for the dose are ready to hand. He prescribes the ideal time, this very evening after supper when the moon is in the ascendant and the hour propitious. Nicia eagerly promises to make Lucrezia take it.

The next step is an important forward movement in the *epitasis*. Callimaco points out that the first man who takes Lucrezia afterward will die within eight days. Expressing his pained disappointment in humorous scatology,[15] Nicia declares, You can't slip that over on me! But the doctor is prepared with a solution: let somebody else sleep with her for one night and so draw on himself the poison of the mandrake. After that you can possess her without danger. Momentarily Nicia avoids the trap. What, is he to make his wife a whore and himself a cuckold? Does he hesitate to do, Callimaco persists, what the king of France and all his lords have done? The husband, by shifting his ground, steps into the trap: Where would I find anybody to commit such madness? Callimaco then soothingly explains that they will search the markets and force the first silly youth they find into Nicia's bed. In the morning he can send him off and have her at his pleasure without harm. Nicia finds the plausible absurdity persuasive and is ready, since kings and princes and even lords have used the doctor's cure.

This complication in the *epitasis* develops renewed suspense, for the real difficulty is how to persuade Lucrezia. Nicia fears that she will never submit, but Ligurio has a devilish inspiration: the way out is through her confessor. But who, Callimaco objects, will suborn the confessor?

Ligurio answers with a diabolical gaiety, You and your money and the wickedness of everybody. In the same spirit the parasite dismisses Nicia's fear that his wife won't confide in her confessor: then her mother will get her to do what they want. Act II, nevertheless, brings back the theme of romance as the anxious lover, trembling with the sudden promise of success, gasps out his emotion, This is killing me!

As the *epitasis* extends into Act III, Lucrezia's mother Sostrata prudently agrees to the scheme if Nicia can find no other way to have children and it does not prey on the conscience. Ligurio (III. 2) discovers new treasures of silliness in the husband, who tells about the fuss kicked up by his wife against his efforts to persuade her to do their bidding. He gropes for intelligibility. She used to be the sweetest person in the world and so easygoing. As he ostensibly comments on her superstition, he actually sketches the firm chastity of Lucrezia. Told that if she heard the first mass forty days at the church of the Servites she would get pregnant, she made her vow and went there about twenty mornings. Then one of those good-for-nothing friars began to cuddle up to her, and now she won't go back. Since then, she pricks up her ears like a rabbit,[16] so if you say anything to her she has nothing but objections.

Ligurio abruptly demands twenty-five ducats to bribe the priest,[17] and he delivers a diabolical little sermon. Priests are crafty and subtle, as you'd expect from their knowledge of our sins, and their own. If you're not experienced in dealing with them, they will outwit you. I don't want you to spoil our little game by talking to him, for a man like you who spends the whole day in the study knows his books but not the world. Thus Ligurio prepares the spectator for a comic situation where stupidity makes Nicia misapprehend everything. The parasite will do all the talking; he will tell the priest that Nicia is deaf.

By withholding the appearance of Fra Timoteo until the middle of the *epitasis*, Machiavelli has inspired a lively interest in a major character. A benevolent piety (III. 3) unifies the features of his public mask. He is unctuous and patient. Away from the view of men (III. 4) he removes it and muses cynically over the paradox that women are at once charitable and troublesome. Swiftly adjusting the mask, he greets Ligurio and Nicia. The bait dangled by the parasite is a large sum for alms. The deaf lawyer expresses a scatological dismay as he forgets his part. Fra Timoteo encourages Ligurio, who begins a test of his pliability. He tells how the judge's grandniece, while at a convent, found herself pregnant. Nicia has pledged 300 ducats to remove this threat of disgrace to the family. The parasite's outrageous suggestion is that Fra Timoteo persuade the Mother Superior to give the girl a drug to make her miscarry. The priest temporizes.

Ligurio points out the many blessings that would follow. Into his mouth Machiavelli puts a theme from *The Prince:* I believe that what benefits and satisfies the greatest number is good.[18] The public mask conceals Fra Timoteo's relish of this casuistry, which he hoards for his own persuasions in III. 11. He leads the parasite on by murmuring piously, Let that be done which you desire, for God and charity. He is compliant and asks for the money so he may begin the good works. Ligurio applauds this demonstration of worldliness, praising Fra Timoteo as the devout man he had thought him. He hands over twenty-five ducats and goes into the church. The priest (III. 5) quizzes Nicia, who, however, having failed to catch Ligurio's drift, is thunderstruck. And Fra Timoteo, fingering the coins happily, rests confident that he can get the better of them.

He welcomes the return of the parasite expectantly (III. 6). The latter, now that he has studied his task, introduces his real proposal. There is, he says, another favor which the priest must do, and Fra Timoteo acquiesces. They go together into the church to consider details, telling Nicia to wait. As the toad said to the harrow! [19] the bewildered husband fussily mumbles in one of the Wellerisms that mark his speech. Once alone (III. 7) he shows how far he lags behind the others. His head is in a whirl because of this idle talk. We agree to say one thing to the priest, and Ligurio says something else. I have to plug my ears like Ogier the Dane [20] and pretend I've not heard his mad ideas. I'm twenty-five ducats poorer, and yet there has been no mention of my business. Here they have planted me, like a numbskull.[21]

Meanwhile, the movement within the *epitasis* has gone forward. Fra Timoteo displays on their reappearance (III. 8) a certain clerical arrogance. He orders the women brought in. Confident of his plans, he promises with the right touch of humility that if his authority prevails he will consummate the match [22] this evening. He casts a sly gleam, at the apparent slip, toward Nicia. But Ligurio's announcement of the priest's readiness to help causes him again to forget his deafness, and he brags preposterously that he feels a new man eager to receive assurance that the child will be a boy. Weeping for joy, he fulfills the Prologue's description, for the miraculous powers he ascribes to Doctor Callimaco are extended from conceiving the child to foretelling its sex.[23]

In a short soliloquy (III. 9) an amused grimace twists the priest's features as he ponders the question of who is tricking whom. That rogue Ligurio comes to me with the first tale just to feel me out. But if they have hoaxed me, it is a profitable hoax. He foresees no difficulty since Lucrezia is both prudent and good; he will trap her by her very goodness.[24] All women lack brains, and the mother is a fool too and will be a great help. Seeing them approach he adjusts his mask with comfortable assurance.

Sostrata's first words (III. 10) confirm his insolent judgment. She declares, If Fra Timoteo tells you it would not be a burden on your conscience, you should do it without thinking twice about it. But the spectator's interest focuses on Lucrezia. Machiavelli has again shown boldness in dramaturgy by prolonging from the beginning of the *protasis* to the center of the *epitasis* suspense over the appearance of his heroine. Her first words ring with her earlier namesake's sincerest virtue, and yet she values her husband at his true worth. Hence her involvement in the conspiracy promises to complicate the action with a development wholly unforeseen by any of the plotters. I've always feared, she insists, that Nicia's desire for children would make us commit some sin.[25] So I've always been suspicious, especially since what happened when I went to the church of the Servites. But of all the things he has tried, this seems the queerest. To subject my body to this disgrace and to cause a man's death for dishonoring me! I do not believe, even if I were the only woman left in the world, I could do such a thing. Ignoring the chaste disdain, her mother complacently urges her to do only what her priest tells her. But the girl's feelings still oppress her.[26]

His unctuous mask an inspiration of serenity (III. 11)

Fra Timoteo relieves the embarrassment by his professional adroitness. He has looked up authorities, he assures them, and found many things that support them. Incredulous, Lucrezia asks if he is making fun of her. Kind and ingratiating, he asks in his turn, Are these matters funny? Are you just now finding out what I am like? This reproach calms her, and she replies, No Father, but this seems the strangest thing I ever heard of. And so he reasons with her, saying, Many things when far off seem terrible, insufferable, queer; but when you get to know them they turn out to be natural, tolerable, familiar. Hence they say that fear is greater than evil. Now this thing is such a matter. In hope of relief from her anxiety the girl cries out, God grant it!

At this point the priest presses into service the ethical gymnastic of Ligurio in III. 4. He expounds, in a masterpiece of casuistry, the principle that the intention justifies the means, a comic perversion of Machiavelli's observation that a good result justifies the method used to arrive at it.[27] In a matter of conscience, Fra Timoteo explains, you must follow the general rule that where there is a certain good and an uncertain evil, you must never give up the good because of fear of the evil. Now here there is a certain good: you will become pregnant and gain a soul for God Almighty. The uncertain evil is that the man who lies with you after you've taken the potion may die of it. Since the outcome is uncertain, it is wise for Nicia not to take the risk. As for the act—that it would be sinful—that is idle talk. It is the will that sins, not the body. A cause for sinning is to displease your husband, whereas you are merely falling in with his whims; or to take delight in it, whereas you face it with abhorrence. Beyond this, the end has to be considered in all things. Your purpose is to fill a seat in Paradise and make your husband happy. The Bible tells us that the daughters of Lot, believing they had been left alone in the world, had intercourse with their father. Since their intention was good, they did not sin. This rich fusion of ends and means with precise illustration from the Holy Book is an audacious triumph.

Yet Lucrezia is still unconvinced and asks with dismay what deed her priest is urging. She continues to fear adultery as a certain evil. The mother supports Fra Timoteo's exposition with the practical argument that if her husband dies a childless woman is forsaken by everyone. Tapping his breast, the priest swears by this heart consecrated to Our Lord that it is no greater burden on her conscience to obey her husband in this deed than to eat meat on Wednesday, a sin removed by holy water.

It is significant that Lucrezia's scruples are not removed at this point. They are authoritatively silenced and her will mastered. The ironic contrast with her Roman forebear sharpens the pathos. She exclaims, Where are you leading me, Father? He replies with disarming tranquility, Toward benefits for which you will always have occasion to pray to God for me. Full of shame, she surrenders: I'll do what you say, but I don't think I'll live till morning. Fra Timoteo promises to call on the angel Raphael to accompany her and soothingly instructs her to get ready for what he calls "this mystery". Defeated but still doubtful, she begs piteously, May God and Our Lady help me and keep me from evil!

The priest (III. 12) confirms the success of the plot to Ligurio and Nicia. The joyous cuckold again forgets his deafness, and the other comments sarcastically on his speedy cure. The mischievous Ligurio thanks St. Clement for this favor, and Fra Timoteo pounces on the quip, seeing a miracle that would exalt his own church.[28] Nicia ought to put up a votive image, he urges, and share the profits. But the husband, dominated by his humor, is the happiest man in the world. With an ironic pun—if a cuckold can father a child—[29] the priest encourages him. Ligurio closes the action of Act III by despatching the priest to prayer, the husband to his wife so as to keep her on a steady course,[30] and himself to Callimaco for the potion.

Act IV, scene 1, returns the *epitasis* to a still doubtful lover. In a long soliloquy expressing an unhappy mistrust of Fortune, Callimaco vacillates between hope and fear. Is it possible, he asks, to remain alive in this suffering, racked by these cares and yearnings? He imagines himself like a ship driven by contrary winds, its danger increasing the nearer the port. Nicia's stupidity gives him hope, but Lucrezia's prudence and strong will make him despair. The repeated emphasis on her prudence, after Fra Timoteo's persuasive success of III. 11, suggests the remote possibility that the victim might alter the direction of the conspiracy.

Callimaco bursts into a self-catechism that traces a lover's irresolution. If you do win her, what then? Do you not know how little happiness lies in the things man desires in comparison with what he imagined he'd find? On the other hand, the worst that can happen is to die and go to hell. Are you ashamed to go there? Face your destiny, and fly from evil; or if you can't fly, endure it like a man. In every part of his body, he feels, such longing to be with her, just once, assails him that he is completely overwhelmed. My legs tremble, my bowels flutter, my heart is plucked from my breast, my arms go slack, my tongue becomes mute, my eyes dazzle and my brain whirls. These

64

are the stigmata of true lovers from Catullus and Petrarch.[31] The intensity with which Machiavelli portrays the sentimental antithesis in the hero of *La Mandragola* strongly reasserts its romantic center.

In the crucial dialogue of IV. 2 between the lover and the parasite, Machiavelli modulates the Petrachan exultation of the one with the agent's practical attention to details. Callimaco exclaims, Oh blessed friar, I'll always pray to God for him. Ligurio snickers: Fra Timoteo will expect something more substantial than prayers. Money? The lover will gladly give the 300 ducats promised. He exclaims with naive surprise at the news that the husband had already paid the priest for making him a cuckold. But Callimaco is still ecstatic with gratitude, asking, By what merits do I deserve such grace? I'll die from pure happiness.

Ligurio observes these raptures with amused cynicism. First joy, then grief—this fellow somehow insists on dying. But have you got the potion ready? So Callimaco has; in reality only a glass of hippocras, it becomes as the counterfeit physician utters the patter of his role, a sovereign cordial excellent to quiet the stomach and cheer the brain. Suddenly he covers his face at a disastrous thought. If he is with the others, he can't be the one they put in Lucrezia's bed. The trusted agent has a solution. He will get the priest to play the doctor. Callimaco is to throw a ragged cloak on his back, come with a lute and sing a ditty at the corner of the house and screw up his face in a grimace. A false nose will complete the disguise. The others will seize him and put him in the bed. The rest he will have to do himself!

Now Ligurio advises a course of action that opens up other possibilities. He urges Callimaco before he leaves to reveal the trick and show Lucrezia the love he feels for her. Show her, he suggests, how she can be your friend without scandal, or your enemy with great loss to her reputation. To this cynical treatment, he argues, she will certainly submit. Thus Ligurio increases the tension of the *epitasis* by opening up several different lines of action. Will the conspiracy bring the lover complete satisfaction in a single night's seduction of Lucrezia? Will the parasite's reading of her character prove accurate, and will Callimaco have the brutality to force her to remain his reluctant mistress? Or will her prudence, as he suspects, twist the outcome another way? These questions must wait for answers upon the *catastasis*.

The anxious lover, filled with new hope and yet self-distrustful, needs the narcotic of action. He entrusts Siro (IV. 3) with the potion for Nicia's wife. Tortured by impatience, he reveals in a soliloquy (IV. 4) continued fear that something will block his happiness. If so, he will drown himself in the Arno, or hang himself, or throw himself from that window or stab himself on her doorstep. Ligurio's return with the disguised priest (IV. 5) renews his hope. The parasite brusquely orders them to abandon their ceremony and assigns every man to his place.

Alone (IV. 6), Fra Timoteo wrestles with his conscience, and silences it. With comic disingenuousness he concedes that bad company leads a man to the gallows as much for being too easy-going as for being wicked. God knows, he protests, I never harmed anybody. I kept to my cell, saying my office and looking after my flock. Then this devil Ligurio came to me, and made me dip my finger into sin, then my arm and finally my entire body. But he finds comfort in the thought that the responsibility belongs to many. He therefore welcomes the parasite's return (IV.

7) with relief, and the tone reverts to satire of Nicia. They laugh at the disguise of the judge, a short nightgown that does not cover his posterior, with a short sword beneath it, and on his noodle some canon's hood. They draw aside to overhear the folly of a husband almost fatalistically determined to share his unwilling wife.

He begins (IV. 8) with the conventional antifeminist tirade of the wrong-headed spouse. How many silly protests has that foolish wife of mine made! She still had scruples about going to bed. He mimics the pathetic struggles of her doubtful soul as mere perversities: How can I do it? What are you forcing me to do? Alas, mother! Nicia snorts that he expects women to be fussy, but she's driven him out of his wits. He even jests at her surrender: I know he will thrust his dibble into mother earth,[32] and before I leave such sport I'll say with Monna Ghinga,[33] I saw it myself, with these hands. He will not release the kidnapped youth until manual proof has established his virility. He strikes the pose of the braggart cuckold, *cornutus gloriosus*. In his disguise he seems to himself taller, younger, leaner; there's not a woman who would demand money for going to bed with him!

At Ligurio's salute (IV. 9) the braggart cloaks his fright with the boast that if he had not recognized them at once, he'd have given them his well-known thrust with his dagger. Then the parasite orders his troops to their positions: on the right wing the doctor, on the left himself, and between the two horns (as the appropriate place for the cuckold) the judge, with Siro as rearguard. The password, another tease of the wittol, is St. Cuckoo because he is the most honored saint in France. Callimaco enters singing,

> May the devil get in your bed,
> Since I can't get in myself!

*They spin him around and lead him into the house.*

To bring Act IV to an end (scene 10) the priest steps forward and addresses the audience directly: Spectators, don't find fault, for tonight no one will sleep. In effect, his statement indicates that the *epitasis* will continue without interruption from Act IV into V. During the interval, Fra Timoteo goes on, I shall say the church service; the judge will wander from bedroom to parlor; Callimaco and Lucrezia—he pauses to strengthen the little flourish—will *not* sleep. This maintains the uncertainty of the audience as to how the trickery and the violation of the chastely unwilling wife will turn out. In the humorously intentional dissipation of dramatic illusion, Machiavelli has employed the obliging cleric for a preparation of the *catastasis*. In a method of suspense used by Shakespeare at the end of Act IV of *Antony and Cleopatra*, the audience again enjoys the tension of alternative resolutions. Will Callimaco rise above the lovers of Boccaccio after scheming only to discharge his lust in a single encounter? Will he follow Ligurio's brutal advice and compel Lucrezia to become his unwilling paramour? Or will the prudent and stubbornly faithful wife become the circumspect and devoted sweetheart? If so, will she exalt his infatuation to the high level of romantic love? Structurally, therefore, Fra Timoteo's role here is to throw the interest forward upon the *catastasis*.

In his masterly exploitation of flexibility Machiavelli prolongs the *epitasis* into Act V by resuming the soliloquy of the priest, a technique used by Shakespeare for the dialogue of Prospero and Ariel at similar points in *The*

*Tempest.* Fra Timoteo tells how he recited Matins, read the life of one of the Holy Fathers, went into the church and lit a lamp and changed the veil on one of the Madonnas that works miracles. He deplores the carelessness of the monks and the decline in the number of devotional images. Once, he muses, we made our vows so that people would behold fresh images, and in confession we exhorted them to consecrate offerings. No wonder that the people are now apathetic! This is the absolute sincerity of a formal piety.

After the flight of Callimaco in the morning (V. 2), the self-cuckolded husband describes with comic tedium how he made the ugly youth strip. He had a big nose and a twisted mouth, but you never saw such handsome flesh. Ligurio jokes about his insistence on ocular proof of virility, and Nicia solemnly brags that he made sure the fellow was healthy before he departed, exploring with his own hands how the affair was going. Such eagerness for cuckoldry inspires a humorous misapplication by Ligurio of a favorite theme of *The Prince:* you have conducted this business with exemplary prudence.[34] Then Nicia joined Sostrata and talked of the boy he could already feel in his arms, the darling! When he returned to the bedroom, he couldn't make that rascal leave, for he seemed tired to death. A spasm of pity for his successful rival turns into rejoicing as he leaves to get Lucrezia ready for her churching.[35] The fatuous cuckold proposes to garland his own horns by the ceremony appropriate to the birth of the longed-for child. This farce delights the priest (V. 3), whom the spirit of pleasure and profit accompanies to the altar to wait for the company. There his merchandise will bring a higher price.[36]

In sharp contrast to this worldly piety, Callimaco's dis-

covery of romance (V. 4) is embodied in a comic peripety
such as Machiavelli endorsed throughout his criticism.[37]
The reversal from despair to exultation in the hero carefully knits the parts of the structure. Before, he cried out
in anguish that death was better than a life of unrequited
yearning; now he is full of joy. The author directs the
torrent of powerful feeling with artful naturalness. He
gives the love scene, impossible to represent onstage,
dramatic force by casting the lover's report in the form of
dialogue. With surprise and delight, the audience shares
his experience of a nobler passion dominating the uncertain alternatives advanced in IV. 2 and 10. This at last
removes all obstacles. The exciting thrill and the unexpected revelation of mutual love shift the mood from intrigue to romantic comedy. Here Machiavelli has placed
the *catastasis*, demonstrating the wide latitude in flexibility of the four-part structure. Lucrezia follows neither
the path laid out by Ligurio nor that suggested by the
priest, but rewards her lover's passion with her own true
love. The counterturn leaves her the dominant personage,
and she is quick to seize command of the future, the devoted girl inspired by a concern for her lover's happiness.
In the history of the theatre, the situation is a triumph for
the emergent heroine.

Callimaco is breathless with adoration. He reports to
Ligurio that with Lucrezia he felt at first satisfied but not
happy. Then he confessed to her. He made her realize
how much he loved her and how happy they could be, with
no scandal. He promised that if God ever did away with
Nicia, he would make her his wife. Besides, she had had a
taste of the difference between Callimaco's virility [38] and
Nicia's. She sighed a while. Then she told me, Your
cleverness, my husband's stupidity, my mother's pliancy

and the wickedness of my confessor have driven me to do what I'd never have done of my own will. So I suppose it has happened through some heavenly plan that has ordained things this way. This, it seems to the audience, is the comfortably pious way Lucrezia defines that Fortune to whose influence on human affairs Callimaco paid tribute in I. 1. Like any religious woman incapable of denying God's will, she calmly accepts it. Therefore she told me, Callimaco goes on, I take you for lord, master and guide. Your desire is my happiness. With the same steadfastness he feared earlier as her greatest defense, she makes the plans for that happiness. What my husband wanted for one night, she said, I want him to have forever. And with her habit of prudence, she directs her lover to become Nicia's friend. Afterward he may come and go as he pleases, and they can meet every hour without suspicion. These words made him all but die of tenderness. He can not describe the least part of what he felt, for he is the happiest man in the world. If this felicity does not fail through death or time, he asserts, I'll be more blessed than the blest and more sublime than the saints. This is the language of undying passion.

The play now hurries to its *catastrophe* as Machiavelli gathers all his personages together. Commending God's way to Lucrezia (V. 5) Nicia is somehow aware of a new quality in her, and with easy wiliness she distracts the attention of the group by an affectation of domineering. This boldness amazes him, for last night she almost swooned with fear. To the priest's properly pious hope (V. 6) for a fine boy, she replies with a cheerfully ambiguous acceptance. She hardly needs the comedy of Fra Timoteo's assurance that it is God's will. The husband now gives romance the support of firm friendship by introducing his wife to her lover. Playing up in a perfection of irony, she puts into practice the priest's casuistic instructions in III. 11, and gravely takes Callimaco's hand. I value him highly, she says, and he must be dear to us. Thus she completes the establishment of the *ménage à trois* or triangular household of her lover's desire. With a dignity matching Lucrezia's Callimaco receives from Nicia the key to the house and promises to use it when it is opportune. Finally Fra Timoteo shepherds the happy flock into the church and turns to dismiss the audience. *La Mandragola* comes to its close in the reconciliations and joy of romantic comedy. To the end there is a beautiful balance between the satire of Nicia's absurdities and the trials and triumphs of devoted lovers.

# Chapter 4

## THE DEVIL'S DISCIPLE: MACHIAVELLI, CARDINAL POLE AND JONSON

The devil incarnate—thus a great prince of the Church stigmatized Machiavelli and voiced the moral disapprobation that became the conventional response to the Florentine Secretary's name in England as on the Continent. In addition, the churchman advanced two vastly different interpretations of Machiavelli's writings that also achieved an international currency. The first of these was that in its prescriptive maxims [*The Prince* was a serious treatise on political science.] The other and contradictory view held that it was a political satire in its communication of a meaning which was the very opposite of what it seemed to say. The seminal little book on statecraft, thus, challenged the ingenuity of Englishmen, and some of the subtler spirits among them boldly explored the three aspects defined by the prince of the Church. One was Ben Jonson, well known early in his career as "Monsieur Machiavelli". In his art we can trace the powerful and varied impact of the Florentine, for a lifelong study of his work extending from *Every Man out of His Humor* (1599) to *The Devil is an Ass* (1631) marks this tutelage. The close relationship invites the conclusion that if

73

Machiavelli was the devil, then Jonson was the devil's disciple.

The spokesman of moral denunciation was Reginald, Cardinal Pole, archbishop of Canterbury under Queen Mary in 1556-58. In *The Defense of the Unity of the Church,* which he addressed to the Emperor Charles V in 1536,[1] he sought to alert that monarch to the new danger in Europe. This was so urgent that he would divert the power of Catholic Christendom from the battle with the Turks and consecrate it to the liberation of England from the embodiment, as he described him, of Machiavelli's prince, King Henry VIII. The transformation of that ruler from a pious defender of the faith to a heretic monster was the work of his wicked and servile minister, Thomas Cromwell.[2] Pole reports a conversation with Cromwell that is, in effect, an apology for a tyranny in government which defies all religious scruples. This immoral policy, Pole charges Cromwell with declaring it the duty of the minister to forward.[3]

In the course of this report, Pole places in Cromwell's mouth a literal interpretation of *The Prince* as a treasury of political science. The practical statesman found in it a collection of maxims on government which proved to be of the greatest immediate usefulness. He offered to send the other a copy of the work, whose author based his advice on experience in public affairs. Cromwell insisted that the brief statement of an experienced man was worth more than all the volumes of speculating philosophers. For its value in everyday concerns, he preferred such a book to Plato's *Republic,* which remained to that day unrealized in the world of living men. Pole tells us, in short, that Cromwell, reading *The Prince* for its literal message, became an attentive pupil of Machiavelli through whom his royal master had tested the recommended policies in the government of England.

When he himself examined this treatise, however, Pole recoiled in horror from it as the work of the devil. He devotes most of his polemic to this second interpretation of Machiavelli, moral aversion and denunciation. He found, he said, that the work undermines religion, obedience and virtue. He therefore read it painfully despite its appealing style, for verily it was written by the finger of Satan. In contrast to the Holy Book written by the finger of God, which teaches men to live in harmony through the rules of righteousness, this abolishes all piety and by setting man against man opens up the road to ruin. It portrays a very special ruler who seems like the son of the devil himself. The cardinal solemnly warns Charles V to guard himself against the poison that transformed Henry VIII.

Prejudice causes Pole to vulgarize Machiavelli by suppressing in his summary the patriotic fervor that was a primary inspiration of *The Prince* as well as the objective analysis and all the sardonic examples of men's ambitions. The result is to reduce the subtle clarity of the exposition to moral caricature. The most ironic instance of this vulgarity, considering the dedication of *The Defense* to the monarch of Spain, is the omission of the Florentine's bitter praise (at the end of chapter 18) of Ferdinand the Catholic for his successful religious hypocrisy,[4] a glaring misinterpretation in a work addressed to his grandson and successor. Another aspect of vulgarity lies in Pole's failure to explain that he was summarizing and attacking in the main only one chapter of the book's twenty-six, chapter 18 on "In What Way Princes Ought to Keep Faith." [5] By leaving the impression that this contained the whole of

Machiavelli's doctrine, he both distorts and obscures the purpose of his author. This wrenching of truth in the interests of moral disapproval served as a model for all later defamers of Machiavelli.[6]

Taking up Machiavelli's advice on religion, Pole cites with alarm the detailed examples of men who lost life or power for keeping faith in all matters. He then denounces the author's emphasis on the transcendent value of prudence, sullenly noting his calm rejection of religion when it is a disadvantage and his counsel that the ruler by always seeming pious may avoid harm. He censures giving the highest place to craft and prudence in the conduct of government without regard to religion or virtue. This, he protests, is the doctrine advanced by Cromwell in his praise of Machiavelli's treatise. In horrified amazement, Pole declares that Machiavelli regards the actual practice of religious virtues as ruinous, and approves of them only when one gains an advantage by doing so.

He pounces on the famous symbols of the lion and the fox as summarizing the entire system taught by *The Prince*. To Pole, these are not symbols, but a bestial degradation of politics. Missing the symbolic meaning, he sneers, Why not tigers and bears? They reveal, the cardinal charges, that the Florentine prefers the principality founded on fear to a government founded on love because it is safer and easier to manage. He finds intolerable Machiavelli's position that the prince must guard the secret of his power with the greatest caution, making use of the violence of the lion and the guile of the fox to preserve himself against all changes of fortune. For the essence of his doctrine of government is to teach guile, deception, mendacity and dissimulation.

Pole is outraged, therefore, by what he takes to be

76

Machiavelli's insistence that the prince must know above all how to dissemble, so that he may display virtue or suppress it according to circumstances. On the contrary, the philosophers, he argues, exalted virtue and highly esteemed religion, faith and justice. But the rules Machiavelli outlines for his prince tell him how to use the pretext of religion to indulge his desires and ambitions—the heart of the doctrine taught by Machiavelli and endorsed by Cromwell. This converts the happy state of the ideal ruler into the tragedy of complete disaster, which overwhelms all tyrants and godless men.

Pole next recommends the Emperor's attention to the dilemma posed in chapter 17 of *The Prince*, whether love or fear is more effective.[7] The disciple of Machiavelli, he complains, having adopted this new art of governing, rules not by right of succession or by the love of his subjects, but by fear. This counsel flies in the face of observed and recorded experience. For princes achieve royal power through the amity of the people, and none governs by fear rather than love. Judging a thing by its result, Pole assures Charles V that he can find no prince who by his rule confirms Machiavelli's prescriptions. He concludes, therefore, that the author's impiety is so blind that he who professes to teach prudence can not see the truth.

This conclusion leads, surprisingly, to an exposition of the ironic interpretation of *The Prince*. How, Pole asks, can we account for what looks like blind impiety in Machiavelli? In answering the question, he reads into the book pressed on him by the detested Cromwell a satiric and paradoxically didactic intent. Machiavelli's fellow citizens, he found on a journey to Florence, shared his own impression of the author's blindness and ignorance. But they corrected this impression by quoting in his defense the reply he gave when he met reproof. He said that the counsels in *The Prince* were intended to make a tyrant's rule short. This he desired most of all because he was afire inwardly with the hatred of the very ruler for whom he ostensibly wrote. He put nothing in his book which did not please the tyrant, and yet he also gave him directions that would precipitate his ruin. This, in short, is the explanation of those who sought to account for the apparent blindness of the author. In other words, Machiavelli, while granting the possibility in theory of his maxims, rejected their practical usefulness except as they plunged the prince who followed them into irretrievable disaster.[8] According to this explanation, he was inspired not by love of tyranny but by hatred of it, ironically writing the opposite of what he intended.

In *The Defense of the Unity of the Church*, then, Cardinal Pole expressed views of Machiavelli that flourished in the Sixteenth Century. One was that *The Prince* is a useful handbook of political science; a second was that the work merited only strong moral disapproval; and a third was that it is a political satire written in a spirit of bitter irony. Hence the view that English Machiavellianism, especially the Elizabethan misunderstanding of *The Prince*, is traceable chiefly to the *Anti-Machiavel* (1576) of the Huguenot Innocent Gentillet[9] requires serious modification. Pole's complex response is more characteristic of the intellectual and literary history of the century, and a writer like Ben Jonson might dramatize all three attitudes which he defined.

The ironic interpretation appears in print four years before Pole's *Defense*, dating from the first publication of *The Prince* in Florence in 1532. The editor, Bernardo di Giunta, defends it against widespread condemnation for its alleged tyrannopedia by deducing a sharply contradictory aim. He expresses this by drawing an analogy from medicine: those skilled in that science must be familiar with poisons so as to know how to guard against them. There is no science or art that can not be put to evil uses by evil men. Who can say, for example, that iron was discovered rather to kill men than to defend men from beasts? By means of these analogies, Giunta attempts to show that Machiavelli's real intention was not to instruct the tyrant, but to expose the dangers of tyranny and so to teach the tyrant's victims how to protect themselves.[10] In 1640 the translator Edward Dacres admitted that Machiavelli's work was poisonous, but added that even poisons can be medicinal if carefully used. Hence, "the judicious peruser may honestly make use of it in the actions of his life, with advantage."[11] Thus Giunta's concept and his metaphor reappear in the first printed English translation.

In 1585 Alberico Gentili, a religious exile from Italy and Regius professor of civil law at Oxford, published a book on diplomacy in which he singled out two works by Machiavelli to praise for their value in substantiating historical theory by examples drawn from practical experience.[12] He thus recapitulates the view ascribed by Pole to Cromwell. He calls the Florentine the most distinguished of political writers, and he describes *The Discourses on Livy* as a golden book deserving to be set up as a model. This leads to a ringing defense of one denounced for wickedness and to an emphasis on his extraordinary insight. But in the explanation of his purpose in writing, Gentili restates the ironic interpretation. Machiavelli, he says, was a eulogist of democracy and its most spirited champion. Born, educated and gaining honors in a republic, he was the supreme enemy of tyranny. His aim in *The*

*Prince* was not to teach the monarch, but by revealing his secret counsels to expose him to the suffering people. Are we not aware, Gentili asks, that there are such princes as he describes? That is why it offends rulers of that kind for the works of the man to survive and be published. For the actual purpose of this wisest of men was to instruct the people under the pretext of counseling the prince.

A few years later, Christopher Marlowe showed how the drama gained in complexity and sophistication by exploiting at one and the same time the moral disapproval voiced by the defamers of the Florentine and the satiric interpretation of his writings. In *The Jew of Malta* (1590?) he introduces Machiavelli by his own name and makes him the presenter of the tragedy, a bugbear resembling the devil conceived by Pole.[13] He declares:

> I count religion but a childish toy,
> And hold there is no sin but ignorance. . . .
> Might first made kings, and laws were then most sure
> When like the Draco's, they were writ in blood.[14]

This prologue, with its commendation of fortresses and poisons, clearly owes little to Machiavelli's actual views. It claims in the rich Barabas a disciple whose "money was not got without my means" (1.32). The Jew becomes the protagonist in a struggle for power symbolized by the wealth with which he surrounds himself and which the Christians cheat him out of when they sell his goods for tribute to the Turks. The conflict with morality in this struggle turns on the recurrent term "policy" [15] used in the two clashing senses already noted by Pole, Giunta and Gentili whether public affairs serve the public good or whether they serve private purposes through cunning and deceit.

One episode vividly exemplifies the ironic view of Machiavelli. In revenge for the wrongs heaped upon him, Barabas delivers Malta to the Turks and their captain Calymath. Thereupon made governor by the generous enemy, the Jew is in a position of power over the Christians, with his old antagonist Ferneze helpless before him. He resolves to maintain this dangerous state by circumspect conduct and "firm policy" (V. 2. 36). This laudable determination corresponds to sound political practice. But blind insolence assails him, and intending to make "a profit of my policy" (112) he frees his implacable adversary and then conspires with him to betray the friendly Calymath. Marlowe's implied satiric commentary lies in the fatal disregard by an alleged disciple of Machiavelli of the maxim emphasized in *The Discourses* never to entrust power to a person whom one has wronged.[16] The alliance, therefore, is an invitation to disaster which the judicious spectator, through his perception of the ironic portrayal of the hero, looks forward to and enjoys with sardonic gratification. Here is a double-dealer who unwittingly struts to his confusion by the very means which his policy would employ for self-aggrandizement.

A number of other attempts, all more or less instructive, attest to the currency in the drama of Machiavellian irony. In Francis Beaumont's *The Woman Hater* (1607) Lord Lucio consciously lives the role of a Machiavellian. He affects to be "a great Statesman" [17] and seeks to dress the part by means of nightcaps, jewels and toothpicks. He receives drunken remarks snapped up in taverns by his informers as proofs of treason, and amuses the duke by interpreting the latter's early rising to visit his mistress Oriana as a concern about some weighty plot. While the young duke pursues his infatuation, Lucio remains behind, as he says, "to practise in the State" for the good of the realm. In this effort he appears without toothpick or jewel, but his "forelap hangs in the right place, and as near *Machiauels*, as can be gathered by tradition." Meanwhile, all his own labors and those of his informers bring forth as a traitor only the contemptible courtier Lazarello, a harmless glutton notable chiefly for the hungry pursuit of a fish head. Lucio hands him over to the duke, who frees him as the courtiers enjoy the discomfiture of the great statesman and his informers.

George Chapman has a gallery of ironically ineffectual Machiavels, who illustrate the point that sharp practice blinds the schemer who professes it.[18] In *All Fools* (1599) he adds some piquancy to his borrowings from Terence by recasting one of the fathers, the old knight Gostanzo, as a "wretched Macheuilian."[19] He is deluded by his son Valerio into believing that the latter's wife Gratiana is the secret bride of Fortunio, son of his neighbor Marcantonio. He takes unwarranted pride in the superiority of this young farmer to a youth reared among "the city Artes". Actually the son, barely escaping arrest for debt, is completely unlike the thrifty husbandman of his father's imagination, a swaggerer, gamester and mischief-lover. The comedy lies in a series of ironic situations in which the very shame he ascribes to the neighbor Marcantonio lies in wait for the smug Machiavellian.

His trust in his own politic arts leads him to welcome the wayward Fortunio and his bride on the principle that his own advice and his son's example will mend his faults. This, of course, is the very step desired by all the young people. To them the hoodwinked Gostanzo is "this olde politique dissembling Knight." The tricked father persists in his ineffectual policy. When Valerio feels bound by a promise to his friend Fortunio, Gostanzo scoffs: "Promises are no fetters." A man's tongue exists only "to speake still to his owne priuate purposes." Friendship, which his son honors, is "but a Terme boy"; honesty is "but a defect of Witt." The satiric intriguer Rinaldo, meanwhile, utters the sense of the others by condemning Gostanzo as "a Macheuil,/A miserable Politician." [20]

When Valerio embraces Gratiana, he gapes at the sudden change in his shy clown of a son. He follows the advice of Rinaldo and orders the removal of the girl as a temptation to Marcantonio's house, on the pretext that she is really Valerio's wife. Yet he fears a slip-up because of his honest neighbor's ignorance of "the fine slights and pollicies of the world." This complacency renews Rinaldo's sneer at politicians who owe any success to chance but who when deprived of Fortune's aid are the greatest fools. This is an ironic allusion to Machiavelli's history of Caesar Borgia, who enjoyed a long prosperity at the hands of Fortune, but at last became the victim of her malignity.[21] In fact, the successful contriver is Valerio, who by playing the repentant son tricks the old poser into joining his hand with Gratiana's and commending them to each other. But Gostanzo exults that Valerio by showing the less honesty has displayed the more wit. The son with shrewd irony exclaims of his father's acts, "Why this is pollicie." [22] The father, informed of his son's arrest for debt and brought to the Half Moon tavern where he carouses and orders wine for the old man, faces the exposure of all his schemes. But when Valerio delivers a vinous oration, he dissolves in sentiment and can see only the actions of a "notable wag." [23] He then abandons all stratagems and accepts the situation calmly, paving the way to a happy ending.

Chapman equates the term "Machiavel" with serpent in *The Conspiracy of Byron* (1608) and echoes Pole's infernal identification of the Florentine. He personifies this concept in La Fin, a "discontented Spirite" who incites Byron. Although King Henry IV extends his pardon to the master, he banishes La Fin from the court forever as "*La-fiend*, and not *Laffin*." But the latter adheres to Byron, offering to "creepe,/Vpon my bosome in your Princely seruice." [24] In the sequel, *The Tragedy of Byron* (1608), the hero summons La Fin to court and instructs him to allay the king's suspicions and lock up or burn all papers. Restored to royal tolerance by "loyalty and pollicie," as Henry IV observes, La Fin betrays his master's conspiracy. Rejecting the warning to distrust his servant's letters, Byron is lured to court. Arrested and charged with treason, he still refuses to believe that La Fin will accuse him to his face. Too late he realizes that he has been tempted to break his oath and lose his valor through "the hisse of such a viper." [25] Here the perfidious servant is the devil incarnate.

Chapman's *Revenge of Bussy D'Ambois* (1613) presents a brace of "your Macheuilian Villaines" (as Guise says in derision to King Henry). One is Baligny, lord lieutenant of Cambrai and husband of Charlotte, the high-spirited sister of Bussy and Clermont. The other is the malcontent Renel, whom Baligny employs in his machinations. Exhibiting the devious conduct of a "Politician," Baligny offers to prove his loyalty to the king by the betrayal of father and brother. He sets an ambush for Clermont on the argument that such "treacherie for Kings" is "graue, deepe Policie." [26] Ironically the plot collapses, and the trap closes on Clermont and Guise only when the royal will stiffens the flabby deviousness of the betrayer.

The anonymous *Alphonsus Emperor of Germany*,[27] once ascribed to Chapman, includes a simple ironic portrayal of the politician in the secretary of the emperor. This is Lorenzo de Cyprus, who seeks above all "to be an outward Saint, an inward Devill." [28] He bids Alphonsus learn six maxims which are the kind of travesty of *The Prince* made by Pole and by Marlowe in the Prologue of *The Jew of Malta*.[29] The first of these is that "A Prince must be of the nature of the Lion and the Fox." Others are that a prince must above all things seem devout, but to keep a promise or an oath is dangerous to his rule; that a prince is safer when feared than loved; and that "To keep an usurped Crown, a Prince must swear, forswear, poyson, murder, and commit all kind of villainies; provided it can be cunningly kept from the eye of the world." Here Alphonsus demurs since a monarch must rely in these things on agents who can be corrupted. Therefore, Lorenzo rejoins, learn the sixth and last maxim: "Be alwaies jealous of him that knows your secrets," and hence credit few and cut off at once those whom you suspect. He points to a box of poisons given to him by a Neapolitan, whom he thereby sent to his grave. Since his pupil is apt, Lorenzo falls victim to his own boasted policy. After memorizing and destroying the notes from which they worked, the emperor repays Lorenzo as he had rewarded his Neapolitan benefactor.[30]

Meriting notice is a prose pamphlet by John Donne called *Ignatius His Conclave* (1611), which stages an infernal competition for Satan's favor between Loyola and Machiavelli.[31] In the mouth of the Florentine's ghost the author puts the hackneyed praise of the art of equivocation, which he prides himself on teaching the Jesuits. He demands the right to stand high in the ranks of those who do harm because he taught perfidy and the dissembling of religion. This is a new version of the moral disapproval that had been Pole's chief response to *The Prince*. But Donne also catches up the theme running from Giunta through Pole and Gentili and represents his personage as asserting that he armed and instructed an oppressed people how to conspire and remove a tyrant. He makes Machiavelli claim, therefore, that from both sides, rulers and ruled, he has made a notable increase in Lucifer's kingdom.[32] Lucifer sees in him a fit instrument to set against Ignatius on the theory that "two poysons mingled might doe no harme,"[33] and so permit him to govern in peace. In this satirical treatise, once again two dominating attitudes toward Machiavelli's work recur.

Meanwhile, the literal interpretation continued to flourish in coexistence with other attitudes. Richard Morison, a public servant under Cromwell, justifies a monarch's interference in ecclesiastical affairs by citing Machiavelli, to whom he appeals also for a description of the self-deception of the common people.[34] Later in the Sixteenth Century Gabriel Harvey praised *The Discourses* for their utility and *The Prince* as indispensable for understanding politics, reflecting Cromwell in his judgment that the latter is superior to any treatise by the utopists, even *The Christian Prince* by Erasmus.[35] It is perfectly natural, therefore, to find that the topic of disputation between Harvey and the public Orator, Dr. Fleming of King's, was a paraphrase of the title of chapter 17 of *The Prince:* "Whether a prince should prefer clemency to severity." On the other hand, the second epigram in his *Gratula-*

*tiones Valdinenses*, composed in honor of Queen Elizabeth on her visit to the Duke of Norfolk at Audley End in 1578, is ironic. Here such clichés of anti-Machiavellianism as "Deceit is my greatest virtue" are materials in a satiric self-portrait.[36] Sir Walter Raleigh also read *The Prince* with literal understanding. He commends the example of Caesar Borgia for performing his cruelty through ministers and so diverting upon them the hatred of the people, whom he later satisfied by destroying the detested minister.[37] This "goodlie pollicie", he reminds us, has had many precedents in all ages. He cites the reign of Henry VIII when the king ruled through Thomas Cromwell.[38]

The most famous English Renaissance echo of Cromwell's pragmatic interest in *The Prince* is Francis Bacon's praise of Machiavelli in *The Advancement of Learning* (1605) for openly declaring what men are accustomed to do, rather than what they ought to do.[39] He endorses the judgment in *The Discourses* of the people as fickle and princes as corrupt,[40] and he approves Machiavelli's insistence that prudence teaches the ruler to maintain a show of virtue.[41] If it does not surprise us that Bacon was aware of the intellectual currents of the age, it remains fascinating to see him reaching back of Cromwell and Pole to Giunta for an ironic explanation of the Florentine's purpose. This he states, with sardonic sportiveness, in biblical language:

For it is not possible to join the wisdom of the serpent with the innocence of the dove, unless men be perfectly acquainted with the nature of evil itself. . . . Nay, a virtuous and honest man can do no good upon those that are wicked, to correct and reclaim them, without first exploring all the depths and recesses of their malice.[42]

Like Gentili, moreover, Bacon commends *The Discourses* for their observations of actual history.[43] Like Cromwell, he applauds the practical good sense of Machiavelli in his study of men and governments and sees in his work a serious effort to preserve states from destruction by bringing them back to first principles.[44]

As for Jonson, it is noteworthy that in his early years as a playwright he acquired a reputation as the devil's disciple. Thomas Dekker identifies the Horace of *Satiromastix* (1602), a transparent caricature of Ben, as *"Monsieur Machiauell."* [45] The fact is that he gave dramatic expression, in three different plays, to each of the three attitudes set forth by Pole. For *Sejanus* (1603) he found in a literal reading of Machiavelli the tyrant's arts that destroy the protagonist. In *Volpone* (1605), however, the ironic judgment is a subtle inspiration for that masterpiece. It was only much later, in *Timber or Discoveries* (c. 1619), that he propounded a moral rejection. The significance of these interpretations is the subject of the three chapters that follow.

## Chapter 5

## THE TYRANT'S ARTS IN *SEJANUS*

*Sejanus* (1603) is a Roman play in which the Roman history of Tacitus and Juvenal has undergone a massive intrusion of Machiavellian elements.[1] The first evidence of this fundamental revision of Latin sources comes early in Act I. Although this opens on a bewildering crowd of persons, the author simplifies the exposition by disposing them into three sharply differentiated groups, each with its focal and unifying center. These are, in order of appearance, the senator Arruntius, the favorite Sejanus and the emperor Tiberius. To Arruntius and his like-minded companions Jonson assigns the function of a chorus, excluded from the wicked court and directly involved in the central conflict only in Act III. At the beginning, therefore, the playwright concentrates interest on titanic adversaries locked in a deadly combat of wits. The chorus interpret this action by means of words and emotions expressed by Tacitus when he pauses in his grim narrative to speak in his own person as a moral judge.[2]

Their indignation over the prevalence of spies at the court, however, is not to be found in Tacitus, in Juvenal, Dio Cassius, Suetonius or any classical historian. It is so important that its utterance is marked off as a "sentence":

> "Tirannes Artes
> Are to giue Flatterers grace, accusers power
> That those may seeme to kill whom they deuoure."
> (*Sejanus*, 1605 Quarto, I. 70-72)

The source is Machiavelli,[3] who had already studied a problem in suspense that did not exist in Roman history: whether such a prince as Tiberius might, by such "Artes," trick such a formidable antagonist as Sejanus into a fatal confidence. Jonson develops this germ of drama by a series of climactic actions based on the devious skill in politics expounded in *The Prince*. For the reversal at the end of his play, he returns to Machiavelli's solution of the problem illustrated by the same adversaries in *The Discourses on Livy*, itself a reinterpretation of Tacitus's *Annals*.

The maxim just quoted shows also the debt to Machiavelli for the remarkable quality of the verse. Jonson preserves the abhorrence of Tacitus and yet suggests an admiration for the mortal enemy who works through statecraft, and thus creates the peculiar tone (more notable in *Volpone*) inspired by a combination of moral sneer and intellectual recognition. The superior wit of monarch over minion derives from a reading of events in *The Discourses* challenged by historians, who puzzle over the various accounts of Sejanus and ask why, with everything to gain by time and caution, he should plot to remove his benefactor.[4] Tacitus and Dio are both guarded; indeed the latter warns that it is impossible for those outside conspiracies to be certain as to what has happened (LIV. 15. 1-4). Tacitus regarded the real conspiracy as a plot of Tiberius and Sejanus against the Roman people (*Annals*, IV. 1), an idea Jonson expresses in the denunciation by Arruntius, the central figure in the chorus, of the "confederacie" (I.

385) of the two; but this is an undeveloped Tacitan relic in the action Jonson unfolds. Suetonius suggests that the favorite was a dupe through whose services and wiles Tiberius destroyed the children of Germanicus and secured the succession for his own grandson (*Tiberius*, LXV.). With no such hesitation, Machiavelli singles out the conspiracy of Sejanus as one of the notable attempts on the life of a prince in the famous sixth chapter of Book III in *The Discourses*, on conspiracies. Jonson's inclination to link Machiavelli with Sejanus in his discussion of the prince in the *Discoveries* shows a thorough knowledge of this chapter. Here he found advice directed to the ruler no less instructive than the precepts of the more celebrated *Prince*, enriched with citations from Tacitus and Juvenal and illuminating the central event of his drama.

The Florentine's aim in his analysis is to teach the prince how to protect himself from the dangers of such machinations. Plotters are lords or intimates of the monarch moved as often by too many benefits as too many injuries; such for example was Sejanus against Tiberius. They had been established by their emperors in such wealth, honor, and rank that they seemed to lack nothing to complete their power except the imperial rule. Ambitious to possess this also, they undertook to plot against their benefactor but met the destruction which their ingratitude merited. Therefore, Machiavelli warns, the prince must guard himself against conspiracies by fearing more those on whom he has conferred excessive favors than those to whom he has done excessive injuries. Those injured by him lack opportunity, but favorites abound in it; and the will is alike, for the desire to rule is as great or greater than that for vengeance. Consequently he ought to give only so much authority to his friends as to leave between it and the principate a certain interval, and in between something else to be desired.[5] This passage Jonson paraphrases in the crucial soliloquy of Tiberius after he has drawn Sejanus into revealing the energy of his ambitions:

> "They are the dreadfull Enemies, we raise
> "With fauors, and make dangerous with praise;
> "The Iniur'd by vs may haue will alike,
> "But 'tis the Fauorite hath the power to strike:
> "And Furie euer boyles more high, and strong,
> "Heat with Ambition, then Reuenge of wrong.
> "Tis then a part of supreame skill, to grace
> "No man too much; but hold a certaine space
> "Betweene th' ascenders Rise, and thine owne Flat,
> "Least, when all Rounds be reach'd, his ayme be that.
>                                             (III. 637-46)

It is hard to decide whether the completeness of the departure from Tacitus is more remarkable than the close adherence to Machiavelli's *Discourses*.

Jonson introduces Sejanus in Act I of the play at the height of his power. While the chorus moralize over the degeneracy of the new order, he demonstrates the swift and calculated efficiency that has raised him to his dominating position. He skillfully appraises the cluster of enemies, arranges an interview with the physician Eudemus, and sells to the highest bidder the office of tribune, as smooth in operation and as inhuman as a machine. To this efficiency and the authority it creates the chorus oppose only a helpless indignation; they lament that the office "*Rome*s generall suffrage gaue is now his sale" (I. 223). The violence of the contrast between the republican days and the evil present when "the noted *Pathike* of the time" (216) could make himself "the partner of the empire" (218) underlines the sinister authority of Sejanus. This menace calls up the question phrased by Arruntius, "Is there any step in state can make him higher?" (242). The answer of Silius, "Nothing but Emp'rour" (244), is a departure from Tacitus: by fixing attention on it Jonson gives the narrative suspense as to whether the usurper may frustrate the "Tirannes Artes" (70) of the prince. The playwright now introduces the concept of lineal succession and makes of Arruntius a spokesman of legitimacy, ready with his sword to protect the heirs to the throne. The horror of regicide expressed by the chorus is a strongly Jacobean, not a Tacitan, emotion.

Tacitus, enemy of absolute power, made no secret of the motive for what he wrote: to leave a record of the evil of tyranny as exemplified in the emperors from Tiberius to Domitian (*Annals*, I. 4-7) [6]. Machiavelli, even in the chapter which follows Tacitus more closely than any other, paints a glowing picture of the empire under the good princes to contrast it with the wickedness under the bad emperors (*Discourses*, I, chapter 10). He does not name Tiberius among the good or bad, but he observes that all emperors (with the exception of Titus) who acquired imperial power by inheritance were bad men, whereas those who acquired it through adoption were good. By implication Tiberius, adopted heir of Augustus, belonged with the latter. In the chapter on conspiracies (*Discourses*, III. 6) Machiavelli recommends to a Tiberius the steps he should take for protection against a Sejanus. [7]

Catching up Machiavelli's prescriptions, Jonson goes further and brings the sentiments of the alienated chorus into harmony with contemporary theory of the duty of subjects. For example, *An Homilie agaynst disobedience and wylful rebellion* (1572) teaches that "kynges and princes, as well the euyl as the good, do raigne by Gods ordinaunce, and that subiectes are bounden to obey them" (A ii^v). Even against "euyll gouernours: God forbyd" men should revolt, for "a rebell is worse then the worst prince, and rebellion worse then the worst gouernment of the worst prince" (B i^v). We can only "paciently suffer and obey suche as we deserue" (B iii^v), for "God (say the holye scriptures) maketh a wicked man to raigne for the sinnes of the people" (B ii): wherefore, "let vs turne from our sinnes vnto the Lorde with all our heartes, & he wyll turne the heart of the prince vnto our quiet & wealth" (B ii^v-iii). This declaration of hereditary absolutism received the uncompromising sanction of King James in *The True Law of Free Monarchies* (1603). The monarch, possessing unlimited authority over the goods and the lives of his subjects, is answerable for his acts to God alone, who "hath the only power to unmake him": even his crimes ("how wicked soever") do not make it "lawfull to them to shake off that curse at their owne hand, which God hath laid on them." [8] From the *Annals* to *Sejanus* we go from the horror of tyranny to the horror of tyrannicide.

At this point in the drama, however, the favorite moves the action forward with machine-like precision. The friendly loyalty feigned to and won from the physician Eudemus and the cold impassionation of the Princess Livia, wife of Tiberius's son Drusus, are ambitious steps effortlessly taken. The impression of colossal force deepens as Sejanus dismisses Eudemus with a cynical penetration of men's motives: "Ambition makes more trusty slaues, then Need" (366). A titan exulting in his titanism, he welcomes the prospect of teaching Fortune a lesson for her neglect. Here Jonson subverts the stoical indifference urged by Juvenal in the tenth Satire by means of Machiavelli's advice to the ambitious man (in chapter 25 of *The Prince*) to assault the goddess and dominate her. With prudential calculation Sejanus addresses not to Venus, but to Pallas his prayer for aid in learning (through Livia) the secrets of her husband. He looks to "wit" (373) to see him through.

When Tiberius comes on stage, therefore, chorus, protagonist, and action alike have prepared the spectator for disaster. Yet the emperor, from the beginning, is alert to the power of Sejanus and is thus no feeble antagonist. By flattering his vanity the favorite seeks to increase his own predominance; Tiberius parries the attempt by taking refuge in dissimulation. The 1605 Quarto emphasized with full notes (C2, n. a and n.c) the acid gibe of Tacitus that the emperor counted dissembling a virtue: Dio interprets this as due to his great fear of Sejanus (LVIII. 13. 1). But Jonson exhibits the tactic in the light of the warning to princes in Machiavelli's *Discourses* (III. 6) that dissimulation is a necessity for defense against the greatest of enemies, a conspiracy. They should seek to understand its exact character very well before they make an effort to avenge it and should measure carefully the circumstances of the conspirators against their own. If they find it great and powerful, they should never expose it until they are prepared with sufficient forces to crush it: by acting otherwise they uncover their own ruin. Therefore they must diligently practice dissimulation, lest the conspirators, seeing that they are discovered, and driven by necessity, act regardless of the outcome.[9] In *The Prince*, Machiavelli immortalizes this prescription in the famous image of the fox. The ruler, he notes, needs to be a fox so that he may know how to recognize traps. A prudent monarch, therefore, cannot and should not observe faith when such observance is to his disadvantage. Innumerable modern examples show that the prince who has best known how to act as a fox has come out best. But the one who has this capacity must be a skillful pretender and dissimulator.[10]

Thus, Tiberius feigns impatience at the servile prostration of Roman senators while Sejanus urges that such adoration is not blasphemy before godlike Caesar. Observing this, Arruntius voices the Tacitan theory of complicity in despotism between the flatterer and the monarch pretending anger; he directs the response of spectators according to the intention of the author: that Sejanus should firmly believe in this "confederacie" (385) is the purpose Tiberius has sought. The latter's insistence that he is only "the seruant of the *Senate*" (393) seems to Cordus rare dissimulation; from Arruntius it wrests the Machiavellian tribute, "Princelike, to the life" (395). The minatory comment, summed up in the gnome of Sabinus—"When power, that may command, so much descends,/Their bondage, whom it stoupes to, it intends" (396-97)—inculcates an awareness that the superiority of Sejanus is only apparent and that the counter-intrigue by Tiberius will be through indirection and subterfuge.

The emperor's piety ("Looke vp on vs, and fall before the gods," 375), therefore, must not deceive spectators, for it is an expedient borrowed from Machiavelli's advice to the prince to make a calculated parade of religion. The condemnation by Arruntius of the indifference of the gods "in these impious Times" (IV. 279) accords with Tacitus's attribution of the conspiracy of Tiberius and Sejanus to the anger of Heaven against Rome, whereas the consistent association of the emperor with religion is unhistorical. Suetonius explicitly declares that Tiberius denied a belief in the gods and was negligent about religious observances (*Tiberius*, LXIX). Much later in the play, Jonson puts the sentiment into the mouth of Terentius as a warning not to be, as Sejanus had been, "carelesse of the gods" (V. 599). The skeptic of Tacitus and Suetonius has become the ostentatiously pious prince of Machiavelli. On his first appearance Tiberius not only discourages the "flatteries" of prostration as to a god (I. 375), but also refuses to build temples for adoration of himself on the ground that it is a form of "pride": we, he sternly reminds the senate, "are mortal" (473, 477). Accordingly he protests, during the interview with the favorite about policy and state, on behalf of religious rites and religious thought (II. 175, 181). The reason he gives for his departure for Campania is not pleasure, but the dedication of temples (III. 671-75). The final note he sounds in the catastrophic "Epistle" in Act V is a reminder of his piety, which makes the killing of Sejanus a sacrifice to the gods (643-44).

Jonson's subversion of Tacitus here seems to derive from the counsel of Machiavelli in chapter eighteen of *The Prince*, "In What Way Faith ought to be Kept by Princes." Whether or not he possesses the virtues of compassion, humanity, honesty, faith, and religion, the ruler must seem to do so. He must say nothing that is not full of these five qualities, especially religion. For men in general judge more by their eyes than by their heads; everybody is fitted to see, few to understand. Ferdinand of Spain is instanced in chapter twenty-one as the example of a prince who put religion to use for the sake of great enterprises and turned to a pious cruelty so as to overawe and

97

manage his subjects.[11] Jonson emphasizes the appearance as opposed to the reality of Tiberius's piety when the latter removes his "masque" in the safe privacy of the interview with the favorite. (II. 279).

The perception of this disparity introduces a strong intellectual element in the use of Tacitus. Thus, in the first lengthy speech by the monarch (I. 439-502), the meaning conveyed by the playwright lies in the calculated deception of his language. With becoming but actually mock humility, he describes himself as the "creature" of the senate, to which as "a good, and honest Prince" he owes his office; the only glory he aspires to is to be "truely a Prince." At the climax of this indirection he utters a maxim drawn from Tacitus speaking in his own person, "Contempt of fame begets contempt of vertue" (502). Jonson, by transferring it to the monarch detested by the historian, achieves an incidental irony which may appeal to the informed reader, but he stresses its primary value as a maneuver in the mortal combat with Sejanus. As the favorite leads the claque of loud flatterers, the muted chorus emphasize the craft of Tiberius: "more cunning, and fine words" (506). With fulsome praise the emperor formally recognizes "our *Seianus*" as the "associate of our labors" (519, 529) and tantalizes him with the promise of public honors for this "great aide of *Rome*" (528). The irony is delicious when Tiberius expresses a disarming concern to persuade the usurper to accept them. But a subdued ominousness is implicit in the irony since the mood of the present occasion is a direct foreshadowing of the "Epistle" scene in Act V.

The exaltation of Tiberius's minion is a sinister effect contrived by the emperor to outwit his enemies. The chorus, thrown off by the devious move, are almost speechlessly indignant; Arruntius can only protest, *"Cae-sar"* (541). Drusus, son of the emperor, explodes a volley of angry questions, denouncing a Sejanus now puffed by pride to the dimensions of a *"Colossus"* (564). He strikes the favorite in a buzz of acclamation for this expression of the senate's resentment. In other words, the political stroke contrived by the emperor produces deviously calculated results. It diverts upon Sejanus the violent opposition of Drusus and the senate, and upon Drusus the pent-up hatred of the ambitious schemer. The lesson from Machiavelli that Jonson employed for the maxim on the tyrant's arts at line seventy of Act I serves to guide the spectator's interpretation of events, especially the real aims masked by the ambiguous practices of the antagonist.

In Act II, therefore, Sejanus studies retaliation against Drusus. In the seduction of Livia, the control of the deceptive fervor of his language by elaborate rhetorical patterns warns the spectator to maintain an ironic attentiveness. The physician Eudemus secured and Livia corrupted, Sejanus sets the fatal trap for Drusus with their connivance. The trivial scene that follows, in which the doctor prescribes cosmetics for the princess, has a dramatic function in the maintenance of an intellectual detachment that differs fundamentally from the emotions appropriate to tragedy. The abrupt contrast of these frivolous details to the deadly action anticipates the vein of serious farce in *Volpone*,[12] and the ironic plight of characters whose expectation is in disharmony with the issue.

"Light *Liuia*" (II. 398), as Sejanus sneeringly names her, has unwittingly aided the usurper. The vein of serious farce continues in his boasts that adultery is "the lightest Ill" (150) he will commit and in the sardonic comment on the foolish gullibility of his mistress. The

99

method employed by Jonson is instructive: he adapts the words of Seneca's *Thyestes* to a wholly original dramatic purpose. The lust that is the driving motive for these actions is much greater than sex and greater even than vengeance over Drusus; it is the lust of a human being for superhuman power. The hyperbolic irony of the plot to use a personal vendetta as a step in the imperial ambition prepares the spectator for the inevitable checkmate. The challenge to the gods as Sejanus exhorts his soul to

> Tell proud *Ioue*,
> Betweene his power, and thine, there is no oddes,
> Twas only Feare, first in the world made Gods (160-62),

is a blasphemous aphorism in sharp contrast with the piety of the emperor. In setting insolence against cunning, Jonson develops suspense as to the practical issue. The chorus had feared that the orthodoxy of Tiberius's utterance was a mask for conspiracy; hence an element in the suspense is the offchance that Tiberius may enlist our moral sympathy as well as our intellectual admiration. Is the chorus right? Will the hated favorite connive with the evil monarch to victimize the Roman state? Does the emperor wear merely the semblance of virtue? Will Sejanus, greater virtuoso in depravity, beguile and betray the monarch? Or will the cunning of the master overmatch the cunning of the minion? When? These questions are implicit in the interview between the adversaries about "pollicie, and state" (171), which is one of Jonson's more considerable additions to the narrative of Tacitus.

This dialogue (II. 163-370) follows the dramatic outline of the tyrant's maxims in Seneca, but the essential material comes from Machiavelli.[13] Jonson transfers the

100

maxims from the Senecan tyrant to his protagonist, who uses them to overcome the reluctance of the emperor for actions which (in the words of Tiberius) "nature, bloud, and lawes of kinde forbid" (170). Structurally the exchanges here look back to the first dissembling appearance of the emperor in Act I when he maneuvered, cautious and inscrutable, for a defense amidst the dangers of the court; and they look forward to his "Epistle" to the senate at the end of Act V. The brutal tactics counselled by the favorite, waxing urgent and then confident as the seemingly humane Tiberius feigns complete submission to the bolder spirit, stand out in grim and ironic reminiscence when Tiberius has judged that Fortune favors a decisive counter-stroke. In Act II Jonson assigns to Sejanus the exposition of amoral "pollicie" or "slight" as he defines it in line 266, in harmony with the ironic conception of the role: accordingly it is Sejanus who insists on the propriety of the tyrant's stratagems, whereas it is the reluctant emperor who actually applies the methods that enmesh the contriver in ruin.

Tiberius opens the interview with a disarming condescension. Encouraged, Sejanus advises the suppression of enemies by any means: "State is inough to make th' act iust, them guilty" (173). This echoes, not Seneca, but *The Discourses*, where Machiavelli provides the only explicit statement of the famous assumption basic to *The Prince* as well. It is very necessary, the Florentine writes, that a reprehensible deed should be justified by its effect. If that is good, it will always justify it. For the one who uses violence to destroy, not the one who uses it to mend things, must be reprehended.[14] Persuaded as though he were the prudent organizer of a state whom Machiavelli had in mind and whose intention it is to govern not in his own interests but for the common good, Tiberius prepares for active effort, working through his agent. At first this is simple assent to the ruthless methods argued in pithy rules. He takes cajoling care to request the advice of his "comfort" (165), who confidently and blindly gives precisely the instructions Tiberius wishes him to apply, to strike down Silius and Cordus in the senate. In a triumph of the candor that disarms, he seems to remove "our masque to thee, our deare *Seianus*" (279). The sardonic ambiguity of the Greek quotation on his exit suggests both his impenetrability and a superior wit. The irony gleams conspicuously through the self-satisfaction which Sejanus takes in his success at frightening the monarch into crushing the favorite's enemies, "Which I alone, could not remooue with safety" (393). A satiric reversal of the precept out of *The Prince*, this would teach the minister how to use the tyrant to destroy opponents.

The dramatic function of the chorus on its reappearance in Act II is the restatement of a theme iterated throughout the play, the isolation from ordinary humanity of the titans locked in a struggle for survival. Act III seems designed in part to show that the author has taken seriously the advice of Horace to give the chorus a strenuous part in the action.[15] First Silius and then Cordus are both interpreters of the action and actors in the plot; the survivors return to the primary purpose of commentary. This stresses the ambiguous policy of Tiberius. On the one hand he works through his favorite to destroy obstructive senators like Silius; on the other he exhibits a noble mastery of grief over the death of Drusus and commends to the senate's care the issue of Germanicus. Arruntius calls him "*Sphinx*" (65) whose "Subtlety" (147) dominates the occasion. Sejanus openly exults over the death of Silius, whereas the emperor deplores "this sad accident," which has forestalled his intended mercy to the "noble *Romane*" (344, 346); and he agrees to save a portion of the estate for the dead man's family: therein, as Lepidus notes, "the *Prince* shall shew humanity" (362). The cupidity which Tacitus ascribed to the emperor in these events (*Annals*, IV. 20) has been displaced by a dictum from *The Prince*.[16] In this series of episodes full of rapid action and frequent shifts of emotion, he is the master of the situation, diverting the heavy odium to his minister.

The second dialogue between Tiberius and Sejanus (III. 488-585) has a salient difference from the first. Here Jonson portrays a favorite so exultant in his confidence that he ignores potential danger. The emperor, on the other hand, is careful to defer to his "Dearest head" (501) and ultimately traps the swelling conqueror into disclosing the ambition that leads to his ruin. Presenting his claims to be "worthy his alliance" (514), he argues that as "*Caesars* friend" (520) he deserves to be Livia's husband. The monarch forestalls any penetration of his mask by the craftily non-committal exclamation of surprise, "H'mh" (515), and contents his "Most-loud *Seianus*" (531) with the flattering but empty promise to consider the proposal. His warning about the pitfalls of such an exalted marriage seems to show an almost paternal solicitude, and he lulls the favorite when he declares that he not "Aduerse" to "*Liuia's* designments" or "thine" (567), "our lou'd *Seianus*" (572), and pledges public benefits to "make thee aequall to vs" (570). The trickery of the insolent man by the appearance of helpless dependence and friendly anxiety is another aspect of Jonson's rewriting of Roman history. He interprets the emperor's decision to follow his

103

favorite's "late aduise" (581) and seek the relaxations of Capreae as an aspect of dissimulation.

The favorite's exclamation when alone on stage, "Dull, heauie *Caesar!*" (586), indicates a blind misjudgment of his despised benefactor. Whereas the Sejanus of the *Annals* at this point in his career went in fear of his life, Jonson's figure congratulates himself on a stratagem which, since direct attack is suicidal, will imprison the "Voluptuous *Caesar*" in fleshly excitements and thus betray his "stupide powers" to "Security" and the neglect of "*Publique* Cares" (599-601). The playwright has found a clear explanation for what Tacitus leaves enigmatic in Machiavelli's chapter on conspiracies in *The Discourses* (III. 6). The passage that centers on Sejanus and Tiberius says that the lust for rule blinds men and then blinds them further in the conduct of the plot, for if they knew how to go about their wickedness with prudence it would be impossible for them not to succeed. But Sejanus, blinded by ambition, allowed himself to be outmaneuvered and exposed.[17]

Since the narrative of Tacitus ends here and since Dio, Suetonius, and Juvenal do not tell the exact course of events, Jonson has no historical warrant for shifting the initiative so decisively to the aroused but still prudent monarch, who shows none of the fears and inward tortures, the vacillating and hesitation of his original. Jonson portrays an alert and energetic prince who weighs the danger from the faction of Agrippina against the threat of Sejanus's ambition and who when he finds that Fortune smiles takes instant action. The discernment of Tiberius in the play rests on the chapter in *The Prince* on the reliability of ministers. One way of knowing a minister never fails the prince: when you see him thinking more of himself than of you and in all his action seeking his own advantage—you know you can never trust him. The one who directs the government ought never to think of himself, but of the prince, and should never remember anything that does not concern him. Jonson's monarch, confirmed in his distrust by Sejanus's self-aggrandizing demand for Livia's hand, conceals his intention by persevering in the journey to Capreae and seizes the opportunity which Fortune has offered.[18] He counter-schemes by setting Macro against the favorite on the principle that "while two poysons wrastle, we may liue" (654), a sardonic echo of Sejanus's trust in ambition for the loyalty of the physician Eudemus (I. 366).

The two interviews between protagonist and antagonist record turning-points in the plot closely associated with fundamental shifts in feeling. Instructed by Arruntius and the chorus, spectators have learned to look on events with emotional detachment, despite the residual Tacitan gloom, and to enjoy the status of ironical observers. The duel enacted in their presence inspires the pleasure of intellectual recognition rather than suspense of interest or emotional sympathy for the oddly matched contestants. Despite the shrill denunciations (from Tacitus and Juvenal) of the chorus, the Tacitan monster emerges as the successful Machiavellian prince whose conduct of the duel and whose defensive skill in dissimulation arouse a sardonic admiration. Jonson, like Aristotle, lays great stress on surprise and on the peripety, which brings about an action just the reverse of that intended by the agent Sejanus. The chief function of the chorus is as commentator, satirically observant but not anticipating the surprises of events. The play seems to take a course, in spite of the refractory materials of history, radically transforming it from a "tragedy" about the "fall" of Sejanus into a vulpine comedy of wits engaged in deadly opposition, which spectators appreciate with objective and intellectualized responses.[19]

Act IV is remarkable for the absence of the protagonists; nevertheless, the action suggests a gradual domination of events by Tiberius. Jonson makes free departures from his source in order to intensify the menacing power of the favorite, which the chorus regard as unassailable. Thus he holds spectators in suspense as to the outcome of the duel with the emperor. The news that Sejanus has saved the life of Tiberius at Spelunca increases this anxiety. The apparent triumph, however, drives Macro to strike "the foremost blow" (92), the nature of which and the moment he keeps secret. The betrayal of Sabinus, although it is ineffectual as a defense for Sejanus, serves to deepen the dismay of the chorus, speaking for normal well-intentioned humanity in the perilous struggle. In Tacitus, Sabinus had denounced both the emperor and the favorite; Jonson centers his outspokenness on Sejanus. The favorite's impiety shocks Arruntius into admonishing the sleeping Jove: "Must vile *Seianus* pull thee by the beard?" (267) True, Silius, Cordus, and Sabinus have perished. But the opposition to Sejanus grows; Macro waits to strike; on Capreae Tiberius lays his plot to overreach him.

The arrest of Agrippina and her sons, by which Tiberius (working through Sejanus) has removed a dangerous faction, is a new shock to Arruntius. It is apparent proof that "our Night-ey'd *Tiberius*" can not see "his minion's drifts" (363-64); in exasperation he would almost welcome the spectacle of the "Mungrill" Sejanus leaping for the emperor's throat (366). Lepidus reminds him that they owe "Zeale, And Duty, with the thought, *He is our Prince*" (371-72). Arruntius retorts, "He is our Monster"

(373), "An Emp'ror only in his lusts" (376). He substantiates the sentiment by the famous catalogue of alarming relaxations contrived by Tiberius on Capreae. He has abdicated his office to a hideously wicked minister and "with all his craft, become the Ward To his owne Vassall" (403-04). Lepidus thereupon outlines an explanation unwarranted by history but valuable in foreshadowing the catastrophe. The emperor, he argues, has observed and parried the ambitious schemes of the favorite. For instance, the successive contradictory letters sent from Capreae to the senate "cannot bee Empty of practice: Tis *Tiberius* Art" (453). Jonson uses them to arouse uneasiness among the followers of Sejanus; Dio explicitly declares that their effect was to make the favorite waver between extreme elation and extreme fear (LVIII. 6.3). Prudently avoiding "an open Contestation," Lepidus continues, the emperor follows "this doubling line" through "*Subtilty*" (464-65) and so keeps the advantage. Meanwhile, Tiberius,

> By his employments, makes him odious
> Vnto the staggering Rout, whose aide (in fine)
> He hopes to vse, as sure, who (when they sway)
> Beare downe, oreturne all Obiects in their way.
>
> (IV. 469-72)

In this exposition the "Tirannes Artes" denounced by Sabinus at I. 70 have become praiseworthy deeds whose result justifies them. Jonson reflects a knowledge of the procedure of Cesare Borgia, who gave full power to the vigorous but cruel Remirro de Orco in the effort to pacify and unite the region of the Romagna. Knowing that the severity of his minister had generated hatred, the duke decided to purge the minds of the people and gain them altogether for himself by showing that if any cruelty had

107

occurred it did not originate with him but with his minister. He exhibited in the piazza the decapitated body of Remirro with a piece of wood and a bloody knife beside him. The savagery of the spectacle caused the people to remain at one and the same time astonished and satisfied.[20]

Lepidus's intellectual rehabilitation of the moral "monster" is too shockingly novel for Arruntius to accept. Why, he asks, should not "a politique Tryanne (Who can well disguise it)" (IV. 474-75) choose the direct path of accusation and legal execution? Lepidus stresses the need of cunning, for "his Feare Would neere be masq'd" (477-78). Act IV closes on the confusion among the ominously uncertain followers of Sejanus, who find reassurance in Tiberius's praise of their master as *"The Partner of his Cares, and his Seianus"* (484). On the face of it this is a flattering repetition of the emperor's condescension at his first appearance in the play (I. 529), but the touch of irony given it by Lepidus's analysis creates a grim expectancy in the reader. The playwright can be observed feeling his way through an experiment in dramatic effect. Again restraining the audience from tragic sympathy with the protagonist, he induces a detached and objective state of mind necessary to the enjoyment of the struggle where power contends with guile, wolf with fox.

How will the favorite meet the new crisis? Infatuation blinds him. He derides the piety urged by Terentius, in a travesty of Machiavelli's advice:

> What excellent fooles
> *Religion* makes of men! Beleeues Terentius,
> (If these were daungers, as I shame to thinke them)
> The *Gods* could change the certaine course of *Fate?*
> (V. 69-72)

His unlimited "desires" (10) tempt him to challenge Olympus; he worships Fortune alone and impious even in the ceremonies of piety grudgingly agrees to calm the fears of his adherents by sacrifice to her. She averts her face; he ridicules the "peeuish gigglot" (206) and ignores the meaning of her indifference. To such unlimited desire for acquiring more than the capacity to get, Machiavelli had traced the variations of Fortune and the instability of things. He says (in *The Discourses*) that since the desire to acquire is always greater than the power to do so, the result is a dissatisfaction with what one possesses: from this there arise the variations of Fortune. Hence the Florentine advises men never to risk all their Fortune with only part of their forces, for such procedure would not be wise.[21] Sejanus ignores at the very time the emperor profits by these counsels of prudence. In the soliloquy after the dismissal of his followers, a momentary perception of danger yields to the habit of gloating over success: "all the world haue seene/*Ioue*, but my equall; *Caesar*, but my Second" (263-64). In this mood he struts to his confusion.

Meanwhile the emperor, acting through his secret agent Macro, has set a fatal trap. The first unexpected blow, calling the senate together in the temple of Apollo, strikes sudden fear into Sejanus lest it "hath some streine of Engin in 't" (298). Too late the insolent man ingratiates himself with his followers and renews their slipping loyalty. Can he disarm Macro? On the contrary, the latter counters his pretense of friendship with hints of high honors to be presented to him in the senate, where they will be "more full, and striking" (344). Exultant and curious, Sejanus presses him to explain "the business meant" (357). Macro's thrust thus comes at the effective moment: "The *Tribun-*

*iciall* Dignity, and Power" (363). Sejanus forgets all caution in proud jubilation; he scorns the "prodigious Signes" from those whom "fooles call *Gods*" (390-91) and by setting out for the temple steps into the trap.

To Arruntius and Lepidus, however, the apparently strengthened position of the favorite is a source of bitter comment. Arruntius's epithet "huge *Seianus*" (433) matches the term "*Colossus*" used earlier by Drusus (I. 564) in an ironic reversal: the one marks a step in his rise, the other his overthrow. The unanimous sycophancy of the Conscript Fathers is not suggestive of impending catastrophe, and Lepidus expresses amazement at "this rising" (440). Arruntius sarcastically describes it as a way "to make his fall more steepe and greiuous" (441). In the same ironic vein the fawning of the senators implies an illusory achievement by Sejanus of greater dominance. This apparent restoration to power recalls to Arruntius and Lepidus the earlier mood of all-encompassing danger. As in Act I, the chorus are conspicuously apart from the throng that hails the conquering hero, and as before give expression to a moral detachment. But instead of the monstrous efficiency of Sejanus at his height, it is Macro whose ominous action symbolizes the impending trap: he orders the doors of the temple closed.

The "Epistle" of Tiberius (V. 546-649), which the assembly clamors to hear, becomes in Jonson's reconstruction the dramatic correlative of the executioner's sword.[22] The emperor has tricked his enemy into an ambush which he has set with such skill as to conceal its deadliness until he has completely disarmed the victim. To convey this interpretation, Jonson again assigns to the chorus a didactic function. Thus, when Tiberius disclaims any wish to retaliate for the libels on his retirement to Capreae "*since*

110

*in a free State (as ours) all men ought to enioy both their mindes and tongues free,"* Arruntius defines his aim by whispering, "(The Lapwing, the Lapwing)": the comparison is to the bird which, by crying at a distance from its nest, lures searchers away from it. The emperor then draws attention to his promotion of Sejanus from obscurity to greatness, and the senators exclaim, "How! How!" He notes the danger to a monarch in loving one subject at the risk of hatred of all others. The effect of this cryptic statement Arruntius describes in the words, "This Touches, the blood turnes." Nevertheless, the emperor protests that the merit of *"our Seianus"* makes the favor he enjoys offensive to no one; the senate breathes relief, "O good, good." Yet Tiberius wishes that Sejanus had been less zealous against Agrippina and her sons since that *"loyall fury"* makes his own *"clemencie"* now seem *"but wearied cruelty."* This thrust excites the admiration of Arruntius: "I thanke him, there I look'd for 't. A good Foxe!" Craftily conceding that the favorite's severity might be interpreted as *"particular ambition,"* the emperor counts the steps by which Sejanus climbed to the height where he aspired *"to be our Sonne in law."* At this thunderbolt the senate murmurs uneasily, and Arruntius inclines to accept Lepidus's praise (in Act IV) of Tiberius's art.

For the moment the emperor calms this uneasiness by pretending to reject any suspicion of imperial ambition in Sejanus. The senate releases a sigh, "O he has restor'd all, List." Troubled nonetheless by reports of reliable informers, the emperor is unable to escape the conclusion that he has placed his benefits ill: so that in the choice of Sejanus, *"either wee were wanting to the GODS, or the GODS to vs."* The carefully prepared and yet sudden revelation is like a fiery blast, and Arruntius describes the effect of

111

panic: "The place growes hot, they shift." The emperor justifies his change of attitude by sound statecraft, by *"those needfull Ialousies of state, that warne wiser Princes, howrely, to prouide their safety"* and that teach a constant vigilance toward even the humblest enemy, but much more toward *"those great ones, whom their owne emploid fauours haue made fit for their feares."* The flatterers break from the ring about Sejanus as Arruntius comments, "Gods, how the leaues drop off, this little winde!" Haterius, kept "most miserably constant" by gout, adds farce to the calamitous scene. The blow falls and wrings a cry of incredulous despair from the confident protagonist caught in his enemy's snare.

Stripped of power and isolated by the arrest of trusted followers, he is at the mercy of the senatorial mob whom the cunningly sanctimonious emperor begs leave to remind of their pious duty: *"how much they hurt the innocent, that spare the guilty: and how gratefull a sacrifice, to the gods is the life of an ungratefull person."* The crushing irony of the pose is unanswerable. Macro leads the fallen favorite to the hideous dismemberment. The "Epistle," famous but unsubstantiated by the records, becomes in Jonson's interpretation a cleverly manipulated weapon that destroys the insolent protagonist. When the stage has emptied, Arruntius and Lepidus remain behind to deliver a kind of epilogue that clarifies and reiterates the central issue, the triumph of statecraft over power by the successful application of those "Tirannes Artes" (I. 70) on which the chorus had fixed our attention at the beginning of the play.

112

## Chapter 6

# VOLPONE: THE COMEDY OF MACHIAVELLIAN IRONY

In *Volpone* (1605) Jonson gives a satiric salute to the author of *The Prince* when Sir Politic Would-Be advises Peregrine to conform his behavior to the "lawes o' th' land" since "NIC. MACHIAVEL" was "of this minde." [1] This farcical distortion is in harmony with the echoes of the Florentine that resound in the comedy. The satiric reading of that author by his fellow dramatists was, indeed, a congenial challenge to the ironist in Jonson. As it happened, his researches for *Sejanus* proved a useful preparation also for a comedy of intrigue. Having assimilated to Roman history the chapter on conspiracies in *The Discourses*, he perceived the rudiment of a drama in the repeated warning of the danger always present when one confederate draws into his plot another who at any time may turn out to be treacherous.[2] This danger underlies the entire action of the play, and the "Argument" sets the tone, from the very beginning, for an ironic enjoyment by the spectator of the cross-plots and the reciprocal temptations of master and parasite.

In Act I, scene 1, a new day gilds the treasure chest which is the precious shrine that opens on Volpone's "saint"—that is, "my gold"—and he falls before it in mocking adoration:

> Haile, the worlds soule, and mine; . . .
>     Thou art vertue, fame,
> Honour, and all things else! who can get thee,
> He shall be noble, valiant, honest, and wise—

Mosca breaks in with an unctuously pat epigram in which the faintest trace of malice is a characteristically sly enjoyment of the master's confident trust:

>         Riches are in fortune
> A greater good, then wisdome is in nature.

From this point to the unmasking soliloquy of Act III, scene 1, the parasite arouses an intense speculation in the "attentiue auditors" to whom the playwright appeals for understanding.[3] The problem hinted at is the reliability of a trusted servant: whether devoted service to his master or devoted self-service characterizes his actions.[4] Volpone ignores this dilemma by reason of his conviction that he has shared his plot only with a man whose fidelity he has thoroughly tested for a long time and (more important) whose end is the same as his own. His candid trust, furthermore, violates prudence and defies the warning to beware a simulated loyalty in a fellow plotter.[5] He also relies on Fortune, seizing the opportunity for "the cunning purchase of my wealth" and complacently welcoming "all delights" to which she calls him. This blind confidence in the benignity of a notoriously fickle deity is a comic transposition of the fatal insolence of Sejanus, and it inspires an ironic reflection in the audience.[6]

In the same mood, Volpone prides himself on using "No common way" to increase his riches, whereupon Mosca, with the same sly enjoyment, comments that his "sweet nature" abhors the miser's way of coffining men alive

> In some kind, clasping prison, where their bones
> May be forth-comming, when their flesh is rotten.

This delicate mockery is the first hint of the *catastrophe* and suggests that the fellow conspirator has already planned his fox-trap, waiting to spring it as fickle Fortune turns her smile on him. He seeks to dull the magnifico's awareness by imprisoning him in the kind of voluptuous bondage in which Sejanus sought to trap Tiberius. He defines the character of a sensualist who, as he flatters his master, does "know the vse of riches", and yet he invites the audience by his indirection to share his private joke. The sudden appeal for the master's generosity "to me, your poore obseruer" loses conventional flatness in its delusive hypocrisy.[7] The same tone informs his pathetic picture of Volpone as living on amidst an infinity of presents long after his own death:

> And that, when I am lost in blended dust,
> And hundred such, as I am in succession.
>
> (I. 2. 119-20)

The deliciously tell-tale insincerity keeps alive the speculation as to what unexpected realignment of forces the dissembling servant can muster against the unsuspecting master.

Jonson combines this mockery with the exaggerations of caricature in the series of sketches with which Mosca welcomes the legacy-hunters. Ostensibly seeking their good will, he plays on their greed and credulity and at the same time anatomizes the corruptions that blacken their conduct. He assures the first of these, the advocate Voltore (I. 3), that his "desert" is the reason for Volpone's favor. In calculated deception of language, he then draws a portrait of a venal lawyer who merits derisive tribute as one able to

> Giue forked counsell; take prouoking gold
> On either hand, and put it vp.

The swelling gull royally promises, "we shall requite it."

Next, Corbaccio (I. 4) tempts Mosca to inflate caricature with mordant hyperbole. The "old rauen" in his grossness and senility—the deafness, the croaking voice, the cackle, the spectacles and the cane for shuffling lamely along—is an especially egregious *commedia dell' arte* pantaloon. The parasite has told his master,

> You know, this hope
> Is such a bait, it couers any hooke;

and he demonstrates the power of avarice by a shameless proposal. Stimulating Corbaccio to a competition in greed, he displays Voltore's present and persuades him to name Volpone the heir to his wealth and thus disinherit his own son. The moral ugliness of the intention stands out conspicuously against Mosca's recital of Bonario's virtues, and the dodderer deepens this by the cynical pretext that he will thereby multiply the inheritance of the youth. Here the physical decay is a manifestation of spiritual decline, a spectacle savored by Volpone as his own blind-

116

ness creates a double irony apposite to speaker and subject alike:

> What a rare punishment
> Is auarice, to it selfe?

Finally, the merchant Corvino (I. 5) provides Mosca with the occasion for restating the theme of voluptuousness on which he builds the temptation of his master. The parasite greets the jealous husband with a summary of Volpone's career as a sexual sinner who has scattered his bastards profligately and keeps only his monstrous sub-parasites as "his family". But the legacy-hunter, tricked by Mosca's example, first delivers a series of hollow sneers at the helpless senility of the supposedly dying man. Then he inadvertently provides the sensual bait that Mosca dangles before Volpone in the image of his beautiful wife. Tantalized, the voluptuary momentarily undermines the conspiracy that the two have richly exploited, by his haste to follow the lure. Leaving the safety of his sick-bed to enact the triumphs of the mountebank scene (II. 2), he surrenders to Celia's beauty, wounded at heart. He places himself (II. 4) at the mercy of his "better Angell," [8] as he calls Mosca, and presses his keys on him, together with his "Gold, plate and iewells, all's at thy deuotion." The temptation has completely submerged the prudence especially necessary to the judgment of a fellow conspirator.

This unwitting surrender to the latter's plot inspires a comment marked by the characteristic delicate indirection when he tells Volpone, "I would/Escape your *epilogue*." He promises, of course, to aid his master with all his "art", Jonson's subtler term for the hackneyed "policy" of stage Machiavels. Volpone understands it as a maneuver to enmesh Celia, whereas the audience sees also that it denotes Mosca's secret purpose. It is a matter of interest that the burning impatience of the stricken voluptuary is an ironic rejection of the solemn caution in *The Prince* against any traffic with one's subjects' women.[9] Perhaps Corvino's trading of wife for wealth shows that in the playwright's judgment the Florentine underestimated human greed.

Toward this unwitting partner, Mosca again adopts the satiric tone employed in the introduction of the legacy-hunters. His description of "some yong woman" (II. 6) to "preserue" Volpone, preferably "Some simple thing, a creature made vnto it;/Some wench you may command," is an ironic summary of Celia's character which the husband endorses. When he hesitates, though only briefly, to prostitute his own wife, Mosca utters a moral sneer behind which lurks the intellectual pleasure of manipulating a gull: " 't had beene done before,/But for your scrupulous doubts." Missing the derision, the other agrees, with unconscious irony, "I, plague on 't,/My conscience fooles my wit." Consequently he insists on full credit for the scheme, begging the parasite to swear that the suggestion was of "Mine owne free motion." From entirely different motives these conspirators collaborate to set the stage for the voluptuous entanglement of Volpone.

Mosca clarifies the hints of double-dealing by a soliloquy (III. 1) in which he removes his mask. With animation and a contemptuous ease in the miming of his role, he expresses a confident delight in the success of his performance. He commends his "most prosp'rous parts", concedes that "Successe hath made me wanton" and humorously fears the growth of self-love. His definition of "true Parasites" is an ironic subversion of the test put forward

118

in *The Prince* to tell the faithful servant from the flatterer.[10] Free of cramping restrictions, Mosca says,

> O! Your Parasite
> Is a most precious thing, dropt from aboue,
> Not bred 'mongst clods.

Such a "fine, elegant rascall" is an accomplished dissembler who can

> Present to any humour, all occasion;
> And change a visor, swifter, then a thought!

This serpentine flatterer possesses an inborn talent for intrigue: he "doth practice it/Out of most excellent nature." Such unmasked self-interest enlivens the ironic speculations of the audience in the midst of Volpone's amorous siege.

Jonson at once substantiates these claims. He meets the son of Corbaccio (III. 2), and Bonario (whose name means simpleton) denounces a parasite for the commonplace vices of servility, sloth, flattery and gluttony, which Mosca in his soliloquy had scornfully renounced. Pretending an injured innocence, he protests to heaven that such imputations are "eas'ly stuck on vertue, when she's poore." He plays with insolent skill upon the young simpleton with that practical hypocrisy which Machiavelli had singled out for notice in the diplomacy of Ferdinand the Catholic.[11] Mosca's virtuous defense, supported by tears and oaths by St. Mark, disarms Bonario. Thereupon the beautifully constructed façade of dissimulation deceives the youth into becoming an unwitting confederate. Mosca admits that "strong necessitie" forces him to get his meager bread and his poor raiment with obsequiousness. But he denies that he has performed any base offices such as

> Diuiding families, betraying counsells,
> Whispering false lyes, or mining men with praises,
> Train'd their credulitie with periuries,
> Corrupted chastitie, or am in loue
> With mine owne tender ease, . . .
> Let me here perish, in al hope of goodnesse.

The bold irony of an actual assertion of deeds done, under an apparent repudiation, deludes the credulous Bonario into forgiveness. The climactic hyperbole of dissimulation occurs when Mosca betrays Corbaccio's intention to disinherit his son. He does this, he smoothly explains, through disinterested "hatred of wrong", moved thereto by the "goodnesse and true vertue" of the youth. The latter's guileless disbelief that his father could be so unnatural prolongs Mosca's amusement in hypocrisy. This disbelief, he urges, bespeaks "Your pietie" or filial duty and "your owne simple innocence," an ironic translation of the name Bonario that inspires a secret laugh. Nevertheless, he has made the son ready to eavesdrop on Volpone and Corbaccio and serve as his agent. As a consequence, Bonario when troubled by "doubt" (III 7), is able to make free of Volpone's house.

Meanwhile, Corvino has dragged Celia (III. 7) to the sickroom, to Mosca's feigned consternation: " 'did ere man haste so, for his hornes?" The husband assails her with an appeal to virtuous scruples whose hollowness the parasite emphasizes by an ironic endorsement. The obedience due to a husband from his wife, her obligation to assist him in his affairs and her loyalty—all should make her eager for this charitable prostitution. As for "honour", which she pleads, it is only a breath, "a mere term/Inuented to awe fooles." As for her "fame", that objection is farcical: Volpone cannot reveal the deed and Mosca is bribed into silence. The lurking Bonario underlines this conspirator's misplaced trust! As for "heauen, and saints", who (as she protests) will not be blind to sin, Corvino retorts that "if I thought it were a sinne,/I would not vrge you." But this, he argues, this is

> A pious worke, mere charity, for physick,
> And honest politie, to assure mine owne.

Honest polity—the paradox is a ludicrously garbled reminiscence of *The Prince* and *The Discourses*. The entire dialogue between husband and wife is a domestic recapitulation of the first interview between Tiberius and Sejanus (*Sejanus*, II. 163-70), where the clinching sophism is the famous principle that the end justifies the means.[12] Corvino's way of restating it is, "the necessitie of those meanes,/For my recouery." Thus does the scholarly Jonson make an ironic assimilation to the dramatic moment of Machiavellian thought.

How base those means are, Mosca stresses with brutal candor as he ushers the husband in to Volpone as one "come to offer,/Or rather, sir, to prostitute—" Here the wittol interrupts with comic officiousness, "Thankes, sweet Mosca," before the parasite can add, "His owne most faire and proper wife." Significantly, his reminder to Corvino that "now you' haue put your fortune in her hands" stresses for the audience the tension created by the fragility of his counter-intrigue. All this time the mag-

121

nifico has thoroughly appreciated a dissimulation so assiduously abetted by its victim, and he adds a touch by the pretense that the girl has come too late to be a "comfortesse" in his dying condition. With the words, " 'Tis a vaine labour, eene to fight, 'gainst heauen," he mocks Corvino's headlong plunge into moral subversion.

Alone with Celia, Volpone assures her that only her beauty could force him to leave his "practice". He thus unwittingly confirms the success with which Mosca's counter-intrigue has diverted his mind and his energies from the conspiracy.[13] As she begs on her knees for the bounty of death—a comic Lucrece whose name means joke—he refuses any longer "To play with opportunity." Ironically, however, Fortune has changed even as he persists in following his original course. She turns against him as Bonario rescues the girl.[14] The structural climax, thus, embodies Machiavelli's theory of the goddess; for *The Prince*, while counseling a bold assault on Fortune because she is a woman, warns that occasion as well as opportunity must offer grounds for success.[15] The hypocritical grief of the self-wounded Mosca (III. 8) over the result of what he calls his "error" disarms Volpone, who extends a comically appropriate sympathy, "Woe, on thy fortune." Mosca's spirit is sardonic as he savors a private delight from the teasing question, "Who would haue thought, he would haue harken'd so?" The malicious epigram, "Guilty men/Suspect, what they deserue still," prolongs his master's fears and his own enjoyment.

Mosca, nevertheless, seems to direct the return of Corbaccio and Voltore (III. 9) to a revival of the conspiracy against the legacy-hunters. On his report of Bonario's attack, the father justifies his immoral deed by moral indignation:

> This act, shall disinherit him indeed:
> Here is the will.

Overhearing this, Voltore shakes the plot by suspecting Mosca of trickery. The parasite quiets him by an appeal to greed, swearing by his "conscience" that

> My onely ayme was, to dig you a fortune
> Out of these two, old rotten sepulchers.

The satisfaction of the advocate is crucial, for they depend on him to prepare the defense of Volpone from the accusation of Bonario. Now eager to do so, he calls for all to meet at the Scrutineo for the trial. Responding to Mosca's suggestion that he pray for their success, Volpone expresses in a wry maxim—"Neede makes deuotion: heauen your labor blesse"—his deepened reliance on a treacherous confederate.

For the parasite's plans throw an ironic light on the imprudence of this reliance. In outlining the tactics for the defense (IV. 4), he draws the gulls to the support of Volpone in a wider and more dangerous plot against the state. In a republic already corrupt, as Machiavelli showed, the great respect for a citizen of long standing may inspire him to a daring act against its interests.[16] In harmony with this view, Mosca rehearses the plotters in their performance of the "lie" at the trial, that is, their malicious connivance in a miscarriage of Venetian justice. Before the state's Avocatori or four magistrates in the Scrutineo, Voltore's circumstantial distortions (IV. 5) succeed in fixing on Bonario the charge of parricide and on Celia the reputation of a harlot. The husband Corvino's ready falsehood idiotically clinches this and also gives him the first taste of the public shame which is his punishment. Justice defrauded by the false evidence, the Avocatori, indeed, actually demand what witnesses the plaintiffs have to support their accusation (IV. 6). "Our consciences," Bonario lamely asserts; and Celia parrots in rote-like silliness, "And heauen, that neuer failes the innocent." The Avocatori are quick to reject such "testimonies" as without legal standing. The false appearance of the supposedly dying defendant confirms the miscarriage of justice plotted by the conspirators and their gulls acting in a harmony of collusion.[17] Voltore's outrageous presentation of the truth which the hearing will not allow closes the case against the innocent:

> See here, graue fathers, here's the rauisher,
> The rider on mens wiues, the great imposter,
> The grand voluptuary!

This fraudulent demonstration leads at once to the arrest of Celia and Bonario. Ominously, however, the Avocatori postpone the sentence till a later sitting, so that the plot against the state remains full of danger.

Nevertheless, Volpone's confidence, though shaken by the anxieties of the trial, returns (V. 1) as he parodies the trinity by three draughts of oblivious wine. This drink has also a satiric function since the exhilaration he experiences is more than vinous. Jonson clearly marks the steps in a comic peripety in which he complicates the action by means of a *catastasis*. The triumph of injustice at the trial is not enough, and Volpone now yearns for a victory of folly. In his sudden intoxication, he proposes to defy anew the legal machinery of the state. He rushes to set going, for laughter's sake, some "rare, ingenious knauery", fatally convinced that he will again succeed.

The ensuing consultation with Mosca (V. 2) parallels the second dialogue between the emperor and the favorite in *Sejanus* (III. 488-585). Whereas Tiberius sought to lure his prey into a trap and then close it on him,[18] Mosca addresses himself to the exquisite problem of tempting the fox from his hole and then catching him in a snare. The master's certitude that "Good wits are greatest in extremities" invites the parasite's flattering description of their thwarting justice: that, he praises as the "master-peece" of their conspirational art. The implied challenge falls on ready ears, for Volpone is determined to surpass earlier triumphs in venality. Mosca nervously entices him by urging that Voltore, for the pains he has taken, deserves —"Well—to be cosen'd." The master snaps this up, blindly persuaded that his servant shares his own enjoyment:

> but for thy sake, at thy entreaty,
> I will beginne, eu'n now, to vexe 'hem all.

In his anticipation of renewed delight in the restored conspiracy, Volpone's infatuation leads him to confer the power of decision on Mosca. First he is to spread the news of the magnifico's death and so bring the birds of prey flocking about "full of expectation." The second step, a climax of Mosca's patient treachery of maneuver, is "to haue it rauish'd from their mouthes" by the designation of the parasite as sole heir. Now Fortune smiles on the perfidious confederate, and he seizes the occasion by encouraging his master to delight in the satiric dividend: " 'twill afford me a rare meale of laughter." He wisely follows the latter's instructions to "Play the artificer now, torture 'hem rarely." The expectant legatees (V. 3) suffer an impotent fury of disappointment as he tallies his riches. These are so splendid and the trick so successful that the audience waits eagerly to see whether prudence will restrain a tell-tale gloating. The veteran dissembler, schooled by the double hypocrisy toward gulls and tormenter alike, conceals his happiness in the apt ascription of it to the last lucky turn of the wheel of chance:

> Good faith, it is a fortune throwne vpon me—
> *Item*, one salt of agat—not my seeking.

Thus Mosca's security is impregnable, and Volpone unconsciously signifies the fact by his salute to the parasite as "my fine diuell."

As he offers thanks to the clients for the gifts tendered in Act I, now triumphantly displayed together, Mosca reveals the conspiracy in one climax of the moral structure of the play. He blunts their indignation by literal denunciations in which the moral directness receives a crushing force from his sardonic reminder of unavailing bribes. The energy and point of these appalling sketches of degeneracy draw from his beguiled fellow the tribute:

Rare, MOSCA! how this villainy becomes him!

The entranced Volpone is ironically made wanton by a success against which the parasite had uttered a self-warning in his unmasking soliloquy (III. 1). Commending "my wittie *mischiefe*" he sends him out to flaunt his triumph, not only proclaimed heir but a wholly new person dressed in "my habit of *Clarissimo*." An insidious zeal for unrelenting torment of the legacy-hunters blinds him to the subtle changes taking place about him. Having once triumphed

126

outside his safe chamber, he fails to vary his conduct as Fortune varies.[19] He moves the arena of the conspiracy from the friendly couch to the dangerous city, insolently eager to "pursew, as well as plot" and not lose "this feast."

To relish the chagrin of his victims he desires some unobtrusive disguise. Thus Fortune provides the opportunity for which Mosca has waited, and he is quick to exploit it. He offers to get his master the costume of a commendadore or lowly sergeant, obscuring his aim by a cunning test of the other's confidence: in vexing the gulls in such a humble guise he must look for curses, and Volpone retorts (as he hoped he would) that the delusive fox is always cursed. Thus one regards the costume as a means of ranging safely beyond the now too-narrow walls of his sickroom, whereas the other sees in it a maneuver to lure the fox out of his hole. Mosca promises (V. 5) that before he will permit him to reenter it, he will make him come to some agreement or "I'le make him languish, in his borrow'd case." But the unlimited desire for acquiring what one lacks the capacity to get, a theme from Machiavelli [20] dramatized in *Sejanus*, overwhelms prudence, and exultation becoming insolence he plans "To cosen him of all." With complacent good humor, the treacherous confederate adds that the ruin of his fellow is not sin but "a cheat/Well plac'd": this is his "FOXE-trap."

The collapse of the legacy-hunting has produced a change of heart in the advocate Voltore (V. 10). This makes Volpone sharply aware of danger which he lightly disdained: "I' am caught/I' mine owne noose." The Avocatori, moreover, show a venality which he has failed to take into account. Thus they look up to the heir of the magnifico not as a parasite, but as "a man of great estate, now left." Too late the fox perceives one error (V. 11):

127

> To make a snare, for mine owne neck! and run
> My head into it, wilfully! with laughter!

But he persists in the fatal error of a blind reliance on the treacherous confederate. This is shaken by the report of his household that Mosca drove them out and took the keys, a symbol of dispossession that makes Volpone stagger under bitter self-reproaches. His torment of the gulls for the sake of merriment has proved "a mischiefe to me!" He is now merely "a vile wretch" who could not "beare/My fortune soberly." After this tardy recognition of Fortune's variability, he casts about in desperation to improvise some scheme that will "Vn-screw my aduocate, with new hope." Ironically he still places trust in Mosca.

In the second trial-scene (V. 12) Volpone's successful appeal to the credulity of Voltore revives expectation. Meanwhile, however, the faithless conspirator has become a formidable enemy since as a "gentleman" he is "A fit match" for an Avocatore's daughter. To the audience, it is a delicious irony that Mosca, made rigid in his decisions by greed and a blind confidence in his luck, ignores the admonition that if circumstances change, one previously enriched by Fortune must change too or be ruined.[21] The first climax of the satiric catastrophe occurs when his shrewdness fails as he seeks a compromise with Volpone: "(Wil you gi' me halfe?)" This is an ironic violation of Machiavelli's warning against trusting a man whom one has wronged.[22]

Indeed, even though the desperate Volpone humbly offers half his goods, triumphant greed makes the parasite strut. He grandly rejects any settlement: "I cannot now/ Affoord it you so cheape." He caps this by the public denunciation of the false commendadore's "insolence", a satiric thrust whose self-description is ironically apt. Finally, his silent acquiescence in the Avocatore's order of the whipping jolts Volpone with the consciousness, too late, that the trusted confederate has betrayed him. The insolent conspirator, delusively secure in his triumph, nevertheless has made in his turn a fatal error of miscalculation. The magnifico's pride is beyond a parasite's comprehension. Volpone, though trapped, is yet resolute; and he throws off his disguise with the words, "The *Foxe* shall, here vncase," experiencing a grim satisfaction in the exposure of "this, auarices foole." His enemy illuminates the depth of his delusion first by his honest amazement and then by honest indignation. The infatuated man at last perceives that Volpone, tricked out of his lair and helpless before the magistrates, is determined to bring their plot down in ruins, not now the fox-conspirator but the wolf-avenger. At the moment of ill-timed recognition, Mosca curses him: "Bane to thy wooluish nature."

## The Structure of "Volpone"

The structure of *Volpone* is another aspect of Jonson's debt to Machiavelli, exhibiting a creative awareness of the flexibility inherent in the four-part design. Its *catastasis* comes at Act V, scenes 1 and 2, where Volpone commits the fatal error that plunges all the conspirators into disaster. The resolution of the action, accordingly, brings events at the end of the play into complete harmony with the moral framework. That the author was perfectly conscious of this departure from the conventional reconciliations of comedy we know from the Epistle. There he warns that "my CATASTROPHE may, in the strict rigour of

129

*comick* law, meet with censure, as turning back to my promise"—that is, "to informe men, in the best reason of liuing." He designed it, he says, deliberately and might easily, had he wished so, have "varied" it. His explanation is that "my speciall ayme" was "to put the snaffle in their mouths, that crie out, we neuer punish vice in our *enterludes*, &c." Yet he felt obliged to justify his "liberty" by citing classical precedents for endings of comedies that are "not alwaies ioyfull." He brings the discussion to a close by a restatement of "the office of a COMICK-POET, to imitate iustice, and instruct to life"[23]—the didactic theory ascribed by Donatus to Cicero. A responsible understanding of this office dictated the resolution that would frustrate an immoral conspiracy and a plot against the state and punish their contrivers. The moral framework, consistently invoked by the ironic commentaries of Volpone and Mosca, has a perfect structural complement in the four-part design.

Thus the counterturn at the beginning of Act V centers with appalling irony on the inflation of spirit which the inflation of language has prefigured.[24] A genial comedy of legacy-hunters fleeced and deluded, of the simpleton Bonario duped, of the witless Celia kindling jealousy in her husband with a handkerchief and indeed of the whole brilliant mountebank scene of II. 2-5 [25] vanishes in the subtle change of mood. The miscarriage of justice in the first trial scene, as Jonson manipulates the structure in harmony with his didactic aim, demands a punishment equal to the gravity of the crime. Even so, the wiles of conspirators working at cross purposes inspire still a sometimes sympathetic and a sometimes ironic amusement.[26] In the face of this almost uniformly maintained

130

double focus, the terrible exposure and disgrace of the protagonist seem to transform the play into a comic imitation of a tragedy, with the moment of Volpone's hubris clearly marked.[27] In the short soliloquy of V. 1 he seeks in a strong draught of wine release from the anxiety of the trial. The physical exhilaration is the objective equivalent of an intoxication of spirit in which insolence becomes wanton. Blind to the counsels of prudence, he succumbs to the temptations of Mosca, and the wise gods having seeled his eyes he struts to his confusion.

This coincidence of hubris and *catastasis* is the mature triumph of the experiment at the end of Act IV in *Every Man in His Humor*.[28] It is not the only phase of the four-part structure that Jonson sets against the five-act division in *Volpone*. The *protasis* leaps across the end of Act I and runs through II. 1 in a continuous dramatic movement. It introduces the conspirators and defines their relationship. It shows how they mulct the greedy clients, tricking Corbaccio into disinheriting his son. It presents Mosca's first tentative attack on the voluptuary with the praise of Celia.

The success of this stratagem leads into the *epitasis* at Act II, scene 2, and it runs to the end of Act IV in a flow of events uninterrupted by artificial act divisions. Early in this part, Jonson again follows a trial in *Every Man in His Humor* by introducing a main character for whose presence he has already excited interest, here the beautiful girl Celia. Lured from his sickbed, Volpone entertains her and satisfies both a curiosity and a talent for acting in the mountebank scene, where she, a comic Desdemona, drops her handkerchief at his command. Abandoning the profitable deception of the legacy-hunters, he is wholly mastered by an emotion that ought to be nobler but is not: he is in love.[29]

Even as he plays the pimp, Mosca unmasks his real character and glories in his serpentine success. As Celia's own husband hungrily snatches at the chance to use his wife as a bribe in the legacy-hunt, the seduction of the girl moves from the overpowering of honor by greed in Corvino to the threat to rape her. But deliverance comes at the hand of Bonario, which the parasite prepared by inviting the youth to eavesdrop on Corbaccio and Volpone and by then leaving him to wander at will. The frustration of the voluptuary is at the point of becoming a public disgrace at the first trial. But the venal lawyer Voltore, at home in the venal court, diverts upon the guiltless pair the task of proving their charge against a dying old gentleman. Bent on prosecuting the innocent, the magistrates nevertheless portentously defer their verdict. Volpone has won a precarious but heady freedom at the end of the *epitasis*.

Jonson places the *catastasis* at Act V, scenes 1 and 2, complicating the action with an unexpected twist and altering the mood of the play. Restored to the safety of his lair, Volpone yields to an intoxication of blind confidence and puts himself at the mercy of his confederate. This submission precipitates in the *catastrophe* a reversal of roles. It is Mosca who is now enriched by the cunning purchase of legacy-hunting. It is Volpone who, degraded to a menial, sees his parasite exalted to equality with a grandee. But if he has miscalculated his confederate, Mosca has undervalued a magnifico's fierce pride and resolution. The whole conspiracy falls in total ruin as the fox uncases and the Avocatori pronounce their harsh punishments.

132

The conspiracy and the structure are not the only affinities of *Volpone* with Machiavelli. The first climax in the *epitasis*, with a comic Lucrece threatened by rape, recalls the attack on the wife in an earlier comedy. Jonson's portrayal is a satiric variation of the moment in *La Mandragola* when the appropriately named Lucrezia, though herself mustering all the serious objections, submits to the arguments of husband, mother and confessor. In the temptation of Volpone, Mosca begins with nicely calculated praise of Celia:

> a beautie, ripe, as haruest! . . .
> Bright as your gold! and louely, as your gold!
> (I. 5. 109, 114)

At the sight of her Volpone forgets his gold and turns to Mosca in the helpless hope of the Petrarchan swain:

O, I am wounded. MOS. Where, sir? VOLP. Not without;
Those blowes were nothing: I could beare them euer.
But angry CVPID, bolting from her eyes,
Hath shot himselfe into me, like a flame;
Where, now, he flings about his burning heat,
As in a fornace, an ambitious fire,
Whose vent is stopt. The fight is all within me.
I cannot liue, except thou helpe me, MOSCA;
My liuer melts, and I without the hope
Of some soft aire, from her refreshing breath,
Am but a heape of cinders.
(II. 4. 1-11)

133

Similarly, Callimaco found that the extravagant applause of the wife of Nicia Calfucci tempted him from Paris to observe her in Florence. Captivated in a like manner by the married girl whose looks exceed description, when he saw her at last, he too burned in hopeless love and feared his death: "Io son morto," he expired in agitation.[30] In his soliloquy at IV. 1,[31] he too vacillated between hope and fear, exclaiming, Is it possible to go on living in this suffering? In every part of his body such longing for Lucrezia assails him that he feels helpless. His legs tremble, his bowels flutter, his heart is plucked from his breast, his arms go slack, his tongue becomes mute, his eyes dazzle and his brain whirls. The juxtaposition of the passages in the two plays suggests that Jonson found a rich comic resource in the satiric allusiveness of Volpone's raptures.

Like the magnifico Callimaco turned to a parasite, Ligurio, for assistance (I. 1, 3). Both agents persuade their masters to adopt a disguise (*Volpone*, I. 5; *La Mandragola*, I. 3). Counterfeiting a mountebank, the magnifico urges the wondrous oil of Scoto, which cardinals, princes and the grand duke of Tuscany value (II. 2). Callimaco, though he disclaimed the arts of the charlatan, asserted nevertheless that his potion was prized by French lords and by the French king (II. 3).

Meanwhile, the virtue of the wives in both plays portends the defeat of their lovers. Celia never stirs abroad except to go to church (II. 5. 46). Lucrezia, reluctant to leave her home, offered prayers in church for her childless marriage (II. 2 and III. 2). Corvino's fear of the law, which restrains him from killing the mountebank (II. 6. 10-11), resembles Nicia's dread lest the trick with the potion get him into trouble with the grand jury (II. 6).[32] Again, Corvino's eagerness for the horns of a cuckold, on

134

which Mosca remarks as he hurries to prostitute Celia, recapitulates a theme of *La Mandragola*, the husband's absurd insistence on embracing the scheme of the parasite to bring the wife and her lover together. Each husband defies the arguments against adultery, each wife protesting in her fashion and imploring the aid of religion. In the beginning, Nicia jealously rejected the idea of becoming a cuckold; then he yielded to Callimaco's persuasions, especially since great lords and the king of France had set the example by their use of the mandrake potion. So Corvino, jealously angry over Celia's fascination with the mountebank, suppresses his conscience with his wit and begs Mosca never to betray to Volpone his "scrupulous doubts" (II. 6. 89).

Preparing him for the immodest proposal that he prostitute his own wife, Mosca describes her character with sardonic contempt as "some simple thing, . . ./Some wench you may command" (II. 6. 57, 59). Fra Timoteo, likewise complacent about his powers of persuasion, was contemptuous of Lucrezia as a good woman but like all her sex of simple mind (III. 9). The varied attempts on her chastity that Machiavelli distributed among husband, mother and priest, Jonson concentrates with ironic emphasis in Corvino. The crucial argument of Fra Timoteo was a biblical casuistry turning on the relationship of ends and means: where an end was good, as in this case, adultery was no sin. Besides, Lucrezia's first duty was to please her husband and fill a seat in paradise (III. 11). Similarly, Corvino dismisses "honour" as "a breath" (III. 7. 38); Celia's fear for his reputation is groundless; if he thought her act a sin, he would not urge her. Instead, it is "A pious worke, mere charity" (65), a kind of "honest politie, to assure mine owne" (66). In spite of her refusal

135

she may "redeeme all, yet" by obeying him (131). His decisive argument is that loyalty to him demands that she recognize "the necessitie of those meanes,/For my re- couery" (35-36). Both comedies, thus, echo the cele- brated maxim from Machiavelli's political writings.

Jonson, as though stimulated by the name of Machia- velli's heroine, goes back of him to his model in popular literature and perhaps in Livy and Ovid. He transfers to Corvino the threats of a Tarquin in the heated demands that Celia yield to his wishes or he will deface her beauty and expose her to public disgrace. She endures this vile usage, seeing herself as his "martyr" (III. 7. 107), pa- thetically offering her life to satisfy him and sinking on her knees in supplication, a comic Lucrece. Machiavelli's wife and Jonson's both trust heaven. Lucrezia, in a bril- liant intuition of romantic comedy, comfortably accepted her new happiness as "the will of heaven"; [33] and Celia, consistent to her "humor", remains aggressively simple in chaste belief. In another consultation of the original source suggested by the Italian author, the Catullan rap- tures of Callimaco, presented sympathetically (especially in IV. 1 of *La Mandragola*), become a cynical travesty in Jonson's adaptation of a song of the Roman lyricist, "Come, my *Celia*, let vs proue, /While we can, the sports of loue" (III. 7. 166-83), with its wholly Volponian thesis that it is no sin to enjoy a clandestine love.

There is some slight evidence that Jonson, omnivorous plagiary, discovered materials for *Volpone* in *Clizia* also. Corbaccio's disinheritance of Bonario repeats a theme in Machiavelli's comedy, where one of the offenses against his family that the infatuated Nicomaco threatened to commit was to deprive his son Cleandro of a fortune by handing it over to his worthless creature Pirro.[34] This

136

opposition between two generations suggests the possibility of an introduction into *Volpone* fleetingly of the theme of youth in conflict with age, which was a dominant motive in *Clizia* and becomes one in *Epicoene*. In the Italian play, the seventy-year-old Nicomaco sought possession of a helpless girl, while Cleandro suffered the torments of a romantic love for her. Whereas Volpone presses his autumnal lust, Bonario follows the path of romantic adventure and rescues Celia from a fate that is, as she takes some pains to stress, worse than death. The removal of the last obstacle to their union, Corvino's restitution of the girl to her father with her dowry trebled, may owe something to Nicomaco's warning that he would repudiate his wife and return her estate (III. 1). Altogether, Jonson seems to show in *Volpone* a more extensive knowledge of Machiavelli than *The Prince* and *The Discourses*.

## Chapter 7

## *THE DISCOVERIES:* JONSON'S MORAL REJECTION OF MACHIAVELLI

Later in his life Jonson expounded the moral construction of Machiavelli that Cardinal Pole had proclaimed. This occurs in *Timber, or Discoveries Made Upon Men and Matter* (c. 1619, printed 1640), a gathering of notes from the author's reading and reflection that group themselves around such topics as life, literature and government. The work in its extant form seems to be a rough set of lecture notes, a state of things explained by Sisson as due to Jonson's presumptive service in 1619 as deputy for Henry Croke, the regular professor of rhetoric at Gresham College in London.[1] Such fruits of a long and zealous combing of books may go back twenty years to 1599,[2] even before *Sejanus*, where our first certain evidence of the dramatist's profound interest in Machiavelli appears. If we bring together the scattered jottings on the topic of statecraft in *The Discoveries*, we find a coherent if fragmentary treatise on the art of government. A single consistent theme runs through them, in a uniform prose style, so that we can trace a consistent development of thought.[3] The apology for the Jacobean monarchy and the attack on the political writings of the Florentine Secretary make this essay an animadversion directed against the one authoritative writer whom Jonson names, Machiavelli. The spirit of the tract is the moral repugnance of Cardinal Pole lightened by occasional touches of the characteristic sardonic irony.

These are not random notes, therefore, but taken together form a considered refutation of the Italian's ideas. This is the nature of the tribute which the latter now exacts from an old and devoted student. Hence, one source for Jonson's putative essay "Of Statecraft" looms large: *The Prince*. A chief interest of the section of *The Discoveries* on the question whether cruelty or clemency suits the prince better is the proof that the author read the text in the original.[4] His language is closer to the Italian than to the Latin of the frequently reprinted translation by Sylvester Telius in the *Princeps*.[5] For example, in the section on cruelty in which Jonson names Machiavelli only to refute him his statement that "such are to be honour'd, and lov'd"[6] clearly comes from a reading of "quelli . . . si debbono onorare ed amare"[7] rather than "honorentur ac didigantur" (*Princeps*, IX. 3). In the same section the passage, "Such let the *Prince* take heed of, and not doubt to reckon in the List of his open enemies" (p. 598), comes from "da quelli si debbe el principe guardare, e temerli come se fussino scoperti inimici" (II. 40) and not from "ab istis Princeps sibi cavendum putet, ac inter eos, qui iam aperti sunt hostes" (IX. 3). These details, though trivial, are suggestive of Jonson's method.

His zeal for the subject, not surprisingly, has led him on occasion to draw on Telius rather than the original of Telius. Take, for example, the following: "*There* is a great variation between him, that is rais'd to the *Soveraignity*, by the favour of his Peeres; and him that comes to it by

139

the suffrage of the people. The first holds with more difficulty" (p. 598). This comes rather from the Latin, "Qui optimatum subsidio principatum subit, difficilius quam populi suffragiis eò euihitur, sustinebit" (IX. 2), than from the Italian, "Colui che viene al principato con lo aiuto de' grandi, si mantiene con più difficultà che quello che diventa con lo aiuto del populo" (II. 39). Moreover, the title of chapter 17 of *The Prince* in Telius begins, "De Crudelitate et Clementia," whereas Machiavelli has "*De crudelitate et pietate*": Jonson's marginal rubric is "*Clementia*" and the text has "*Clemency*" (p. 599). Again, the rubric, "*Firmissima verò omnium basis jus haereditarium Principis*" (p. 598), comes rather from the title of chapter 2 in Telius, "De Ius Qvi Haereditario iure obveniunt principatibus," than from Machiavelli's heading, "*De principatibus haereditariis.*" Telius is on the whole fairly accurate, but he omits one large part of the original, the section of chapter 18 that explains how princes are compelled to break faith with their pledged word and how honesty in negotiations is to be restrained. Jonson's familiarity with the omitted portion shows that he was reading the Italian with care. The upshot is that the studious poet, relying mainly on the language of his author, found now and then in the Latin translation an expression or a turn of phrase which he worked into his own essay.[8]

Despite the implied agreement with official condemnation of Machiavelli, there are gleams of the characteristic derision that sparkled so magnificently in *Volpone*. For instance, the praise of clemency and the dispraise of cruelty, although in apparent opposition to the teaching of the writer who inspired these notes, catches the muted irony of the Italian. Chapter 7 of *The Prince*, on the subject of new dominions acquired by the power of others or by Fortune, tells how Duke Caesar Borgia sacrificed his Sejanian minister Remirro de Orco. Borgia had worked through Orco to give the province of Romagna an efficient but harsh administration. Machiavelli observes that since he knew Orco's past severity had aroused hatred, he decided, in order to free the minds of the people and win their compete adherence, to show that if any cruelty had taken place it had not been ordered by him, but was due to the harsh nature of his minister. One morning he found an opportunity and had him hacked in two and displayed in the public square of Cesena. The ferocity of the spectacle inspired in the people both astonishment and satisfaction (II. 31). Jonson says, "*A Prince* should exercise his cruelty, not by himselfe, but by his ministers: so hee may save himselfe, and his dignity with his people, by sacrificing those, when he list, saith the great *Doctor* of *State, Machiavell*" (p. 598). The sardonic allusion to his author calls to mind the writer of a *De Regimine Principium*, the great doctor of theology St. Thomas Aquinas; and it illuminates the political citation with a flash of implied comment that shows the old ironist again at work. This satiric salute to the master of statecraft is the kind of verbal flourish that delighted Swinburne when he declared *The Discoveries* superior to Bacon's *Essays*.[9] The same spirit flashes in the nickname Jonson fixes on his author: "the said St. *Nicolas*" (p. 599).

Once Jonson made a literal application of Borgia's policy in order to dramatize the machinations of Tiberius in the play *Sejanus*. Now, although the emperor and his favorite make a conspicuous appearance in *The Discoveries*, they are no longer the figures in Machiavelli's *Discourses* or Jonson's drama; they are the wicked prince and

141

his minion as presented by Tacitus.[10] Of monarchs who make an arbitrary use of their power, he writes that "It is dangerous offending such an one; who, being angry, knowes not how to forgive." For they destroy whole countries since "All is under the Law of their spoyle, and licence." He proceeds to offer a specific illustration that does indeed promise briefly to follow the interpretation of Machiavelli and of his play, but returns to orthodox history. Princes who neglect their office thus, he says,

their fortune is often-times to draw a *Seianus*, to be neere about 'hem; who will at last affect to get above 'hem, and put them in a worthy feare, of rooting both them out, and their family.

But the moral he draws moves from the fundamentally Tacitan concept into a new direction:

For no men hate an evill *Prince* more, then they, that help'd to make him such. And none more boastingly weepe his ruine, then they, that procur'd and practic'd it. The same path leades to ruine, which did to rule, when men professe a Licence in governing. *A good King* is a publike Servant (p. 601).

This rises from the Latin gloom to a hopefulness original with the Englishman.

Jonson renews the moral abhorrence with which Cardinal Pole had shrunk from Thomas Cromwell's approbation of *The Prince*. Pouncing on the dilemma expounded by Machiavelli, whether it is better to be loved than feared, he sees no contradiction. For a monarch, he explains, exhibits no virtue that "becomes him more, then his *Clem-*

*ency*" (p. 599), and the lenient ruler finds his safety rather in the love of his subjects than in terror. The effect of this pleasant picture is to obscure the Florentine's nice, objective discriminations and to debase a treatise on statecraft into a flattering, unreal account of politics such as Cromwell had derided in the theorists. Even so, the recognition in chapters 17 and 18 of *The Prince* that clemency may have a practical usefulness strengthened Jonson's point of view. He disapproves a ruler's suppression of the people by his severity: "It is then, most gracious in a Prince to pardon, when many about him would make him cruell" (p. 599). In like manner, Machiavelli had observed of the ruler who exhibits lenity when men feared oppression: as men who receive benefits from one from whom they expected evil feel under a greater obligation to their benefactor, so the people soon become better disposed toward him than if he had become a prince through their favor.[11] Of considerable interest is a related passage in *The Discourses*, where the author, weighing the two motives of love and fear, declares that the man who makes himself loved will prevail as much as the man who makes himself feared; but the latter will be more often followed and obeyed than the former.[12] The dilemmatic mode of argument so characteristic of Machiavelli has likewise proved useful to the disciple.

Jonson's method in the statements that he singles out for ascription to their author is to make a generally accurate paraphrase (as in *Sejanus* [13]), and then reject it. This practice extends to minute details. Thus his retort to the great doctor of state on the subject of love and fear is, "But I say, he puts off man, and goes into a beast, that is cruell" (p. 599). The politic man as beast is a reminiscence of Machiavelli's insistence that the successful

143

prince must learn to cultivate the virtues of an animal as well as those of a man (II. 64). The habit of oblique reference to passages that he wishes to condemn, rather than direct quotation, runs through the sections of *The Discoveries* on statecraft. The result is that the Florentine is almost omnipresent even when never mentioned and when the view expressed is a moral one. Particularly where he has made his orthodoxies thickest, Jonson seems to glance at a favorite source and chooses the at least amusing method of refutation by silent allusion. How far the intellectual distance is between the earlier *Sejanus* and the later prose essay appears from the following lines, declaimed by Silius just before his suicide has frustrated the malignancy of Tiberius:

> Since I haue done thee that great seruice, *Caesar*,
> Thou still hast fear'd me; and, in place of grace,
> Return'd mee hatred: so soone all best Turnes,
> With *Princes*, do conuert to iniuries
> In estimation, where they greater rise,
> Then can be answer'd.[14]

In the 1616 Folio edition, line 303 of the 1605 Quarto was changed to "With doubtful Princes" [15] in harmony with the change in the author's attitude from an approval of Machiavellianism to a moral rejection.

Machiavelli, it must be remembered, devoted chapter 19 of *The Prince* to the avoidance of contempt and hatred. He reached the conclusion that rulers should order their agents to do those things that might make them detested, but should themselves do those that give satisfaction. He also reinforced his conviction that a ruler ought to value the nobility but at the same time not make himself hated by the people (II. 66 and 69-70). Jonson endorses the theory by implication, characteristically expressing it in this work with monarchic rapture: "the merciful *Prince* is safe in love, not in feare" (p. 599).

A representative example of close but unacknowledged indebtedness is the passage on the difference between a prince "rais'd to the *Soveraignity*, by the favour of his Peeres; and him that comes to it by the suffrage of the people" (p. 598). Simpson printed in the notes the pertinent sections of chapter 9 of *The Prince*, on the civic principality.[16] The brilliant metaphor "chi fonda in sul populo, fonda in sul fango" (II. 41) attracts into Jonson's terse English not only the sense of the aphorism, but also, surprisingly, the praise of the people eloquently asserted by the Italian: "Nor let the common Proverbe of (Hee that builds on the people, builds on the dirt) discredit my opinion" (p. 599) closely renders "e non sia alcuno che repugni a questa mia opinione con quello proverbio trito" (II. 41). The monarchist and rabble-hater has momentarily become a democrat by a kind of literary contagion. The zealous scholar, turned for an instant into the sobersides plagiary, neglects even to seek his author's source.

Jonson found more congenial a scorn for "the beast, the multitude" (p. 644).[17] He says,

The *vulgar* are commonly ill natur'd; and always grudging against their *Governours:* which makes, that a Prince has more busines, and trouble with them, then ever *Hercules* had with the Bull, or any other beast: by how much they have more heads, then will be rein'd with one bridle. There was not that variety of beasts in the Arke; as is of beastly natures in the multitude; especially when they come to that iniquity to censure their *Soveraign's* actions (p. 593).

But even this censure reflects the calm bitterness of Machiavelli's judgment of the universal badness of men. A pertinent example is in chapter 17 of *The Prince*. It may be said of men in general (he writes) that they are ungrateful, fickle, hypocritical, dissembling, fugitives from danger and covetous of gain. As long as you benefit them, they are entirely yours, offering you their blood, their wealth, their lives and their children—when the necessity is remote. The prince who has relied solely on their words finds himself unready with other preparations and therefore ruined (II. 62). Jonson's familiarity with *The Discourses* when he wrote *Sejanus*,[18] especially the long analysis of the ingratitude to the monarch of those benefited by him, makes it likely that he read further to reinforce his agreement with his author's harsh judgment. Machiavelli concludes that the people always show the same disposition to avarice and bad faith (II. 462) and that they fight because of ambition, a passion so powerful in the hearts of men that it never leaves them no matter what heights they attain. For nature has created men so that they desire everything but are unable to achieve it; desire is always greater than the power to acquire, and the result is a discontent with what they have and a dissatisfaction with themselves (II. 190). Most interesting is the considered estimation that the people are "un animale brutto" (II. 150), ferocious and savage, subdued by imprisonment and servitude and when freed unable to provide itself with food and shelter, so that it becomes an easy prey to the first one who seeks to chain it up again. This is "la moltitudine sciolta" (II. 234) or ill-natured vulgar of Jonson.

Perhaps a more conventional derivation from Machiavelli appears in the warning, among the reflections on the bestial populace, about the evil of calling the prince's decisions into question: "Then all the Counsels are made good, or bad by the events" (p. 593). The famous maxim about ends and means finds its first expression in *The Discourses:* It is very fitting that when the deed accuses him, the end excuses him; and when this end is good, as in the case of Romulus, it will always justify one (II. 131). The playwright had already assimilated the precept to the argument of the favorite in *Sejanus*, where he reasons that "State is inough to make th' act iust, them guilty" (II. 173). In *The Prince* it appears in the advice that in the actions of all men, especially of princes, from which there is no appeal, one must consider the end (II. 66). A jocose employment of the locution occurs in the casuistry of Fra Timoteo in *La Mandragola* and in the arguments to Celia by Corvino in *Volpone*.[19] Jonson's version is closer to the Florentine's language than the famous Jesuit dictum that the end justifies the means.

Even the picture of "the mercifull *Prince*, . . . safe in love, not in feare" of his people, afraid of no treasons and "guarded with his owne benefits" (p. 600) owes not a little to Machiavelli's sardonic emphasis in chapter 20 of *The Prince* (on fortifications) that the ruler's best fortress is the love of the people.[20] This is a distillation of the pleasant account in *The Discourses* of the Golden Age of the Roman Empire. Then the monarch, surrounded by reverence and glory and beloved by a people happy in its security, exalted nobility and virtue. Then good princes ruled securely among subjects no less secure in a world filled with peace and justice, where nobility and virtue were held in the highest esteem.[21]

Another common theme is the need for the monarch to be a patron of learning and the arts. Jonson's belief in a "consociation of offices" (p. 565) between the ruler and the professors of learning catches up an idea in chapter 21

147

of *The Prince*, which explains how the monarch may gain reputation. He should be a lover of excellence, advancing the skillful and honoring those who are outstanding in every art. Indeed, he should offer rewards to those who seek to improve the state and so give an example of humanity and munificence (II. 84). Jonson naturally places emphasis on learning, observing that "It is the greatest part of his Liberality, his Favour: And from whom doth he heare discipline more willingly, or the Arts discours'd more gladly, then from those, whom his owne bounty, and benefits have made able and faithfull?" (p. 565). Here the two writers seem to think as one.

Both authors see the necessity, as Jonson puts it, for "a reputation of *Honesty*" (p. 566). He comments on the usefulness of "dissembling our knowledge of ability in our selves and avoyding all suspition of arrogance, ascribing all to their instruction, as an *Ambassador* to his master, or a *Subject* to his *Soveraigne*" (p. 566). This is a reminiscence of well-known and morally condemned maxims from *The Prince* on the imperative need at one and the same time to practice dissimulation and to win esteem for integrity.[22] But the Jacobean tamely declines upon the more decorous commonplaces of Vives.[23] Jonson and Machiavelli agree, furthermore, that the ruler should not fleece his subjects. The former declares, "Hee is an ill *Prince*, that so puls his Subjects feathers, as he would not have them grow againe: that makes his *Exchequer* a receipt for the spoyles of those hee governs" (p. 602). Machiavelli solemnly warns the prince rather to be a miser than rob the citizens, and one of his prudential maxims is that men will forget the death of a father more easily than the loss of a patrimony (II. 60 and 62).

Both express a serious concern for trustworthy ministers. Machiavelli devotes chapter 22 of *The Prince* to the problem of secretaries and servants and 23 to flatterers (II. 84-87).[24] How grave a matter this is, Jonson signifies by concluding that "the good Counsellors to Princes are the best instruments of a good Age" (p. 601). He observes the great difference in the "understanding of some Princes, as in the quality of their Ministers about them" (p. 571) some being flatterers and some good men who make the times good. These cogitations recall Machiavelli's juxtaposition in the two chapters just cited of the benefit accruing from good secretaries and the evil from time-servers. A related topic reflects the passage in *The Prince* specifically singled out for comment by Jonson (p. 598), on the ruler's working his cruelty through his agents. He writes, "*I have* discovered, that a fain'd familiarity in great ones, is a note of certaine usurpation on the lesse. For great and popular men, faine themselves to be servants to others, to make those slaves to them" (pp. 597-98).[25] This perception had already provided the Machiavellian spectacle in *Sejanus*, where Sabinus says of the dissimulation of Tiberius,

When power, that may command, so much descends,
Their bondage, whom it stoupes to, it intends.
(I. 396-97)[26]

Equally close is the agreement of the two authors on the vital necessity of prudence, a term that echoes without cessation throughout their advice. Jonson asserts with a Machiavellian boldness that "the Princes Prudence is his chiefe Art, and safety" (p. 594). The Florentine names a series of vices and their corresponding virtues and then advises that since a prince can neither possess nor exhibit all the latter, it is necessary for him to cultivate prudence so as to avoid an evil reputation (II. 58). Prudence, in

149

fact, is a virtue which Machiavelli exalts above faith (II. 65), and it is an excellent guide because it consists in knowing how to recognize the nature of disadvantages and how to make good use of the least harmful (II. 84). The choice of ministers will be good or bad depending on the prudence of the ruler. A prudent prince, therefore, having chosen wise men for his government, ought to give solely to them an absolute freedom to tell him the truth. It follows that any prince who gains the reputation of being prudent may be considered so by reason of the good counselors he has about him (II. 86-87). Jonson phrases this perception thus: "they are ever good men, that must make good the times" (p. 571).

Even the comments on religion, at first glance so antithetical, show the powerful influence of the Italian. "*The strength* of Empire is in religion" (p. 600), Jonson confidently proclaims. Machiavelli is equally emphatic though more intent on political utility. Carefully defining the spiritual qualities a prince ought to display, he cautions that nothing is more important than to seem to practice religion (II. 66).[27] Jonson may (as Simpson believed) wrap his preachment in the words of Farnese,[28] but the powerful sentiment seems to reflect the operation upon him of the more powerful mind of the Florentine. It may be, indeed, that the Englishman's numinous theory of the principate (p. 594) is another sign of careful reading of Machiavelli. The latter is nowhere so solemn as when he expounds the awesome significance of religion, which he praises in *The Discourses* as the basis of a healthy state. The famous chapter 11 in Book I on the religion of the Romans explains how Numa Pompilius, finding a very savage people and wishing to reduce them to civil obedience by means of the arts of peace, turned to religion as the thing necessary above all others for the maintenance of a civilization; and he established it so successfully that for many centuries there was never so great a fear of God as in that state.[29]

Similarly, Jonson notes the wise use of superstitions to inspire an awe of the ruler:

Hence the Persians gave out their Cyrus, to have beene nurs'd by a Bitch, a creature to encounter il, as of sagacity to seeke out good; shewing that *Wisdome* may accompany fortitude, or it leaves to be, and puts on the name of *Rashnesse*.

(pp. 594-95)

Machiavelli concludes that the religion introduced by Numa was a primary cause of the felicity of the Roman government. He finds, therefore, that as the observance of divine institutions is the reason for a government's greatness, so the disregard of them produces disaster. For where there is no fear of God, either that kingdom necessarily comes to ruin, or it must be sustained by the fear of a prince who supplies the lack of religion (II. 140). If the ruler offend, Jonson comforts the reader, "he hath his Discoverer" (p. 600). His enthusiasm in such utterances as, "*After God*, nothing is to be lov'd of man like the Prince" (p. 594), is approached by the Florentine only in the patriotic ardor of the exhortation to the princes of Italy with which he brings *The Prince* to its eloquent close (II. 91-93). The fact remains that a strong tincture of Machiavellianism colors Jonson's anti-Machiavellian treatise. Although often implied and oblique, its pervasive influence shows how profound was this aspect of the playwright's debt.

## Chapter 8

## JONSON ON COMEDY

In his pronouncements on comedy, Jonson throughout his career disparaged Terence and expressed a preference for Plautus. At the same time, nevertheless, he repeatedly called attention to the existence in his own plays of the four-part structure of Terence, which Machiavelli had adapted from *Andria* for the design of his original comedies. Moreover, in the numerous comments on his art that he scattered through his plays, Jonson showed, in terms borrowed from Donatus and Scaliger, how they conform to this structure. As for his pronouncements, they are generally of two very different kinds. Some resemble the apologetic prologues described by Donatus, whereas others imitate the critical expositions in which Machiavelli explained his dramatic practice.[1] In *Every Man out of His Humor* (1599) the Grex or chorus of Asper, Cordatus and Mitis freely discuss the argument and structure of comedy in the long induction and in the shorter commentaries between the acts and at the end of the play. We may disregard their best-known utterance, a definition of "humor", and examine the theory of comedy they put forward. This play, Asper declares, seeks to "oppose a

152

mirrour,/As large as is the stage, whereon we act," [2] in which the audience will see the time's deformities anatomized. Like Machiavelli, Jonson employs the idea of a *speculum consuetudinis* which Donatus, crediting it to Cicero, bequeathed to the Renaissance.[3] The author's hope, Asper explains, is to appeal over the head of the people to

> attentiue auditors,
> Such as will ioyne their profit with their pleasure,
> And come to feed their vnderstanding parts.
>
> (III. 435)

The self-conscious invitation to the discriminating few bases the plea for their approval on the Horatian platitude about the didactic and aesthetic purposes of art. Jonson is confident of making their eyes, at least, "Flow with distilled laughter" (III. 436).[4]

The discussion that follows is not unlike the critical essays of Machiavelli in its effort to define the art of comedy. The drama presented by Asper, Cordatus declares, is "somewhat like *Vetus Comoedia*." This is cryptic, and Mitis tries to pin him down by demanding whether the author observes all the laws of comedy in it. He means "the equall diuision of it into *Acts*, and *Scenes*, according to the *Terentian* manner, his true number of Actors; the furnishing of the *Scene* with GREX, or CHORVS, and that the whole Argument fall within compasse of a dayes business." Significantly, Cordatus at once rejects the authority of Terence and his practices. When Mitis protests that they are necessary if a comedy is to be "authentique" the other claims that such a test of authenticity

153

would be valid only if the laws he asserts "had beene de-liuered to vs *ab initio,* and in their present vertue and perfection" (III. 436-37). But this is not the situation.

Cordatus then traces the evolution of comedy from its primitive beginning to the *"Poeme"* of Aristophanes, which "appeared absolute, and fully perfected." But it changed under the innovations of Menander and Plautus, who excluded the chorus, changed the persons "and aug-mented it with all liberty, according to the elegancie and disposition of those times, wherein they wrote." Signifi-cantly again, Cordatus makes no mention of Terence in this brief sketch of the development of comic art. The evolving pattern of the drama leads Cordatus to demand for modern writers the freedom "to illustrate and heighten our inuention as they did; and not to be tyed to those strict and regular formes." This criticism of the rigid divi-sion into acts and scenes (associated with Terence) is part of a general rejection of conventions which "the nicenesse of a few (who are nothing but forme) would thrust vpon vs" (III. 437). Thus Jonson argues the need for a more flexible structure, such as he had already intro-duced in *Every Man in His Humor* (1598).

At the end of Act I Mitis suggests that the author ought to lengthen the act so as to place a didactic emphasis on Macilente's reproof of the covetous farmer Sordido. Cordatus bases his objection to this statement on dramatic principle, arguing against the prolongation of the scene on a stage devoid of action. But Mitis insists that "propriety" requires a lengthened scene. The appeal to decorum leads Cordatus, again defending the author on critical grounds, to dismiss the other's purely didactic interpretation. He asserts that a drama must keep decorum solely by dra-matic propriety. In other words, he is the spokesman for

154

the view firmly held by Jonson (which accords with Machiavelli's) that a play must maintain a single consistent illusion.

On the other hand, Mitis objects to the length of Act II, scene 3, on the theory that the presentation of a series of humors in a series of single scenes would be more effective. Again Cordatus bases his demurrer on dramatic principle. It is, he contends, "an obiect of more state, to behold the *Scene* full and relieu'd with varietie of speakers to the end, then to see a vast emptie stage, and the actors come in (one by one) as they were dropt downe with a feather, into the eye of the spectators" (III. 479). The submission of Mitis to an aesthetic judgment here lends emphasis to Jonson's concern to maintain a constant ebb and flow of dramatic movement with the assistance of variety.

After Act III, scene 6, Mitis has seen enough of the comical satire to voice a fundamental objection to the kind of play he is watching:

the argument of his *Comoedie* might haue beene of
some other nature, as of a duke to be in loue
with a countesse, and that countesse to bee in
loue with the dukes sonne, and the sonne to loue
the ladies waiting maid: some such cross wooing,
with a clowne to their seruing man.

(III. 515)

He thus describes the pattern of romantic comedy which Terence had perfected. Cordatus, making sweeping denial of such claims, narrows the range of comedy within the definition of Donatus: let the critic who seeks to tell what comedy is content himselfe with CICEROS definition (till hee haue strength to propose to himselfe a better) who would haue a *Comoedie* to be an *Imitatio vitae, Speculum consuetudinis, Imago veritatis;* a thing throughout pleasant, and ridiculous, and accommodated to the correction of manners: if the maker haue fail'd in any particle of this, they may worthily taxe him, but if not, why—be you (that are for them) silent.

(III. 515) [5]

By thus restricting the scope of comedy, Cordatus calls for a purely realistic and didactic art that seems to deny the very freedom he had demanded against the niceness of a few. In theory, then, Jonson rejects the developments just praised in Menander and Plautus and condemns the balance of satire and romance which, after the example of Machiavelli, he had maintained in *Every Man in His Humor.*

This aesthetic dead end may be due to Jonson's study of Sir Philip Sidney. The latter ignored argument and structure in Terence and read him for moral instruction. Accordingly he concentrates on the derision of satiric types, whose names he takes from the Latin playwright. He begins with the definition of comedy ascribed to Cicero and then restricts its scope to a "ridiculous & scornefull" representation of "the common errors of our life," with the aim of dissuasion from the vices portrayed. The "right vse of Comedy," therefore, is to depict "the filthines of euil" in the "actions of our life." The list of satiric types recalls Machiavelli's: an avaricious old man, a crafty servant, a flattering parasite, and a braggart soldier; Sidney finds names for them in Terence. Jonson, in abandoning the intention to excite genial humor, follows Sidney also in

156

excluding delight and retaining profit only in the laughter which he sanctions. This is "a scornful tickling" at "deformed creatures." The ridicule of Hercules in woman's attire at Omphale's command suppresses the delight in the exhibition of the power of love for derisive laughter at the folly of the spectacle.[6] The limitations of this satiric and didactic theory help us to understand the dramatic limitations of Jonson's play.

Before Act III has ended Mitis recalls Cordatus to one of the freedoms he had earlier claimed. In a complaint grounded on the neoclassical idea of decorum, he says of the attempted suicide by Sordido that "the intent and horror of the obiect, was more then the nature of a *Comoedie* will in any sort admit." The other disposes of the objection by reminding him of the appearance of Alcesimarchus in the *Cistellaria* of Plautus, drawn sword in hand and ready to kill himself but restrained by Silenium and the bawd. The classical precedent satisfies Mitis (III. 622). After III. 8, furthermore, Cordatus suddenly praises the author for his rejection of strict and regular forms and his employment of a flexible structure, calling for close attention to the present phase of the play. "Lose not your selfe," he warns, "for now the *Epitasis*, or busie part of our subiect, is in act" (III. 522). As he minimized the five-act division in the Induction, so Jonson's spokesman here stresses the effectiveness of the four-part design. The placement of the term amidst the stage business of Act III implies a theory of continuous action unimpeded by the pause between acts.

By means of the comments of the Grex at the end of Act IV, Jonson carefully prepares his audience for a comic reversal. Cordatus promises that among all the stage personages "the current of their dispositions shall receiue so

157

quick, and strong an alteration." Mitis, looking forward to the implications of the title *Every Man out of His Humor*, nevertheless has seen "all his actors so strongly pursue, and continue their humors." Cordatus maintains that the peripety of the author is most effective:

Why, therein his art appeares most full of lustre, and approcheth neerest the life: especially, when in the flame and height of their humours, they are laid flat, it fils the eye better, and with more contentment.

(III. 562)

Mitis, speaking for the attentive auditors, waits eagerly for Act V to begin so that he may enjoy the "*Catastrophe* or Conclusion." [7] This is further evidence of Jonson's contemplation in 1599 of the possibilities in a quadripartite structure existing within the five-act division. As to the Induction and the conversation of the Grex in the play, they form a critical essay resembling the aesthetic prologues of Machiavelli in which a practicing playwright recognized and sought a solution for the problems of his craft.

*Cynthia's Revels* (1600), on the other hand, begins with the reportorial prologue described by Donatus.[8] In defense of his labors, the author appeals from the ignorance of the popular stage to the discrimination of the court audience. From it he hopes for understanding and applause of "his *poesie;* which (he knowes) affords/ Words, aboue action: matter, aboue words." Nevertheless, the poet again demands the right of freedom to experiment:

In this alone, his MVSE her sweetnesse hath,
She shunnes the print of any beaten path;
And proues new wayes to come to learned eares.[9]

A classic Donatist tract is the aptest description of "The Apologetical Dialogue" of *Poetaster* (1602), for it exactly meets the grammarian's definition of the reportorial prologue.[10]

The dedication of *Volpone* combines the Donatist and the Machiavellian prologues. The attack on poetasters, thus, is Donatist. But the eloquent assertion of the didactic function of a playwright "to informe yong-men to all good disciplines, inflame growne-men to all great vertues, keepe old-men in their best and supreme state" accords with the views of Machiavelli. The poet, Jonson goes on with a Horatian conviction, is "the interpreter, and arbiter of nature, a teacher of things divine, no less then humane." [11] He again disclaims any intention in his dramatic work of personal attack, however sharp his satire: this is a Donatist point. Thus wavering between personal defense and aesthetic exposition, he reemphasizes the didactic aim "which is the principall end of *poesie*, to informe men, in the best reason of liuing." This promise, he then concedes, he seems to abandon; hence "my *catastrophe* may, in the strict rigour of *comick* law, meet with censure." In defense of the resolution he claims the right to employ a freedom for aesthetic variety which he had already demanded in *Every Man out of His Humor*. He now asserts the rightness of his method as being in harmony with the moral structure of his play. "But my speciall ayme," he says, was "to put the snaffle in their mouths, that crie out, we neuer punish vice in our *enterludes*." Consequently he is led to the conclusion that it is "the office of a *comick-Poet*, to imitate iustice, and to instruct to life, as well as puritie of language, or stirre vp gentle affections." [12] Here Jonson has exploited the Machiavellian essay for a remarkable and instructive statement about his own aims.

159

The Prologue of *Volpone*, if it has less aesthetic interest than the dedication, is free from embarrassing defensiveness and inspires a gaiety precisely because it is Machiavellian in its genial tone. The "true scope" of the poet is Horatian, "to mix profit with your pleasure." This precludes the clowning, the loose writing and the forced action of the popular theatre and presents, instead,

> quick *comoedie*, refined,
> As best criticks haue designed,
> The lawes of time, place, persons he obserueth,
> From no needfull rule he swerueth.

The neoclassical reassurance does not suppress the insistence on a certain liberty. The language, deliberately inoffensive, possesses "onely, a little salt" to inspire hearty laughter.[13]

Prologue I of *Epicoene* (1609) restates the right of the author to exercise an aesthetic freedom:

> And though all relish not, sure, there will be some,
> That, when they leaue their seates, shall make 'hem say,
> Who wrote that piece, could so haue wrote a play:
> But that, he knew, this was the better way.

Again Jonson relies on the discernment of the attentive auditors. He expands a crib from Machiavelli into a defense of the propriety of his "cates", which are fit and varied enough to please ladies as well as lords, knights and squires.[14] Prologue II restates the Horatian purpose in a flourish of epigram. Then in a more Donatist vein, the author proclaims that he taxes, not persons, but their "crimes"; and in the present play he is aware that the

160

*Poet* neuer credit gain'd
By writing truths, but things (like truths) well fain'd.

Those who distort what he has written for "particular application," make "a libell, which he made a play." [15]

The same defensive spirit marks the address "To the Reader" prefixed to *The Alchemist* (1610). This is a broadside discharged now against the private as well as the popular theatre, and it ends with the caustic renunciation "to doe good on any man against his will," characteristically however denouncing the rude taste of the "unskilfull." [16] The Prologue itself, on the other hand, is Machiavellian in its discussion of comic principles. The performance of the play, for example, requires two hours; the setting is London since the author has found that "No countries mirth is better then our owne," a discovery noted by the Florentine. His *dramatis personae* of "Bawd, squire, imposter, many persons more" is an extension of the cast recommended by the Italian; and the two writers share a belief in the general sameness of men and morals:

Whose manners, now call'd humors, feed the stage:
    And which haue still beene subiect, for the rage
Or spleene of *comick*-writers.

Of course Jonson endorses the didactic and Horatian aim of comedy, which is not "to grieue, but better men" by wholesome remedies that are "sweet,/And, in their working, gaine, and profit meet." Such "faire correctiues" (V. 295), he feels with Machiavelli, will please his auditors.

At the end of Act V, scene 5, there is a highly original treatment of the contemporary concept of propriety. As Jeremy steps forward to the front of the stage to speak the

161

*plaudite*, he admits that his role had, in the preceding scene, declined in importance. But he adds with a twinkle, "Yet 'twas *decorum*." He runs pleasantly through the list of enemies which his transformation from bearded captain to smooth butler has frustrated: Subtle, Surly, Mammon, Doll, Ananias, Dapper and Drugger. He might have added his suddenly returned master Lovewit, whose anger he has changed to reconciliation and the joy of matrimony. From all those named in this ironic recapitulation of self-enrichment, he smugly notes that he himself has "cleane/ Got off," his own fortune no less than his master's transmuted by the alchemist! We do Jonson wrong to miss the playful satire: the force of the reversal that changes Face back into Jeremy is a coincidence humorously exalted to decorum.[17]

The Prologue written for the revised version of *Every Man in His Humor* (1612) is both Donatist and Machiavellian. Rejecting popular formulas, Jonson will instead portray the actual deeds of men using living speech; the personages will be appropriate to comedy

> When she would show an Image of the times,
> And sport with humane follies, not with crimes.[18]

The Ciceronian tag and the decorum, especially in language, are cardinal points in Machiavelli's criticism. These are points also emphasized by the Prologue of *Bartholomew Fair* (1614). The poet warns the king:

> Such place, such men, such language and such ware,
> You must expect: with these, the zealous noyse
> Of your lands *Faction*.

162

These he offers for his majesty's sport, hoping "To giue for a *Fayring*, true delight." [19] With commendable propriety, the author omits the almost mechanical Horatian promise of profit.

The play begins with an Induction that is, in the main, an amusing variation of the Donatist prologue. The bookholder enters with "certaine Articles" drawn up for an agreement between the author and the audience of the Hope Theatre. For their part, they agree to remain in their places, to retain freedom of criticism, but each to use his own judgment and not "censure by *Contagion:*" they are not to expect more than a fair will afford, not to look for real counterparts of the personages, and not to denounce the author for scurrility "because the language some where sauours of *Smithfield.*" For his part, the author promises to stage a new play called *Bartholomew Fair*, "merry, and as full of noise as sport: made to delight all, and to offend none." These provisions agreed to, the comedy is ready to begin. But the author has one last stipulation:

And though the *Fayre* be not kept in the same Region, that some here, perhaps, would haue it, yet thinke, that therein the *Author* hath obseru'd a speciall *Decorum*, the place being as durty as *Smithfield*, and as stinking euery whit.

(VI. 17)

Thus Jonson, as in *The Alchemist*, turns to humorous account that concern for propriety which agitated Machiavelli and other Renaissance dramatists.

Comedy is one of the topics for which Jonson supplied

163

scattered notes in *Timber, or Discoveries* (c. 1619), and these deal with aspects of his art sometimes appearing in the plays. To begin with, the disparagement of Terence recurs twenty years after the emphatic rejection in *Every Man out of His Humor*. In recommending authors for the instruction of youth, he strikes the well-known didactic note, ranking the "*Comicke* with the best, if the manners of the Reader be once in safety." There follows a much more interesting aesthetic antithesis. In Plautus, he claims, "we shall see the Oeconomy, and disposition of Poems, better observed then in *Terence*, and the later." The reason is that the latter thought "the sole grace, and vertue of their Fable, the sticking in of sentences, as ours do the forcing in of jests." [20] This dispraise of the well-knit play of Terence is less surprising, because of the same view in the humoral comedy, than the transference of the appropriate description to the rambling structure of Plautus. In these judgments, Jonson departs from his source, which for the rest he employs faithfully. This is Quintilian, who says that he speaks of Menander and others, not mentioning either Plautus or Terence. Jonson changes the statement to "in the *Greeke* poets, as also in *Plautus*." Quintilian then praises the "oeconomia" or arrangement of the parts in the plays of Menander and his followers, referring vaguely to "plerisque novorum" whose love of "sententias" Jonson has gratuitously ascribed to Terence.[21] This emphatic repetition of the depreciation of the Latin playwright in *Every Man out of His Humor* again raises the question where he studied the economy of the four-part play.

Conversely, Jonson goes out of his way to dispute the judgment of his favorite Horace against Plautus, drawing on Daniel Heinsius [22] for his protest that "it is a hard

Censure upon the parent of all conceipt, and sharp-nesse." [23] Accordingly, he has reservations about Horace's lofty esteem of Terence, reporting incredulously that "he ascribes the Art in Comedie to him alone, among the *Latines*, and joynes him with *Menander*." The English-man is more interested in seeing what may be said "not wholly to condemne *Plautus*" (VIII. 643): Varro, at least, had proclaimed him "the *Prince* of *Letters*, and *Elegancie*, in the *Roman* language" (VIII. 641).

In a discussion of dramatic personages, Jonson briefly explores Cicero's analogy of poetry to oratory. The comic poet, he agrees, closely resembles the orator in the capac-ity in which both excel of "moving the minds of men, and stirring of affections." Comedy even outdoes painting in the lifelike expression of "so many, and various affections of the minde." The examples that substantiate the gener-alization are ones that Machiavelli also had employed.[24] Comedy presents these vivid emotions:

There shall the Spectator see some, insulting with Joy; others, fretting with Melancholy; raging with Anger; mad with Love; boiling with Avarice; undone with Riot; tor-tur'd with expectation; consum'd with feare: no perturba-tion in common life, but the Orator findes an example of it in the Scene.[25]

In other dramatic criticism, Jonson is disappointingly content to submerge his independence of thought under extensive borrowings from Heinsius. Thus he declares, because Heinsius said so, that the parts of a comedy are the same as those of a tragedy. But unlike the essays on dramaturgy that appear in his plays, these remarks con-tain no specific details and no applications: for Heinsius did not condescend to practical considerations. He repeats the assertion that the end of comedy is partly the same as that of tragedy: "both delight, and teach." He now sharply repudiates the constant aim in his own works in his declaration that exciting laughter is not always the aim of comedy: "as *Aristotle* saies rightly, the moving of laughter is a fault in Comedie" (VIII. 643). Here he follows, not Aristotle, but Aristotle as misunderstood by Heinsius.[26] The objects which he now says inspire laughter appear to be Sidneyan; such are "a wry face without paine" or "a deformed vizard" or "a rude Clowne, drest in a Ladies habit, and using her actions." We scorn such representations, he explains, much as the ancient philosophers "ever thinke laughter unfitting in a wise man" (VIII. 643-44). The direct source of these remarks is Heinsius.

Jonson carefully translates Heinsius also in his statements about the fable of a drama, about imitation, and about the unity of action: the last includes the Aristotelian division of beginning, middle and end, a not very instructive utterance. Only rarely does he look up in the *Poetics* any matter derived therefrom by his source. Consequently his limitation of time is neoclassical and not Aristotelian. The action of a comedy, he writes, should

be let grow, till the necessity aske a Conclusion: wherin two things are to be considered; First, that it exceed not the compasse of one Day: Next, that there be place left for digression, and Art.[27]

(VIII. 647)

The undeveloped and yet pregnant suggestions of structure and variety come from Heinsius. The effect of this

166

dependence is to cheat the reader of informative observations given authority by a lifetime of experience in the theatre. Once Jonson argued vehemently for his kind of play; now he indolently neglects the ideal opportunity to substantiate or refute the commonplace generalizations of the Dutch humanist.

In the Induction of *The Staple of News* (1626), however, Jonson reasserts his aesthetic independence, for like *Bartholomew Fair* it dramatizes the genial satire of the Donatist apology. Attired like ladies, four "ridiculous Gossips that tattle betweene the *Acts*"[28] interrupt the Prologue. These bogus women of fashion insist on the privilege of sitting on the stage and being seen, and from this point of vantage they propose to censure noblemen and their wits and poets. After a gibe at the playwright as "rowling himselfe vp and downe like a tun"[29] they seat themselves and let the first Prologue begin. This (for the Stage) is a conventional Donatist appeal for silence so that the actors may not have to compete with conversation and other social exchanges customary at theatres. It then reverts to a more Machiavellian statement of intent: the poet's task is to guide the soul with his pen, instructing youth and keeping age "in the state of truth" (VI. 282). A second Prologue (for the Court) is cast in the difficult form of the Sidneyan sonnet. Despite this formidably literary flourish, it promises a work not smelling of the lamp, which will delight the king since it will "shew you common follies" in close imitation of life (VI. 283), the Donatist-Ciceronian commonplace. The epilogue recalls to the audience another commonplace, the Horatian intent "To *profit* and *delight*" (VI. 382).

Jonson prefixed an argument to *The New Inn* (1631) that begins as a Donatist summary of plot but includes an intimation of the four-part structure. The protasis is very long, running to the end of Act II, which has six scenes. This unusual length was due to Jonson's wish to allow for the introduction of personages who make their first appearance only in II. 6, and it demonstrates the flexibility of the structure. Then the poet calls attention to the second part: "Here begins, at the *third Act*, the *Epitasis*, or businesse of the *Play*," [30] and it runs to the end of Act IV. Of the final part he says, "The fifth, and last *Act* is the *Catastrophe*, or knitting vp of all" (VI. 401). The presence of the technical terms and their easy definitions show that even in the dotages Jonson relied on the proved advantages of this method of construction.

Jonson's last play, *The Magnetic Lady* (1632), has (like the early *Every Man out of His Humor*) a substantial body of information about his dramatic practice. The Induction or Chorus here, like the Grex there, consists of an informed commentator and an ignorant auditor particularly in need of instruction, with a third well-disposed person. These are respectively the Prompt-boy, Damplay and Probee. They begin with an agreement that the purpose of the stage is to please the people, their warrant coming, not from Horace, but surprisingly from Terence.[31] The Boy then asserts that the present play, like any true comedy, will unfold "*In Foro*" or on stage, any matter "conceald within" being "brought out, and made present by report." Authors who fail to do this "never dreamt of any *Decorum*, or what was proper in the *Scene*." [32] Like the expressive statement in the Induction of *Bartholomew Fair*, this denotes a lifetime adherence to a neoclassical principle also dear to Machiavelli. Like him Jonson is now indifferent to "vulgar censure" in the confidence that he will "super-please judicious Spectators" (VI. 511).

For the pleasure and instruction of that ideal audience, Jonson gives his most elaborate discussion of the four-part structure. At the end of the first conventional division of the play, the Boy explains that they have reached the close of "our *Protasis,* or first *Act,*" whose purpose was to make "a faire presentment of your *Actors.* And a handsome promise of somewhat to come hereafter." Damplay grumbles that "there is nothing done in it, or concluded. Therefore I say, no *Act.*" In reply, the Boy embarks upon a detailed exposition of a play's structure:

Do you looke, Mr. *Damplay*, for conclusions in a *Protasis?* I thought the Law of *Comedy* had reseru'd <'hem> to the *Catastrophe:* and that the *Epitasis* (as wee are taught) and the *Catastasis,* had beene interveening parts, to have beene expected. But you would have all come together, it seems. The Clock should strike five, at once, with the Acts.

(VI. 527)

Thus Jonson, at the same time that he keeps the mechanical division of events into five acts, asserts for the underlying four-part structure the superior effectiveness of a higher aesthetic law.

In the Chorus at the end of Act II Damplay asks for an identification of one of the personages, but Probee disclaims on the author's behalf any intention of confusing his stage characters with real ones, citing the example of Plautus and Terence. Damplay's vice of interpretation, he explains, twists a comedy awry from its purpose. This is to hold up "the Glasse of custome" and to exhibit "the daily examples of mens lives, and images of Truth, in their manners," the hallowed Donatist-Ciceronian definition. He adds the Horatian explanation that the poet offers these "for my delight, or profit" (VI. 544-45).

169

The epitasis of *The Magnetic Lady* occupies Acts II, III and IV. The Chorus at the end of IV discuss the purpose of the *catastasis* and its relation to the *catastrophe*. Although a conspicuous device in the series of plays beginning with *Every Man in His Humor*, it receives nowhere else in Jonson's writings a precise definition. At this point in the performance, the bewildered Damplay finds the action of the comedy "pull'd into that knot, by your Poët, which I cannot easily, with all the strength of my imagination, untie." Precisely, the Boy retorts, for the office of an auditor is "to sit still, and expect." Probee amplifies the advice by declaring that the spectators should follow events as the playwright unfolds them, observing the business on foot at the present climax and not losing the right thread. Jonson thus makes the point that ingenious plotting requires attentive auditors. But now the benighted critic objects that the play might have ended with Act IV and so have spared the audience "the vexation of a fift *Act* yet to come, which every one here knowes the issue of already, or may in part conjecture." This, the Boy replies, is to miss the poet's purpose. For it ignores the renewed suspense created by the twist or counterturn in the action called the *catastasis*. Therefore the Boy urges,

Stay, and see his last *Act*, his *Catastrophe*, how he will perplexe that, or spring some fresh cheat, to entertaine the *Spectators*, with a convenient delight, til some unexpected and new encounter breake out to rectifie all and make good the *Conclusion*.

(VI. 577-78)

This is a far more informative description than the one

170

with which Donatus fumbled in his analysis of Terence's *Andria*.[33] The notes in *The Magnetic Lady* form another Machiavellian essay.

Jonson's series of pronouncements on comedy are, then, both defensive, after Donatus, and critical, after Machiavelli. The critical statements all tend in one direction. They claim for the English Renaissance playwright the freedom to experiment with dramatic methods. The most recurrent of these experiments is the attempt to dispose the constituent phases of a dramatic action in the four-part structure. Terence had shown the way in *Andria;* Donatus and Scaliger provided it with a descriptive terminology; and Machiavelli both revived it and employed it with cunning variations in his original comedies. If Jonson emphatically rejected Terence as a model, he nonetheless practiced assiduously the Terentian art of the well-made play. But for this he had the benefit of the Italian's adaptations. In response to the implied encouragement of Jonson's extensive notes, the student of his work should find it rewarding to make a fresh analysis of the design of his comedies along the lines laid down in his dramatic essays. This will now be our concern.

# Chapter 9

## THE DESIGN OF *EVERY MAN IN HIS HUMOR*
### (Quarto)

*Every Man in His Humor* (1598) remains a pioneering achievement in design, as in other ways. In it Jonson introduced to the Elizabethan stage a play built on the four-part structure that cuts across the five-act division in an unimpeded dramatic movement. Moreover, he attempted in the Quarto or Italian version to write a comedy that is, like Machiavelli's, at once satiric and romantic. To that end, he experiments (like Machiavelli in *Clizia*) [1] with the presence of two blocking characters. In the worried father Lorenzo Sr. and in the jealous husband and suspicious brother Thorello he answers the question what makes a blocking character absurd [2] by ascribing his oddness to an amusing obsession or "humor". Equally important, the two old men function as obstacles to the smooth course of true love whose removal the romantic catastrophe requires. Satire makes them gulls who relax a protective vigil over son and over wife and sister. Romance makes necessary, at last, the reconciliation of merchant-father and poet-son, of jealous husband and suspicious wife, and also a wedding to transmute all emotions into joy: Jonson in the mode of Shakespeare.

172

The playwright takes advantage of the flexibility of the structure which he imposes on his incidents by extending the *protasis* into Act II. This method of linking units of the action raises the question whether he did not sense, as Machiavelli's practice suggested, that the five-act division is a largely conventional and literary device.[3] The play begins with a type of character in a kind of situation made familiar by Terence, developed in a slight but seminal enlargement by Machiavelli and fully elaborated by his Italian followers. This is the indulgent but worried citizen-father Lorenzo di Pazzi, Sr. (I. 1) whose son's devotion to study has won favor in "all our *Academies*" (he has studied at the University of Pisa) [4] but who has fallen into "one vayne course," a "humor" for "idle *Poetrie*". This solicitude, of course, makes the audience suspect that an equally traditional object of a parent's disapproval, love, looms even more ominously over the household. The disharmony between the two generations is signalized by the marked difference in their ages,[5] a detail Jonson dwells on with the pertinacity of Italian comedy.

The dramatic movement begins with the delivery to the house of a letter. This comes from a friend of the son, Prospero, addressed ambiguously to Lorenzo di Pazzi; and it falls by merely apparent error into the hands of the father. He opens it with guilty curiosity, explaining self-consciously that he desires to savor the excellence of the style and of the writer's invention. But it is actually a whimsical invitation to enjoy in Prospero's company the entertainment provided by two complete gulls; it contains also practical counsel for eluding the father by some memorable lie, the sort of thing (the writer gaily asserts) in which Lorenzo Jr., as a poet, is very fertile. Dismayed by such words from such a "pretious wit", as the son had described Prospero, the old man deplores his boy's captivity to this "geering *follie*, and fantastique *humour*." He sets himself the hard task of reclaiming Lorenzo Jr. from "so loose a spirit"; and though he will not prevent the meeting between the two, he will meanwhile study some mild means of turning the young man to "a happier shrift." The awkward relationship between the two generations is the basis of the first sub-action of the *protasis*.

Lorenzo Jr. (I. 2) receives the letter from the household servant Musco, who disobeys his master by adding the irritating information that the father has already opened it. Musco's instant decision resolves the classic dilemma of the *servus*, for example Davus in *Andria*. Unlike the latter, he rather favors his young than fears his old master. Welcoming the letter with laughter at its misdirection—"it is able to breake the shinnes of any old mans patience in the world"—Lorenzo determines to join his friend and grace the entertainment by the display of his own favorite gull, his country cousin Stephano.

Jonson anticipates Prospero's exhibition by presenting the second sub-action of the *protasis* in the appearance of his gulls (I. 3), a pilferer of verses, Matheo, and a bogus captain, Bobadilla. The impoverished old soldier credits his humble lodging in the house of the water-bearer Cob [6] to a dislike of being overwhelmed by popularity. When Matheo reports the threat of Prospero's older brother Giuliano to cudgel him, Bobadilla brags that by the life of Pharaoh he would have challenged him on the instant. He then drills the simple youth in a fencing lesson with bedstaves for rapiers. They set out for Prospero's dwelling resolute for a meeting with "*Coridon* his brother," the captain's sarcastic synonym for boor.

For the presentation of the third sub-action of the *pro-*

*tasis*, the scene shifts (I. 4) to the house whither all the young men are bound, that of the merchant Thorello. He complains to his brother-in-law Giuliano of the dissipations of his younger brother Prospero, who (he charges heatedly) makes his house a tavern where he and his wild companions swear, leap, dance and revel night after night. He reveals, moreover, a deeper uneasiness. He fears that since he is newly married to a beautiful woman whose young sister lives with him, any hint of displeasure he might make would cause others to accuse him of jealousy and so "stab my reputation, and good name." The stage for Prospero's entertainment of gulls, therefore, provides an opportunity for other mischief.

The swaggering entrance of Bobadilla and Matheo interrupts the painful comedy of the jealous but peaceable citizen. This changes quickly to farce as the loud boaster, first insulting Giuliano, sneaks away from a confrontation and yet has the last word in the taunt of "Scauenger". His enemy explodes in anger and promises, like a gentleman, to satisfy honor with his sword and "Fill that huge tumbrell slop of yours," the fine loose breeches admired by Matheo. Braggart and nemesis now go separate ways.

Thorello reverts to his obsession, the fatuous conviction that no woman could remain virtuous in the cluster of gallants around Prospero. From this he leaps to the logical conclusion of absurdity that only the occasion has been wanting to make him a cuckold. Therefore he will watch every look and glance, and "My presence shall be as an Iron Barre." At this moment Jonson introduces the wife Biancha and her sister Hesperida going cheerfully about their household tasks. Hesperida, obviously, is the technical heroine of the piece; and there is, therefore, the foundation of romance in the presence of a marriageable

175

girl whose youthful attractiveness deserves better than her declared suitor, Matheo. The happy wife is generous with caresses and endearments for her new husband and concerned, like a comic Desdemona, about the peculiar headache from which he suffers. Whether her talk is simple or subtle, he cannot tell; he broods miserably on the plague of jealousy, which invades and possesses the whole mind.

Solicitous citizen-father, fun-loving poet-son, two vacant youths and a cautious braggart, his quick-tempered enemy and the jealous husband, the presence of whose sister also multiplies interest—these are the humors and the lines of action presented in Act I. The *protasis* includes it but does not coincide with it since there are other introductory details in the offing. Thus Jonson prolongs the dramatic movement in a dynamic disregard of the act division, putting off till II. 1 the introduction of Musco's humor, a very important aspect of this humor play. He now reappears disguised as a soldier, his motive being "to insinuate with my young master" by using any pretext to delay the father and lying like a trooper to prevent his discovery of his son's occupations. The extension of the first part of the structure into Act II links this solidly to I. Musco's words, furthermore, when confirmed by the entrance of Lorenzo Sr. at II. 2, prepare for the initial step forward in the second part.

The *epitasis*, then, begins with Act II, scene 2, as Lorenzo Sr. trudges along pondering some means of countering "my sonnes follie" and leading him back "To reasons manage." His soliloquy on nature and the mind, despite its wisdom, reiterates the comic theme of the appeal to reason by the anxiously unreasonable parent. Musco inadvertently tests his disguise by a sudden appearance. His begging gets him a sermon and employment as the father's servant Portensio. With complacent satisfaction in his costume, he will now be a party to "all his determinations," which he will share with his young master.

Along the street Prospero now appears (II. 3) accompanied by Matheo and Bobadilla. For dramatic suspense Jonson, experimenting with Machiavelli's practice,[7] has cleverly postponed till early in the *epitasis* the entrance of this main character whose acts have already excited interest. When Lorenzo Jr. joins him with Stephano, he greets his friend affectionately, swearing to love the poet's patron "*Appollo*, & the mad Thespian girles the better while I liue for this." But Lorenzo upbraids him pleasantly for misdirecting the letter, saying cheerfully that the worst damage done was to the reputation of the friend. By the evidence of his missive itself, his father regards him as "a damn'd dissolute villaine" and his son as little better for keeping him company. Prospero thoroughly enjoys the large return from a small investment of fun.

The *epitasis* now develops the second sub-action in a performance of the gulls, Prospero's "two *Zanies*" and Stephano, who likewise "hath his humor." The clown who dominates the occasion by his fertile lies is Bobadilla, affecting a gravity which forces him to a silence that gets the attention of all. Reluctant to utter his thoughts, he falls into a melancholy nostalgia and tells of his military valor on St. Mark's day ten years before. As the other gulls gasp with envy of his oaths, Prospero and Lorenzo collaborate in encouraging him to triumphs of solemn absurdity.

The disguised Musco introduces another forward step in the *epitasis*. Catching up with his young master, he must first, so successful is his counterfeit appearance, explain who he is. Then he warns of the coming of Lorenzo

177

Sr. in search of his son. Prospero rallies that perturbed youth by a gay little homily on the superiority of their fresh wits over the father's "old plodding braine" capped fittingly by the concluding formula of a sermon, *"in secula seculorum."* Musco catches the fun-loving spirit with his "Amen, Amen." On Prospero's initiative, they complicate the sub-action centering on father and son by concealment in Thorello's house, where he proposes that they take their ease.

The intentional ambiguity of the letter was the first frolicsome exploit of Prospero, whom Jonson makes from the beginning of this first characteristic play the comic intriguer, delightfully ingenious at all times "to hould vp a iest," as he confesses to his victims at the *catastrophe.*[8] Thus he plays the role of entertainer as he shows off his gulls and expertly compares their points with the example furnished by Lorenzo Jr. With his friend he forms a little society of well-bred young men pleasantly whiling away the tedious hours in mischievous idleness. In this aspect he foreshadows the more significant intriguer, Sir Eugenie Dauphine, in *Epicoene.* Appropriately in a comedy that is romantic as well as satiric, he is also a matchmaker, vigorously prosecuting his friend's suit and clearing away all the not inconsiderable obstacles. As events unfold, he lays new little plots for the fun of it (the point he makes to Dr. Clement), seizing opportunities with a casual ingenuity that accomplishes one triumph of amusement after another. The mischief he inspires, especially at the expense of the sober citizen world on which his feats are a youthful and irreverent comment, becomes the primary source of the joy that irradiates this most light-hearted of Jonson's plays.

The *epitasis* continues in III. 1 without interruption as

Jonson develops the sub-action of Thorello. Even as he counts his money and calls for his cloak to go about his affairs, he fears that his absence will provide the opportunity for "trecherie". Preposterous as he tortures himself with love and fear, he decides not to leave the house. Feeling the need to confide his troubles to a safe ear, he tries to share his secret with his loyal servant Piso, alluding mysteriously to a thing that "sits neerer to my crest,/ Then thou art ware of." But he only succeeds in leaving one clear command, to send him word at once if Prospero brings any gentlemen to the house in his absence, a line of action for future unfolding. He departs in the half-absurd knowledge that there is "No greater hell then to be slaue to feare."

The entrance of Prospero and his companions links III. 2 closely with the preceding scene as Piso sends Cob to Dr. Clement's for Thorello. Meanwhile the gulls again amuse the young men. Bobadilla praises tobacco for its nutritive and medicinal virtues and beats Cob for disparaging the herb, valiant against an unarmed menial, "Body of *Cesar.*" Stephano's part is to practice the oaths and gestures of the soldier, unaware of the attention of the others. They follow Matheo, who has departed to court his mistress, Hesperida, with his verses.

Thorello hurries home (III. 3), magnifying the company with Prospero into "A swarme, a swarme." He sighs with regret:

What meant I to marrie?
I that before was rankt in such content.

He seeks to face the fact, "thou art a cuckold"; and to discover his rival he closely quizzes Cob as to who kissed

179

his wife first; then he dashes out tempestuously. Here Jonson introduces the humorous magistrate Dr. Clement accompanied by Lorenzo Sr. When Cob begs for a warrant enjoining Bobadilla to keep the peace, the former on learning that a denunciation of tobacco was the cause of his beating orders him to jail for abusing the princely herb. Lorenzo Sr., anticipating Hamlet, exclaims compassionately, "Alasse poore *Oliuer*." Thereupon, the justice relents and issues the warrant, a laughable pacific instrument that may, however, serve one coward as well as another, as we see in IV. 2. Dr. Clement turns to the subaction of the anxious father by urging the claims of youth: "What? your sonne is old inough, to gouerne himselfe; let him runne his course, it's the onely way to make him a stay'd man." As for himself, had he twice so many cares, he'd drown them in a cup of sack. This healthy opposition to the other's solicitude by the fun-loving and powerful composer of differences foreshadows the spirit of the *catastrophe*.

Giuliano and Biancha (III. 4) exchange angry words about the company that haunt the house. Her reminder that they are Prospero's friends inspires in the elder brother an almost paternal anxiety lest these "Vnlucky Sprites" tempt him "to all maner of villainy." The crowd of young people swoop in, their little sister Hesperida playing a conspicuous part. She actively promotes the fun of the well-bred young men by encouraging her "servant" Matheo to expend his "wits treasure" on her praises. He recites an elegy pieced together with brazen pilferings from Marlowe's *Hero and Leander*, as the merrymakers smother a laugh at the theft from the dead. Their linguistic mirth as they ring changes on *meretrix* draws Biancha into their range, and Giuliano tries to expel them, pouncing on the silenced Bobadilla. But Prospero is ready with his rapier to defend their gulls, and on all sides they draw their weapons as the women scream. Thus protected, the soldier threatens Giuliano to "pinck thy flesh full of holes." He gravely promises not to kill him. At this point Thorello bursts in, and the gallants hasten away. The husband shouts to know "who enforst this braule", and Giuliano fumes over the "lewd rakehelles."

Having reached the mid-point of the *epitasis*, Jonson exploits the flexibility of the quadripartite structure again by setting in motion a fourth sub-action. Giuliano's sneer at the young men and their gulls as having neither "manhood nor good manners" makes Hesperida bridle. At least she had found "one a ciuill gentleman," Lorenzo Jr. When Thorello derides this "loue of yours," she sighs,

> A loue of mine? in fayth I would he were
> No others loue but mine.

Biancha supports her with a spontaneous tribute to "a gentleman of an exceeding fayre disposition, and of very excellent good partes." This sympathetic understanding of her sister's new feelings only fans Thorello's uneasy suspicion to certainty. This is "my wifes minion," he decides, and searches the house. In this scene Jonson has at last significantly developed the hint of romance in I. 4 and thus has aroused a new kind of pleasurable anticipation in the audience. Although the scene ends with the confirmed jealousy of the suspicious husband, the author gives the claims of love for a moment predominance over satire.

At the Mitre tavern (III. 6) the merrymakers prepare complications in the *epitasis*. Trusting the disguised Musco's loyalty Lorenzo charges him with "this business,"

181

the explanation for which Jonson defers till Act IV, scene 1. When Prospero speaks mysteriously of another "deuise", the audience pleasantly awaits a humorous scheme like the misdirected letter or the exhibition of the gulls. The misgiving of his friend increases the expectation, satisfaction for which does not come till IV. 3. More informatively, Prospero gives the servant a message for "my brother: for theres no other meanes to start him." Speculation whether he means Thorello or Giuliano likewise remains till IV. 3. But the chief business of the scene is to provide impetus to the fourth sub-action. Hesperida's love for Lorenzo is matched by his ardent affection for her. Thus Jonson prepares for the *catastrophe* appropriate to romantic comedy. At the same time, he deepens the sober father's disapproval of his poet son's ways by adding the traditional frivolity of love to other sources of displeasure. Meanwhile, the love affair prospers as the brother, eager to match sister and friend, promises to fetch her immediately to an agreed rendezvous. The young men, furthermore, each take a step to remove the blocking characters, the lover to escape the vigilance of his father and the friend to tempt his brother-in-law from his house. Here again the movement of the action toward romance predominates though not to the exclusion of renewed mischief.

As the *epitasis* continues into the fourth act, Jonson reveals what Lorenzo Jr.'s "business" was in III. 6. Musco (scene 1) reveals to Lorenzo Sr. (as his servant Portensio) his son's knowledge of all his plans, perhaps, since he is a scholar by means of the black art. The possibility of "such a diuelish practice" dismays the anxious father. Musco also pretends that he overheard the son make an assignation with a rich citizen's wife at Cob's house. Certain that the youth has fallen into the frivolous humor of love, the father rushes to the water-bearer's dwelling, a blocking character diverted from the path he had stubbornly followed. Musco goes with Dr. Clement's man Peto to share a pottle of wine at the Mermaid, another thread left dangling till IV. 3.

The second scene resumes the second sub-action of the play in the renewed silliness of the gulls. Bobadilla in particular climbs to strange heights of solemn braggadocio and plummets to sudden disgrace. His bloodthirsty arithmetic causes Lorenzo to express a sly gratitude for not being in Giuliano's shoes, especially since the soldier never yet missed a thrust. Bobadilla generously promises to content himself with bastinadoing the elder brother. That personage here passes across the stage and inspires a new dodge just before the fall: the pretense that it was not the enemy who walked by. Cornered and challenged to draw his weapon or receive a thrashing, the soldier evades the quarrel on the pretext that he cannot fight because enjoined by Cob's warrant to keep the peace. And so he endures his beating and pacifically submits to disarming, his explanation being that since he is restrained by Cob's injunction he may conscientiously refuse combat, or if that proves unavailing he may conscientiously yield to the cudgel. Besides, a planet must have bewitched him into powerlessness to touch his rapier during the scuffle.

In Thorello's house (IV. 3) Prospero seizes every opportunity for gay machinations. He blames Giuliano for the noisy humiliation of Bobadilla: as to the angry squire, "whats a tall man vnlesse he fight?"

He gives an impetus to the third sub-action by the same gift for farcical mischief. As to Biancha's nervousness that some harm might have come of the brawl, he points out that on the same principle her husband's clothes or his wine might be poisoned. Deceived by the verbal trick, Thorello feels ill at once and calls for an antidote, as his pleased tormentor declares, "poysond with a simile." Musco, now wearing the clothes of Dr. Clement's man Peto, gives a surprising twist to the thread of plot left dangling at the end of IV. 1. Here Jonson clarifies the mention by Prospero in III. 6 of a deception to "start" his brother, for the false Peto gives the false message (entrusted to him then) asking Thorello to see Dr. Clement without delay. The jealous husband, and equally, vigilant brother obeys the summons, removing a second blocking character from the difficult course of true love. The new situation enables Prospero to give Musco a more sentimental message to deliver to Lorenzo Jr., that he meet Hesperida and himself at the Friary since in the house "there is no roome for loue to stand vpright in."

Thorello hurries back, again warning Piso to watch Biancha and the gallants, and then dashes out to see Cob. The humor that afflicts the husband now infects the wife, as Prospero had hoped, and she distrusts Cob. Her mischievous brother, exploiting the occasion for new mirth, asserts that Cob's wife is a bawd whose house her husband visits. This invention sends her in pursuit, and by requiring the escort of the trusty Piso she surrenders Thorello's household to the possession of merry youth. Prospero teases his sister on her beauty and charm, then more seriously urges the suit of his dear and respected friend Lorenzo who, he asserts, "hath vowed to inflame whole bonefires of zeale in his hart, in honor of your perfections." Moved by such eloquence she is eager to keep the appointment at the Friary and ready to "blesse my happy starres." Thorello's return threatens their scheme

184

only briefly, for Prospero impishly suggests, when the husband fearfully demands where Biancha has gone, that it is to Cob's. Thither the jealous man hurries at once.

In IV. 4 Bobadilla and Matheo console each other, the former's abjection seeming in retrospect merely a rude touch with soft wood borne with exemplary patience, the latter's flight gentlemanly discretion. Musco's appearance in the clothes of Dr. Clement's servant gives them the opportunity to seek a civilian's revenge on Giuliano in a warrant and arrest. The false Peto, already planning to get money by pawning his apparel, yields to the temptation of further gain and demands five crowns for a warrant. In lieu of the sum, he accepts a jewelled earring and silk stockings and sets a meeting on the Rialto.[9]

This unlooked-for windfall causes Musco to suffer an access of comic hubris. Entrusted with the message for Lorenzo Jr. that is to prepare for the romantic catastrophe (IV. 3), he now usurps the role of a prime mover in the action, and so precipitates a *catastasis* or counterturn in the action. An unexpected comic dividend, this introduces a complication by their agent of which Prospero and Lorenzo remain in total ignorance. Musco proposes to trade the clothes of the doctor's man for a varlet's suit, to act himself as the varlet, and get either more bribes to pawn or money from Giuliano to avoid arrest.[10] In his zeal for fun and gain, he seems about to abandon his necessary role in the love affair. This new uncertainty is the kind of perplexity set forth in the Chorus of *The Magnetic Lady*.[11]

The comic form that Jonson gives this *catastasis* anticipates the use of the structural device so brilliantly exemplified in *Volpone*.[12] If that is a comic imitation of a tragedy, Jonson is content in *Every Man in His Humor* to borrow for the mirthful enrichment of comedy the kind of climax monopolized by tragedy. It complicates the movement of the play with a welcome uncertainty. In tone and in the expectation aroused in the audience its action centers on youth and friendship and love, their happy outcome and the reconciliations with crabbed age which they inspire. The question as to what Musco will actually do, what effect his infatuated confidence will have on the short-tempered and not altogether simple Giuliano, how this twist will affect Thorello and Lorenzo Sr., and above all whether his aberrant conduct will undermine the machinations of Prospero or the happenings at the Friary —these unresolved matters demand a fifth act to unravel.

Lorenzo Sr. and Biancha (V. 1) confront each other before Cob's house, and he mistakes her for the citizen's wife described by Musco in IV. 1 in accordance with the business set in motion by Lorenzo Jr. Then Thorello, in accordance with the scheme of Prospero in IV. 3, swoops upon them, denouncing her as an impudent strumpet and him as a hoary-headed lecher. Giuliano adds to the misery of the jealous husband by informing him of the escape of Hesperida. Thorello groans, "a harlot too?" and blames his wife: "She takes right after her." He hales his suspects to Dr. Clement's.

Stephano, dressed in Giuliano's russet cloak (V. 2), creates an obstacle for Musco when in the varlet's suit he tries to serve a counterfeit warrant on the counterfeit squire. The angry Giuliano roars in, and Musco charges him to keep the peace and appear before Dr. Clement. The audience trembles in a brief uncertainty before his disguise succeeds as Giuliano gives him a fee to arrest Stephano for theft. At first, then, his comic hubris has a profitable consequence. But Giuliano ominously refuses to take back his cloak and forces Musco to escort them to the magistrate's. Now exposure and punishment loom terribly before him. Like the tragic hero, he does not accept his fate without a struggle. He tries to give the fee back to the squire, then to persuade him to take the gentleman's word to appear when called, and finally to accompany him alone without the varlet. Giuliano is firm. Musco, crestfallen on seeing his confident audacities in ruins, fears "I haue made a fayre mashe of it."

In the final scene (V. 3), all the sub-actions converge on Dr. Clement's house, the setting for the *catastrophe*. Despite the noisy confusion, the magistrate shows that Lorenzo Sr., Thorello and Biancha were all gulls at the mercy of a trick. When Bobadilla and Matheo entreat him for redress of the wrongs done by Giuliano, he mocks the military pretensions of the former and dismisses this gull as a bogus soldier. The entrance of the squire with Musco and the ensuing revelation of his disguise and his trickeries concentrate on the servant Dr. Clement's angry attention. However, his pleasure in "a merry knaue" leads the jest-loving magistrate to drink a bowl of sack in salute to his roguery. The spirit of the resolution passes, thus, from stern justice to forgiveness and mirth. The comic retribution reprieves the insolent culprit, and he freely delivers his tale of the day's disguises and intrigues. The climax of his narrative, a complete surprise to solicitous father and vigilant brother, comes with the report of Hesperida's elopement. The magistrate signalizes a sympathy for youthful love by shaking the hand of this agent of joy.

The fourth sub-action of the play, therefore, dominates a catastrophe in which satire has yielded to romance. The eager young gallants and the affianced girl on their entrance win the sanction of their adventures. Although Lorenzo Sr., heavy father almost to the end, bemoans the trouble to his peace by "this dayes worke of yours," Dr. Clement deprecates the reproach as a lapse from sympathetic jubilation and assumes full responsibility for everybody's future. A theme prominent in I. 1 reappears when the exposure of Matheo's thefts inspires an impassioned apology for poetry by Lorenzo Jr. Significantly, Dr. Clement applauds this linguistic humor, giving the authority of his approval to youth, love and poetry.

The magistrate also devises a resolution for the subactions in a general reconciliation from which only the gulls are excluded. He commands them, "I must haue you all friends" and leaves them to make their peace while he takes the lovers aside. Thorello and Biancha kiss and make up after Prospero has explained his mischief: "Fayth I did it but to hould vp a iest: and helpe my sister to a husband." In this romantic function he wins the last necessary assent to the betrothal from Lorenzo Sr., and the softened father urges "a generall content." Thereupon Dr. Clement urges him to resign his "cares", husband and wife their jealousy, Giuliano his anger and Prospero his "wit". Bringing Lorenzo Jr. and Hesperida forward, he bespeaks "a peace offering, heres one willing to be sacrifised vppon this aulter." He leads in wishing them joy and invites all to be his guests and enjoy "the very spirite of mirth." His arm about the shoulders of the young intriguer Prospero, he also proposes a carouse "to the health of this *Heroick* spirite." For in the *protasis* of the comedy, as in the *epitasis* and the *catastrophe*, his machinations set the action going and sustain it. Its satiric no less than its romantic close, Jonson clearly felt, invites the magistrate's admiration and the applause of the audience.

## Chapter 10

## STRUCTURE IN JONSON'S COMIC MASTERPIECES

*Surprise and Irony in "Epicoene"*

Unlike Hamlet in his contempt for the unskillful and his desire for the censure solely of the judicious, Jonson in the prologue of *Epicoene,* or *The Silent Woman* (1609), promises "to content the people" at the same time that his very title is one of the "cates" [1] reserved for lords and knights and the attentive auditors he could rely on to relish his subtlety. He builds an action that paradoxically combines an irony of tone with surprise in the resolution. For this purpose he bends the four-part structure, which he assimilated in *Every Man in His Humor* and also manipulated in *Volpone,* to its extreme limit of flexibility, boldly experimenting with a delayed *catastasis.* Applauded before Dryden and after for its unity, *Epicoene* restores the variety of the earlier play.[2] This consists in amplifying a simple linear pattern by means of a series of constituent sub-actions and related themes appropriate to a comedy of manners, sometimes developed singly and sometimes woven together. Moreover, the gay intriguer

Prospero reappears in Sir Dauphine Eugenie, an advance in being the single sharp focus, with his silent woman, of the play's twin effects of surprise and irony.

The *protasis*, as before, runs through Act I and the first scene of II in a dramatic movement that continues without pause across the conventional act division. I. 1 begins with Clerimont and his friend Truewit in a discussion of the pastimes enabling one to "melt away his time" so that "the houres ha' no wings," an explicit definition of the problem faced by the well-bred and fun-loving Prospero and Lorenzo Jr. in *Every Man in His Humor*. A man may have his mistress, his minion, music, racing, hunting, gambling, even learned jesting, but above all the society of ladies. This discussion establishes the controlling mood of elegance and amusement indulged by young men of wealth, fashion and breeding.

The mention of ladies is Truewit's cue to give Clerimont the latest gossip about "the colledge". The subject forms the first sub-action,[3] the activities of the "new foundation" of women "that call themselues the Collegiates, an order betweene courtiers, and country-madames." Neglecting their husbands, they bestow their favors on "all the *Wits*, and *Braueries* o' the time", the familiar gulls now masquerading as fools intellectual and fools social.[4] As in *Every Man in His Humor*, the primary amusement of the young gentlemen is the exposure of pretenders and all who violate their canons of refined behavior. The president of the college is the youthful matron Lady Haughty, and the triumph of her skill in cosmetics on her "autumnall face" leads to the statement of a theme recurrent in the play, whether in a woman's beauty art is preferable to nature.[5]

190

Truewit also introduces the second sub-action with his mention of the melancholy Dauphine Eugenie, "Sicke o' the vncle". The estrangement of the latter and his nephew, and after the removal of the single blocking character, their surprising reconciliation form the main business of the play. The predominant humor of the old man, Morose, is a hatred of noise, which tempts the idle youths to tease him by seeking loud encounters. The entrance of Dauphine (scene 2) completes the exposition with the report of Morose's zeal to marry and by begetting an heir to disinherit his nephew. Delighted by the uncle's search for a silent woman to be his bride, Dauphine's companions are fertile in schemes to torment him. But the nephew refuses to join them, avowing with suspicious gravity, "He shall neuer ha' that plea against me, that I oppos'd the least phant'sie of his." Struck by a mischievous inspiration for pleasantly whiling away the time, Truewit abruptly departs. Again Dauphine mocks his own solemnity with Clerimont by the casual mention of an intrigue which he vaguely describes as "a businesse", a foreshadowing of the *epitasis*.

The two gentlemen pass to the third sub-action in the wooing of the silent woman by the pretended wit Jack Daw and in the ostentations of the bravery Sir Amorous La-Fool. This rich young upstart arrives (scene 4) to invite the others to his quarter-feast at the home of Captain Tom Otter, where the Collegiates will welcome the silent woman, now first named Epicoene. The titular personage comes upon the audience's attention with a casual ease requiring alertness for the appreciation of the exquisite irony of her part.[6] This moment is significant, for it changes a mild curiosity about Dauphine's business to an awakened confidence in his sly adroitness and therefore in the ironic aspect of the action.

The *protasis* also introduces the antagonist of the second sub-action. From his first appearance (II. 1) Morose is, with his crotchets, his speaking tube for deafness, his "graue head" (II. 2. 29) and especially with his old man's passion for a young girl, an absurdity rich in theatrical tradition. He resembles the seventy-year-old Nicomaco in Machiavelli's *Clizia* [7] and the pantaloon of the *commedia dell' arte*. His aim in life is a delicate and heretofore elusive "felicitie", which he has partly achieved by the elimination of noise in his household.

The very long *epitasis*, beginning with II. 2, catches up and develops the sub-actions set going in the *protasis*. It commences briskly with a step forward from scene 1 as Truewit shatters Morose's quiet with a post-horn, then "thundring into him the incommodities of a wife, and the miseries of marriage" (II. 4. 14-15).[8] Overwhelmed by his loud chatter, Morose calls for physic from Cutbeard the barber, whom he absurdly trusts, and for counsel.

II. 3 reverts to the third sub-action with the presentation of the charming Epicoene and Daw in a recital of his "workes". Jonson here follows the practice he successfully borrowed from Machiavelli for use in *Every Man in His Humor* and *Volpone*, of postponing until the *epitasis* the introduction of important characters for whose presence he has already aroused expectation. Truewit's return (II. 4) resumes the second sub-action. He is eager for praise for tormenting the uncle, but Clerimont scoffs at him for being "ignorantly officious". Dauphine denounces him for blasting his plot to marry Epicoene to Morose. For the attentive auditor, the irony of this revelation lies in the possibility that the nephew deceives his friends by disclosing only part of his intention. But at this point Morose himself proposes to restore the plot, as Cutbeard reports, by defying Truewit's advice under the suspicion that Dauphine inspired it and by marrying the silent woman at once.

The Morose sub-action advances in II. 5 with the presentation of Epicoene to the old man. This kindles in him, as in Machiavelli's Nicomaco, the grotesque anticipation of the felicity which is his life's aim. Enraptured, he babbles like a fatuous Callimaco even while he flourishes his deaf man's tube. An equally powerful source of felicity is the revenge he will contrive against his "insolent kinsman" by frustrating his plots "to fright me from marrying". This very night he "wil get an heire, and thrust him out of my bloud like a stranger." On Cutbeard's reporting his "triumph in his felicity" (II. 6), Dauphine yields to Truewit's proposal that La-Fool move his feast and all the guests to the noise-hater's dwelling for "an excellent *comoedy* of affliction, so many severall noyses." The arrangement of details continues without pause into Act III, and the nephew enjoys by anticipation the irony of Morose's persecution: " 'Twill be a most solemne day for my vncle, and an excellent fit of mirth for vs" (III. 3). The gentlemen prepare for additional merriment by bringing the third sub-action to a climax in a duel between the wit and the bravery. But Dauphine's transition from a reluctance to torment the old man to a mischievous promptitude keeps the auditors attentive to undisclosed possibilities.

One possibility emerges in Dauphine's first great triumph (III. 4), a deception of friends as well as uncle which in its incompleteness opens the way to unforeseen consequences. United to a quiet bride, Morose enjoys his last complacent moment, for the delicate felicity of his

193

posturings proves altogether elusive. Epicoene loudly denounces his expedients and refuses any longer to permit an "vnnaturell dumbnesse in my house, in a family where I gouerne." Too late he realizes that he has sold his liberty to "a manifest woman". Truewit acts as the presenter of the comedy of afflictions by announcing the arrival of many friends "to the celebration of this good houre" (III. 5) and tricks the tormented bridegroom into a boisterous cursing match, Morose's shout the symbol of his loss of felicity.

In III. 6 the sub-actions all converge on Morose's house, which remains the setting until the resolution. Epicoene kisses the Ladies Collegiate as Daw, identified to the husband as "your wifes seruant", presents them. Dismayed as much by the chatterers as by this revelation, Morose is laughably stricken. Truewit reduces the absurdly voluble pantaloon to absurd silence when he again officiously boasts of Dauphine's plot to afflict him with a loquacious wife, the ironic consequence of his own vindictive scheme to impoverish his nephew. In the ironic usurpation of gentility the Ladies Collegiate mock him as "a rude bridegroome, to entertayne ladies of honour in this fashion" and, to the amusement of gentlemen, stigmatize his manners as "meere rusticite." The arrival of still others with the musicians (III. 7) magnifies the tumult, and as the drums and trumpets sound Morose flees to the top of the house pursued by a veritable pandemonium of noise.

After this climax, Act IV begins with a complication of the first sub-action. Clerimont and Truewit (scene 1) take up again the debate whether art is superior to nature in woman's beauty, and Clerimont satirically rejects nature for art, whereupon Truewit entertains him with an Ovidian disquisition on the advantages of the latter. He en-

194

dorses Dauphine's impartiality in the mock confession that he loves all the Ladies, for "men should loue wisely", one for the face to please the eye, another for the skin to please the touch and a third for the voice to please the ear. Truewit promises to make all the Ladies in love with Dauphine. Meanwhile, the collegiates advise Epicoene (IV. 3) in the wise management of a husband and the pursuit of pleasure. The suggestion encourages Daw to give an impetus to the third sub-action as he boasts that certain ones "haue tasted her fauours," a suggestion that carries the *epitasis* into Act V.

In a return to the second sub-action, IV. 4 moves the action toward a resolution. In his extremity Morose as preposterously renounces as he embraced the vengeance against his nephew and gropes for a reconciliation. He offers anything, even a limb, to be rid of Epicoene. But Dauphine wants something more than that and contents himself, with suspicious restraint, with the offer of advice. But fresh torment awaits the uncle when the gentlemen, on Epicoene's cry that he is "a distracted man", seize him and wrangle about a cure. Desperate, he again turns to Dauphine for help, begging him to find out "For how many causes may a man be diuorc'd." And again the nephew's negative reply is suspiciously restrained.

The third sub-action reaches a climax in the satiric "tragi-comedy" of IV. 5, the mock duel between the wit and the bravery. Daw, "a whiniling dastard", humbly receives the kicks he thinks delivered by La-Fool; and the latter, "afraid in a great looke", patiently suffers the tweaks of his nose performed as he thinks by Daw. The Ladies (IV. 6) observe the humiliation of their favorites, but now scorn them as "adulterate knights". Jonson shifts his emphasis to the College as they turn with eagerness to

Dauphine, that "perfect gentleman", in their opinion at once a wit and a bravery. This assault also prolongs the *epitasis* into Act V.

Morose's groping for a reconciliation moves a step further toward a comic climax (IV. 7) when Dauphine asks him whether he had as yet spoken to a lawyer. He had not since the noise and confusion of the court alarmed him. The nephew permits Truewit to thrust him aside and promise a lawyer and a divine to inquire into the state of the marriage. The old man's gratitude is ludicrous: "Doe your pleasure with me, gentlemen; I beleeue in you." The pranksters, of course, propose a comic diversion of this trust into a disputation between Otter and Cutbeard, disguised. This measure, again, prolongs the *epitasis* into Act V.

The *epitasis*, in fact, is remarkable for its Machiavellian extension into the last act of the play,[9] steadily developing each of the sub-actions in fresh comic climaxes. Daw and La-Fool (V. 1) try to suppress their cowardice into oblivion by new brags, under Clerimont's ironic encouragement, that they have both been Epicoene's lovers. Meanwhile Truewit's promised impassionation of the Ladies Collegiate succeeds (V. 2), and they assail Dauphine with attentions, one giving him a jewel, one pressing a love-letter into his hands and one inviting him to her chamber. The two disputants appear in dyed beards and black robes (V. 3). Their long-winded civility to each other exacerbates Morose, as Truewit tricked him in III. 5, into a voluble declamation against legal tumults. Inquiring "for how many causes a man may haue *diuortium legitimum*," they find twelve impediments that nullify a marriage. To Morose's intolerable vexation Cutbeard remorselessly lists the entire dozen. Amidst this verbiage a gleam of hope now and then animates the husband, but the pranksters quickly extinguish it. Thereupon he offers, with comic pathos, to do anything.

On the irruption of Epicoene and the Ladies (V. 4), however, his sufferings take new "varietie and changes". Even the pantaloon's confession of impotence is unavailing, for his wife will "take him with all his faults." A final ludicrous recourse remains. Daw and La-Fool repeat the boast that the bride had been their mistress. Epicoene, coached by Dauphine, seems crushed by shame; Morose is fatuously ready to adore his deliverers. But Cutbeard prolongs the comedy by cruelly dismissing the point as invalid. The husband, uncertain which fate is worse—"Marry a whore! and so much noise!"—is so abject that he finds his only pleasure in "dying in silence." His admission of complete frustration is the turning-point of the *epitasis*.

Dauphine seizes the propitious occasion, and the play jumps to its surprising *catastasis*. Jonson has brilliantly applied the lesson of Machiavelli's *La Mandragola* [10] in holding this part of the structure in suspense until the last effective moment. The nephew offers to free his uncle of the unhappy match in return for a substantial allowance for life and the whole estate of Morose thereafter. The agreement signed, he liberates his uncle by lifting the bride's peruke and revealing the boy who had masqueraded as Epicoene. The equally swift *catastrophe* now provides a neat resolution of the three sub-actions. The comic mortification of the amorous pantaloon is not so harsh as that of Machiavelli's Nicia, but like him he submits humbly to the contriver of the elaborate practical joke at his expense. Truewit now interposes a salute to the intriguer: "Well, DAVPHINE, you haue lurch'd your friends of the better halfe of the garland, by concealing this part of the plot!" And it is he who moralizes the exposure of the other victims of the joke. The cowardly knights Daw and La-Fool stand before the company as egregious liars, and humiliation at last silences the Collegiates. Highly unified and yet various in its action, *Epicoene* perhaps merits Dryden's praise as the pattern of a perfect play.[11]

## The Unified Structure of "The Alchemist"

In *The Alchemist* (1612) Jonson returns to the simpler unified structure of *Volpone* and to the presence, as in *Every Man in His humor*, of two blocking characters whose removal is necessary to a happy ending. But he experiments with complications of the *epitasis*, preparing an ascending series of unforeseen climaxes that culminate in the twist of the *catastasis* at the end of Act IV. As the play begins the dramatic situation is a conspiracy always on the point, like the alchemical "proiection" that lies at its center, of blowing up in ruin. The imminent dissolution of "the venter tripartite" [12] that unites Face, Subtle and Doll in their uneasy collaboration is a theme to which the audience, instructed by the "Argvment", must be attentive. First, any subsidence of "the sicknesse" [13] may bring the absent master back to his house at any unexpected time, and his very coming will destroy the cozenage whose profits are ample but precarious. Second, the deceptions practiced by the cheaters, above all the search for "the stone", [14] are dreams provided for credulous victims, but idle dreams whose emptiness must in the natural course of events be glaringly exposed. From the "Argvment" to the epilogue, Jonson places the audience in the ironic certainty of the hopelessness of Sir Epicure

Mammon's longing "to enioy a perpetuitie/Of life, and lust." [15]

The *protasis*, embracing like *Every Man in His Humor* and *Epicoene* scene 1 of Act II, opens on the recurrent quarrel of suspicious accomplices (I. 1). The butler Jeremy, "translated suburb-Captayne" and charged with the task of drawing victims to the house, threatens to unmask the alchemist. Subtle, transformed from a starving rogue to a well-rewarded practitioner of the black art, stands on defense with a vial of "strong water". Trying to allay the mutual suspicion, their accomplice Doll dances about nervously. Only the advent of the lawyer's clerk Dapper (I. 2) reconciles them, greed once again uniting them in their imposture.

He commences a procession of gulls, and he gives four angels for the promise to materialize the Queen of Faery, who will attend him as a familiar spirit. The collaboration now operates smoothly as the second caller, the tobacconist Drugger (I. 3), contributes his money to the profits. But their *"great worke"* (I. 4), as Subtle declares with mock solemnity, is the long experiment to perfect the philosopher's stone for Sir Epicure Mammon, gull-in-chief. Equally magnificent in his imagination and his credulity (II. 1), he pours out rich vaporings whose unsuspected hollowness is underlined by the comments of his skeptical friend Surly. This completes the *protasis*.

At the beginning of the *epitasis* (II. 2) the triumph of the imposters requires an ingenious subordination of Face to Subtle in another metamorphosis, to alchemist's drudge. Mammon, reposing a childlike trust in Subtle's charlatanry, anticipates the benefits conferred by the stone in lascivious dreams. The distrust of Surly, however, remains (II. 3) an obstacle which the alchemist first attempts to remove by a demonstration of his fluency in the sometimes lofty jargon of "our art". Unmoved, Surly is still a "heretique" believing that alchemy "is a pretty kind of game" whose object is "to cheat a man,/With charming." The conspirators' second attempt to remove him is to give him a message that Captain Face wants to meet him "i' the *Temple*-church", and although he leaves this confirms the skeptic in his suspicion. From this moment Surly's role is to play the blocking character who matches wits with the knaves in a campaign to search out "the subtilities of this darke *labyrinth*." For the audience, it is an ironic pleasure to see this gamester, the only honest man among the imposters and the fools, in the difficult performance of the honest man's duty of uncovering fraud. Jonson suspends the outcome till the *epitasis* reaches one of its magnificent climaxes.

The playwright again follows the Machiavellian practice of introducing important characters in the *epitasis*. The Puritan Ananias (II. 5) refuses to give further contributions from the Sanctified Brethren until they may see "*proiection*", and Subtle sends him off to bring an Elder to make atonement for his wickedness, a forward movement in this part of the action. Drugger (II. 6) prepares the coming of the rich young widow Dame Pliant, a shadowy figure like Lucrezia in *La Mandragola* until the *epitasis* substantiates her part. At this point her description renews the quarrel between Subtle and Face as each demands possession of this fresh victim. The venture tripartite again totters on the brink of ruin, which they avert temporarily by agreeing on lots to determine who gets the girl and who keeps the loot.

They are interrupted when, the *epitasis* continuing without pause into Act III, Ananias brings his pastor,

Tribulation Wholesome. The latter upbraids (III. 1) his more rigid follower by reminding him of the Machiavellian doctrine that the end must be considered in all things:

> Good *Brother*, we must bend vnto all meanes,
> That may giue furtherance, to the *holy cause*. . . .
> The children of perdition are, oft-times
> Made instruments euen of the greatest workes.[16]

In these delusions the greedy pastor is hardly less the perfect dupe than Mammon. In the confrontation of saint and alchemist (III. 2), the two impostors understand each other perfectly, so that Subtle is able to remove the Puritan squeamishness about counterfeiting:

> SVB. It is no coyning, sir.
> It is but casting. TRI. Ha? you distinguish well.
> Casting of money may be lawfull.

In their apparently irreconcilable aims, the playwright cruelly finds an essential congeniality, but the greater rogue renews the gifts from the Sanctified Brethren.

An unpredictable element in the *epitasis* occurs when Face (III. 3), having missed Surly in St. Paul's, has lighted on a new prey, a Spanish count upon whose wealth the cheaters plan an impudently brazen attack. The silly heir Kastril (III. 4), meanwhile, comes to receive a lesson in quarreling and agrees to fetch his sister, Dame Pliant. Drugger's longing to see the Queen of Faery (III. 5) leads to his blindfolding and gagging—with gingerbread!—while Face and Subtle strip him of purse and property. The scene crowds as the action of the *epitasis* intensifies, and they hide the clerk in the privy to clear the room for Sir Epicure.

Jonson again, in the continuity of the stage business, disregards the formal act division between III and IV. Mammon (IV. 1), solemnly warned to avoid theology in his conversation, courts the disguised Doll and scattering gold departs with her to the chamber above where he proposes to enjoy his perpetuity of life and lust. Kastril returns with Dame Pliant (IV. 2) and receives instructions in the duello couched in the terms of scholastic logic. Subtle plies the simpering girl with kisses, and when Face announces the arrival of the Spaniard the confederates revive their bitter rivalry, each now claiming the young widow.

The count, helplessly limited to the Spanish language, offers an irresistible spoil (IV. 3). This unpredictable element becomes the center of one of the swift, successive climaxes that keep the development of action in the *epitasis* high in excitement. Its tone differs in the Quarto and Folio versions. The former maintains the pleasure of surprise by concealing the identity of the Spaniard until IV. 6. The latter prints a marginal stage direction at IV. 3 that identifies him as Surly in disguise. Such knowledge inspires in the audience an irony that enriches the rapid movement of events with suspense whether this blocking character may expose the conspiracy and save its victims. It also increases the comedy inherent in the conspirators' ignorance who their enemy is. They rifle his pockets as he affects an exaggerated and comically suspicious innocence, demanding the sight of the woman promised him. But Doll is still busy with Mammon, and the loud impatience of the count makes them fear lest he suspect some-

202

thing. His use of the word *"vida"* suggests a shocking improvisation: the needed harlot is available in the widow Pliant. This cheapening of wares leads now to a firm agreement on sharing the booty, for Subtle is to have the earnings and Face the girl. In the present necessity of concentrating on the long-awaited *"proiection"*, they hurry the count and the widow into the garden. In setting everything aside to prepare for their explosion, the conspirators make the fatal error of giving Surly the opportunity of blurting out his information and so putting themselves at his mercy.

The *epitasis* rushes to its first climax. The culmination of Subtle's experiments in alchemy has come (IV. 5). His scheme requires that Doll first dash in, victim of a fit of madness because Mammon, careless of the warning against theology, talked about a fifth monarchy [17] he proposed to erect for her. Thereupon a great explosion occurs, wrecking the apparatus for the transmutation of metals. Mammon witlessly takes sole blame on himself as he babbles, "O my voluptuous mind!" He eagerly submits to the penance of donating a hundred pounds to Bedlam, which Face, of course, receives. The conspirators have won a victory [18] over Mammon and the Saints, and they get rid of the disappointed knight.

This triumph fades in the second climax of the *epitasis* as complete exposure threatens them. Surly rushes in (IV. 6) throwing off his disguise, and he seeks to open the eyes of the dazed Pliant to the deceptions of the rogues. When the ignorant Subtle confidently reaches out to pick his pockets as in IV. 3, Surly knocks him down. The suspense of the moment turns on the question whether the honest man will mortify the rogues so soon after their success with their explosion. The alchemist's cries bring Face running, and he calls for the immediate help of the gulls. They sweep in (IV. 7). Greed and credulity overpower reason, so that they turn at Surly's denunciation, not upon their tormentors but upon their savior. Kastril puts into practice the roaring lessons he has mastered and leads the crowd in driving off the scene the first of the blocking characters.[19]

The removal of Surly permits the rogues no rest. The gulls must be satisfied, and the division of spoils takes a new twist as Subtle demands the widow. Jonson now brings events to a third climax, which is the *catastasis* of *The Alchemist*. Doll informs her companions of the sudden arrival of one they had forgotten, the master of the house, surrounded by gossiping neighbors. The conspiracy passes through another crisis threatening dissolution, for the scoundrels confront disgrace as well as ruin from Lovewit, a far more substantial blocking character than Surly. Face hurries to resume his former shape as Jeremy the butler while Subtle and Doll pack up their profits and get ready for flight. Their fate and his role remain for portrayal in Act V.

Lovewit's attention (V. 1) to the reports of his outraged neighbors is due only partly to fear for his belongings and partly to amusement at his servant's "teeming wit". This spirit prepares a genial resolution of the comedy since it is the temper of the pleasure-loving and gay old bachelor Periplectomenus, that friend of fun and youthful love in the *Miles Gloriosus* of Jonson's beloved Plautus. But Face's advantage (V. 2) is slender indeed when Surly, their acknowledged savior now, leads in the gulls (V. 3) to get what satisfaction they can, injured greed and credulity parading as virtue barbarously discomfited. As the butler, Jeremy brazenly refuses them admittance when they pound on the door. There is, however, peril within the house. Dapper, forgotten in the rush of events, cries out for Subtle and Face, whereupon Jeremy and the alchemist call to each other. Sternly demanding the truth, the master is the last formidable obstacle in the way of their scheme. Jeremy removes this blocking character by the ingenious device of drawing him into the conspiracy. At the same time he excludes Subtle and Doll and precipitates the *catastrophe*.

First he promises Lovewit the prize of a rich young widow if he will dress himself as a Spaniard. Then he demands from Subtle and Doll (V. 4) the keys to the trunks in which they have packed their booty. He proclaims the termination of the venture tripartite, showing the others how to escape over the wall at the back of the house. The trunks stay behind, a reward to the new conspirator. Successful in courtship of Dame Pliant (V. 5), the master joins his servant in serene indifference to the renewed attack of the gulls and the officers who accompany them. Surly, his own dream of winning the rich widow now vanishing, bewails "that same foolish vice of honestie!" The skeptic is thus the commentator on the ironic triumph of unabashed roguery. Only Kastril avoids the humiliation of the gulls by the glad acceptance of his new brother. The play ends in the pleasures of reconciliation and romance after the manner of genial comedy. But Jeremy has an epilogue [20] in which he makes an ironic recapitulation of self-enrichment, gaily exulting in having "cleane/Got off", his fortune no less than his master's enhanced by the subtleties of the alchemist.

Modern criticism of *Bartholomew Fair* (1614) rests upon T. S. Eliot's assertion that in it Jonson gets along with hardly a plot at all,[21] a view echoed with various subtleties of iteration by later writers.[22] This claim ignores the presence in the comedy of what is inescapably *there:* a linear structure whose lines remain firm and consistent in spite of the bewildering chaos of the Fair itself. The fact is that Jonson manipulates his favorite four-part design of the action with easy concealment of his art. He reverts to his practice in *Every Man in His Humor* [23] and *Epicoene* of introducing in the *protasis* the several themes or sub-actions which unfolding events gradually substantiate, and Act V ends in the genial *catastrophe* of reconciliation. The *epitasis* begins, as in earlier plays, at Act II, scene 2, and runs to the close of IV. Jonson, however, subtly modifies the *catastasis,* complicating the *epitasis* by the placement of an aspect of his third part at IV. 3 in a fresh experiment with the pattern of comedy. Whereas he relied even in *Epicoene* on a single such perplexity of the action, he now divides and disperses that climax of structure. In so doing he controls events during the confusions of the Fair by a series of five catastatic moments.[24] The last comes as late in the play as V. 5, and each inspires a twist in the action demanding additional scenes for its resolution. We thus observe him, in *Bartholomew Fair,* busy with a refinement of formal dramaturgy that far transcends the example of Terence and Machiavelli.

The *protasis* opens on the respectable burgher household of John Littlewit, proctor, and it presents, with a slight elaboration, the five significant themes of the action. Littlewit (I. 1) introduces the first of these: he has the license ready for the marriage of Grace Wellborn and Bartholomew Cokes. The presence in his house of his mother-in-law, Dame Purecraft (I. 2), is a second theme, for she attracts a procession of suitors that includes the young gentlemen Ned Winwife. The favored rival (I. 3) seems to be the Puritan preacher whom she hospitably entertains, Zeal-of-the-Land Busy. The rich and illiterate Cokes and his betrothed Grace (I. 5) join the household and enliven the *protasis* with a third theme, the compassion of Winwife and his friend Tom Quarlous for her in her superiority to Cokes's folly and her undisguised distaste for the match. Littlewit, however, gives Cokes the box with the license in it and so appears to seal her unhappiness.

The burning desire of Cokes is to see the Fair, a fourth theme that Jonson at once develops. Winwife and Quarlous depart to enjoy the sport there, where, Littlewit announces, his puppet-play will be presented. He and his pregnant wife, Win-the-Fight, outwit the Puritan opponents to a day of merrymaking when she feigns a craving to eat pig at the Fair. Rabbi Busy (I. 6) withdraws his objections so long as the meat "be eaten with a reformed mouth, with *sobriety*, and humblenesse; not gorg'd in with gluttony." [25] In the *protasis*, once again, Jonson disregards the formal act-division and presents a fifth theme in II. 1, effecting at the same time a transition to the earthy vitality of the main setting. This is Justice Overdo's whim of taking as a model an earlier patriot Junius Brutus and assuming the disguise of a fool so he may spy out and record in his black book all the "enormities" of the Fair.

There at the commencement of the *epitasis* the playwright shifts his scene and from II. 2 to V. 5 draws a hilarious contrast between its raucous turbulence and the innocent citizen spirit of the *protasis*. He links this firmly to the *epitasis* with the instant discovery by Overdo (II. 2) of examples of the place's wickedness. The balladsinger Nightingale and his confederate, the cutpurse Edgeworth (II. 4), attract his attention, but misunderstanding the latter's profession he resolves to rescue a worthy youth from evil company. Winwife and Quarlous now arrive (II. 5), and they amuse themselves with the sights and the crowd. Cokes, Grace and his man Humphrey Wasp enter (II. 6) upon a solemn sermon by Overdo against bottle-ale and tobacco, the most pernicious of enormities of whose harm he exhorts Edgeworth to beware. In the press of the crowd that gathers to listen, that proficient thief cuts the purse of Cokes. Angry confusion follows his discovery of the loss, and all accuse the counterfeit fool Overdo. As Wasp cudgels him, that absurd victim of a genuine enormity bellows in pain, "Murther, murther, murther."

The stage business proceeds without regard for act-division as the watch hurry forward (III. 1). With the entrance of the Littlewit household (III. 2), Jonson completes a necessary task of the *epitasis* in concentrating all his personages at the center of the Fair. They ignore its vanities in the reformed manner Busy has directed and only follow the scent of pig from the booth of Ursula, the pig-woman. In III. 3 the author introduces a fore-shadowing of the *catastrophe* in Overdo's ironic intention to treasure the incident of Cokes's loss as mirth for supper. A forward movement of the third and fourth sub-actions occurs (III. 4) when Winwife and Quarlous seize their opportunity, as Cokes and Wasp examine the objects on sale at the booths, to begin the action of detaching Grace from her escort. This is the first artfully casual step in a whole succession of separations in the *epitasis* that scatter the burghers of Act I.

In another exhibition of the fifth sub-action (III. 5) Overdo is again blind to Edgeworth's skill in cutting the second purse of Cokes, but fears instead that he is, by association with the ballad-singer, the victim of "a terrible taint, *Poetry*." Again his intention jocosely misfires as the real thief diverts suspicion to the real justice, whom the watch carry off to the stocks. In a development of III. 4, Winwife and Quarlous take advantage of the tumult and prevail on Grace to remain with them when the others dash away. Having carefully noted Edgeworth's thievery, they threaten to expose him unless he steal the marriage license from the box now carried by Wasp. Furthermore, they now compete openly as acknowledged rivals for her hand. In an advance from III. 2, John and Win Littlewit (III. 6) determine to enjoy the sights of the Fair in defiance of Busy. Unable to restrain his zeal, the Puritan denounces the "Apocryphall wares" all about him, overturns Joan Trash's gingerbread booth with its figures of St. Bartholomew, and is seized by the watch and hurried to the stocks. Win, having indulged too liberally, needs urgent relief; John and she depart to ask Ursula for a facility.

The *epitasis* continues in IV. 1 with no interruption of dramatic action. Overdo lies in the stocks. The madman Troubleall, deranged when removed from his place in court by the Justice, reminds the watch by his demand whether any act has the latter's warrant that his honor is "a very parantory person." So they release the counterfeit fool and Busy as well. Cokes (IV. 2), separated from his companions like Grace in III. 4, has lost his way and falls an easy prey to the thieves. Moving the third sub-action forward from III. 5, Jonson sets Quarlous against Winwife (IV. 3) in a wrangle over Grace. To settle the quarrel, she proposes a lottery in which each writes a name on a slip of paper and gives it to the next person happening by. This is Troubleall, who chooses one slip, the secret remaining in his and Grace's possession. Here Jonson has placed the first *catastatic* moment of the play, complicating the action with an unexpected twist.

Winwife and Grace leave Quarlous behind to watch Edgeworth try his skill, a separation of the rivals to the decided advantage of one of them. Wasp (IV. 4) plays at the drunken game of vapors and neglects the box from which the cutpurse filches the license. This is a second *catastatic* moment. Not only has the precious document passed from Wasp to Edgeworth to Quarlous, but that gamester now has the necessary means of validating a marriage no matter who has won Grace. The brawl that ensues over the accomplishment of Edgeworth brings in the watch, who now arrest Wasp. His disappearance leaves Dame Overdo, wife of the Justice, at the mercy of the bawd Captain Whit, who applies to Ursula for a utensil to provide the same relief for her as John sought for Win. The comic naturalness of this domestic crisis has divorced husband from wife amidst the ribald chaos of the Fair since Littlewit leaves her (IV. 5) while he prepares the puppet-show. These separations act together as a third *catastatic* moment.

The contrast that has set citizen against Fair reaches a scandalous climax as Win's companions, the bawds Knockem and Whit, welcome her and Dame Overdo each as "a Bird o' the game" to serve the throng of clients. Meanwhile, Quarlous (IV. 6) searches for Troubleall to find out whose name he had chosen. In the stocks Busy, rejoicing in his afflictions, employs his leisure to prophesy "the destruction of *Fayres* and *May-games*, *Wakes*, and *Whitson-ales*." Overdo in his fool's habit is at last put in

210

beside the rabbi. Unable to get an intelligible answer from Troubleall, Quarlous adopts a disguise closely resembling the madman. Dame Purecraft, herself separated from her household, sees the counterfeit and at once fixes on him as her choice: "I loue him o' the sudden." It is the fulfillment of the prophecy in I. 2 that she would find happiness only with a lunatic. Coming at the end of Act IV, this is still another *catastatic* moment.

Scene 1 of Act V brings all the personages of the comedy together again at Lantern Leatherhead's booth for the puppet-show, but in the new combinations prevailing after the separations that began at III. 4. Overdo (V. 2) has abandoned the fool for the disguise of a porter in the pursuit of additional absurdities like giving redress to Troubleall. But the first sub-action to find a resolution in the *catastrophe* is the rivalry of Winwife and Quarlous. Still playing the madman, the latter learns from Grace that Troubleall chose Winwife's slip. In this disappointment Dame Purecraft offers ample consolation, not only in her renunciation of Puritan familiars but also in her fortune. No Romeo he, Quarlous does not defy his stars: "There's no playing with a man's fortune!" He accepts and has the license of Cokes to make sure of her. The Justice caps his good luck by mistaking him for the real Troubleall and signing a blank charter by way of redress. Thus Jonson, as he broke up and dispersed the aspects of a single *catastasis* in a series of catastatic moments, precipitates not a unique *catastrophe* but first one and then another of its constituent elements.

The playwright meanwhile elaborates the fourth theme when Littlewit (V. 3) shows the puppets to Cokes and explains his "Motion" of the story of Hero and Leander conflated with Damon and Pythias. V. 4 picks up the thread of IV. 5 as Mistress Overdo and Win Littlewit, in

"Greene-gownes" and "Crimson-petticoats" (IV. 5. 92-93)
and their faces masked, take their places near the unsuspecting husbands. Leatherhead now enacts the puppet-
play to its noisy climax. This draws Busy (V. 5), zealous
to overthrow the players and shouting, "Downe with
*Dagon,* downe with *Dagon.*" Edgeworth makes a hilarious
proposal: let there be a disputation between the Puritan
and the puppet. And so Busy contends with Dionysius, his
"base noyse" set against the latter's "treble creeking" until
the preacher yields: "I am confuted, the *Cause* hath failed
me." Converted, he joins the other spectators and so
brings his part in the second and fourth sub-actions to its
*catastrophe.* His apostasy is the prelude to a comic
peripety as Overdo in effect ties up the fifth sub-action.
He throws off his disguise, for "It is time, to take Enormity
by the fore head, and brand it; for I haue discouer'd
enough." This last strategic moment of the *catastasis*
precipitates a complete reversal of his expectations.

He promises the disguised Quarlous (V. 6) and Edgeworth his protection, and the folk of the Fair tremble in
his presence. But Winwife, when the Justice tries to rescue Grace from a stranger, boldly asserts his new alliance
with her. Overdo can no longer suppress his catalogue of
enormities. Possessed by an utterly consistent absurdity
he prides himself on being "The example of *Iustice,* and
*Mirror of Magistrates.*" He accuses Leatherhead of being
a "professor of *Puppetry,* little better then *Poetry,*" and
also Busy, Knockem, Whit and his masked companion. On
uncovering her face, he reveals the "twelue-penny" lady,
"my greene *Madame,*" as Littlewit's wife. In the consternation, the other masked woman suffers a nausea, and
begging for a basin and for Justice Overdo, discloses that
she is *his* wife. Horror silences him.

Quarlous thereupon steps forward with an ironic exposure of the enormities. The Justice's innocent young man is a cutpurse; his ward Grace is the gift of Winwife; Quarlous himself has won the widow Purecraft; waving the blank charter, he uses Troubleall's slogan to confirm his words: "here's warrant for it." He reminds the crest-fallen magistrate, "you are but *Adam*, Flesh and blood! you haue your frailty." [26] Jonson now assigns to him the suggestion for a convivial resolution in harmony with the spirit of comedy: "forget your other name of *Ouerdoo*, and inuite vs all to supper. There you and I will compare our *discoueries;* and drowne the memory of all enormity in your bigg'st bowle at home." Caught up in the mood of general reconciliation, the Justice declares that the young gentleman's judgment will prevail. Thus Jonson unifies the several themes of the action advanced in the *protasis* in this comic *catastrophe*. Littlewit's license has gained happy spouses for Grace and Ned; his interlude pleased all, even converting a Puritan to sound sense. Win has enjoyed excitements more delicious than pig. Cokes, though he has lost Grace and all his money, is content with his toys and gingerbread. Dame Purecraft has found the perfect husband in the now confident gamester. Not least, Overdo has learned the salutary lesson that he is not so much the Junius Brutus of his conceit as the fool of his disguise, a fallible Adam indeed. Nevertheless, the final note struck by the comedy is the genial harmony created by the relaxations of supper and friendship.

# Chapter 11

## BACK TO SATAN: *THE DEVIL IS AN ASS*

Late in his career as a playwright, Jonson seems to turn
again to Machiavelli, this time to his tale of *Belfagor*.[1]
This fable neatly combines two medieval themes, that
wives are the most terrible of human afflictions and that
human cunning can outwit the hellish powers.[2] The author also infuses the story with a nostalgia increasingly
felt by the arch-devil Belfagor, an infernal longing no less
profound than man's desire for a celestial home. As the
narrative begins, Pluto resolves, in his good-natured fair-
ness, to test before he accepts it the assertion made by the
majority of damned souls that the cause of their misery is
their wives. He sends Belfagor into the world to marry
and verify the facts.

Despatched with an ample allowance for a ten-year
stay, he takes the name of Roderigo di Castiglia and
chooses Florence for his inquiries because of its lively
commerce, where since he does not understand it, he is
easy to swindle. There he marries a noble and beautiful
wife Onestà, and having assumed a human shape he becomes a victim of human passions and falls helplessly in
love with her. Onestà, whose pride exceeds Lucifer's, gets
him to squander his wealth on her relatives and by her

214

own caprice and extravagance proceeds to ruin him. The devils who accompany him as servants find her such an imperious mistress that they gladly return to hell. Roderigo, indeed, is throughout his earthly sojourn better and less crafty than the human beings around him, an innocent spirit in a devilish world.[3] Before long he is bankrupt and forced to flee from his creditors. Saved from their pursuit by the farmer Gianmatteo, he confides his story with other-worldly ingenuousness to this shrewd rescuer and promises in gratitude to make his fortune. He will do this by taking demoniacal possession of girls and then quitting them when Gianmatteo pretends to exorcise him.

Twice he performs this trick and enriches Gianmatteo on the proceeds, always showing a sympathetic concern for his rescuer's benefit. The latter has become so famous that when the king of France sends for him to cure his daughter, he is forced to go in spite of Belfagor's threat to do no more for him. On his arrival in France the king tells him that the penalty of failure will be hanging. Gianmatteo first tries, with human hypocrisy, to wheedle Belfagor into departing, and this failing he stages the exorcism with much ceremony. It includes a concealed brass band. He approaches the girl and begs the devil to leave her. Belfagor refuses. The farmer then gives a signal to the band, which strikes up with a horrid din. Disturbed, Belfagor asks what was happening. "It's your wife come to find you!" Gianmatteo answers. The terrified devil leaves the girl at once and returns to hell, a sound witness to the miseries of marriage. The mockery of the author establishes as the real devils, not the visitor from hell, but the human beings among whom he moves, the true arch-devil being the crafty Gianmatteo.

The homesickness for hell that weighs on Belfagor in

215

Machiavelli's story becomes perhaps the most powerful emotion felt by Jonson's demon in *The Devil Is an Ass* (1631). The playwright makes explicit what Machiavelli only implied and renders it the unhappy duty of Pug the devil to survey his own incompetent efforts to live among men on their terms with a growing consciousness of their superior diabolism. If he tries to trick a foolish husband and comfort his love-starved wife, he is foiled by her and beaten by him. If he retaliates by informing him of her interview with her lover, he gets only more physical pain and perceives in disgust that by serving morality he has profited the cause of hell but little. If he emulates the other servants in pursuit of the maids, the excitement makes him easy prey of a thief—more cudgeling. On observing the manifold deceptions about him in human society, he groans in dismal admiration. Yearning for his infernal home, he implores Satan to call him to hell again and free him.

The *protasis* begins with a roaring Satan and the devil Pug standing in Hell-Mouth discussing the latter's careless demand for permission to spend the month on earth to which every petty demon is entitled. He boasts—before the event,

> Within that terme, the Court of *Hell* will heare
> Some thing may gaine a longer grant, perhaps.[4]

Satan laughs at the "foolish Spirit": what would he do on earth? Pug can not foresee but hopes to report something that will win him the admiration of "the Court of *Hell*." This is *Belfagor's* Council of Hell (Panella ed., I. 701-02) with Jonson's characteristic adjustment to the English

216

stage. Satan inquires what particular harms Pug may do, warning him against the superior cunning of mankind:

> You are too dull a Diuell to be trusted
> Forth in those parts, *Pug*, vpon any affayre
> That may concerne our name, on earth.

For the "reputation" of the "state of *Hell*" must be protected, especially "Heere about *London*." The spectacle of the innocent spirit in a devilish world, specifically a sophisticated city, is another prominent motive common to both writers. Pug now begs for only a fortnight and a Vice to accompany him. This is Iniquity, bearing into the play the atmosphere of the moralities [5] with his fourteeners and his tale of enticements of youth. This choice sobers Satan, who points out the disadvantage of such an outmoded person on earth, where men's ingenuity in vice is so prolific that they threaten to

> put downe ours. Both our breed and trade
> Will suddenly decay, if we preuent not.
> Vnlesse it be a *Vice* of quality,
> Or fashion, now they take none from vs.

He therefore dismisses old Iniquity as "not for the manners, nor the times" and sends Pug alone "To doe the Common-wealth of Hell some seruice" on earth, where vices are most like virtues. He is to enter the body of a cutpurse and get his clothes from the hangman, ordered to "spye/Amongst mankind" for a single day: thus he goes into the world for a set term like Belfagor although Jonson's adherence to neo-classical rules reduces the ten

217

years allowed the latter. He is to become the servant of the squire Fitzdottrel, a silly dotard with a young, beautiful and unloving wife who repeats the situation in *La Mandragola*.

Fitzdottrel, having longed for a devil to help him find hidden treasure, takes Pug at once into his service (I. 3). The gentleman Wittipol, loving his wife Frances (I. 4), completes the triangle. Yet the lover has met her only once: he says,

> I ha' not seene her,
> Since I came home from trauell.

The circumstance recalls the plight of Callimaco at the beginning of Machiavelli's play (I. 1). He trades his cloak for permission to speak with the wife.[6] She like Lucrezia and Celia in *Volpone* reluctantly obeys her capricious husband (I. 6), and like Lucrezia also she succumbs half against her will to the temptations of adultery. This is a logical extension by Jonson of Machiavelli's tally of the afflictions of marriage suggested by the outrageous whims of Onestà. Frances submits to the odd suit of a lover in the presence of her spouse. Wittipol urges a consideration very prominent in *The Prince* (chapter 25) and in *La Mandragola* (III. 11), especially the advice to young men to take Fortune by storm: love, he argues,

> no lesse then *Fortune*
> Helps th' aduenturous.

Then Jonson fumbles the *protasis* by the unnecessary anticlimax of I. 7, which prepares for the fraud that cheats Fitzdottrel.

He moves with his old skill, however, to the *epitasis* in II. 1. The squire's lust for wealth makes him the credulous gull of the projector Meercraft, whose racket is to promise to drain the fenlands, of which Fitzdottrel will become the duke. The husband now sets Pug the task of guarding his wife. The willing devil (II. 2), having appraised the marriage and the project, admits,

> My *Chiefe* was i' the right. Can any feind
> Boast of a better *Vice*, then heere by nature
> And art, th' are owners of?

His first service to hell will be to cuckold his master by assisting the wife and her lover. This ingenuousness recapitulates the innocence of Belfagor in his dealings with Gianmatteo. Pug is, moreover, the victim of his human integument's senses in the presence of her "most delicate damn'd flesh": so Belfagor fell helplessly in love with Onestà. He expects also to win the confidence of the wife by encouraging her, a sympathetic concern resembling the solicitude of Machiavelli's devil for the farmer.

But Frances, perfectly aware that he is a spy, cleverly contrives to send Wittipol, through the unsuspecting devil, a message how to approach her. When he betrays Fitzdottrel's command, Pug realizes, to his alarm, that his too-simple zeal in what he saw as his infernal duty has actually seduced him into telling the truth. He offers to connive in deceiving the husband and moves to receive the wife's rewarding kiss. She traduces him, however, by diverting upon him the suspicion of Fitzdottrel, whom she still has every intention of traducing also. The result of Pug's first attempts, thus, is to be outwitted by the human wife and cudgeled by his human master (II. 3). Belfagor likewise, once he assumed an earthly shape, was out-maneuvered and frustrated by Onestà. Pug departs in chagrin, easily chastised by the simpleton, who exalted by the hopes kindled by Meercraft's design, needs concentrate only a corner of his feeble mind on the humiliation of the devil. The crestfallen Pug (II. 5), fearing as Belfagor feared at the hands of Gianmatteo worse punishment because of a human hypocrisy beyond his infernal understanding, is tempted to seek refuge from the world in the safety of hell. He hesitates since to leave Fitzdottrel now "Were a contempt against my *Chiefe*, past pardon."

In response to the message sent through the innocent Pug by Frances, Wittipol appears (II. 6) in the chamber window of his friend Manly in Lincoln's Inn, opposite to the gallery of Fitzdottrel's house. Here she emerges. A love scene follows marked by intimate caresses and capped by one of Jonson's delightful songs. Pug mutters with wounded pride and frustration:

> The *Diuell* is an *Asse!* fool'd off! and beaten!
> Nay, made an instrument! and could not sent it!

He seeks to avenge the rebuff and the trickery by informing the husband even though this course will preserve domestic morality. Fitzdottrel thereupon interrupts the love scene (II. 7), gets a coward's satisfaction for the dishonor by striking his wife and then thanks the devil for redeeming all. Pug, however, feels a sense of failure now that he has discharged his malice:

> my conscience
> Tells mee, I haue profited the cause of Hell
> But little, in the breaking-off their loues.

220

The act division between II and III shows a decline from Jonson's earlier practice in the presence of a strong pause in the *epitasis*. Meercraft schemes to fleece Fitzdottrel of a ring and 100 pieces of gold, and Pug appears on only two occasions. In III. 5 his master entrusts to him the diamond ring to purchase his wife admission to the Academy of Lady Tailbush, Meercraft's confederate. The projector immediately devises a way of stealing it, for Jonson's Londoners find Pug as easy to swindle as Florentines found Belfagor. The devil, burning "to haue a little venery" (III. 6) and prompted again like Belfagor by the cravings of his flesh, leaps to assail Pitfall, Lady Tailbush's woman. In the excitement of the chase he hands the ring to the disguised Trains, Meercraft's servant. Too late remorseful for this easy cozenage by the projector and his man, he bewails his simplicity:

> *Satan* himself has tane a shape t' abuse me.
> It could not be else!

He would

> Run from my flesh, if I could: put off mankind!
> This's such a scorne!

But he must fulfill his term. In humiliating anticipation he feels the cudgel of his master and innocently calls for succor to Meercraft, the very person who contrived the theft.

In the house of Lady Tailbush (IV. 4), Pug observes how Fitzdottrel's ring passes from Meercraft to Wittipol to Frances, and notes the cheats and hypocrisies of the Academy. This moves him to exclaim at the superior devilry of mankind:

You talk of a *Vniuersity!* why, Hell is
A Grammar-schoole to this! [7]

So Belfagor's companions learned that hell was far more
tolerable than the imperious household of Onestà. The
additional torment that awaits Pug makes him declare
that all his days in hell were holidays to this. Fitzdottrel
exhibits him as his wife's *"Escudero"* or squire, and Lady
Tailbush renames him fashionably as De Vile. Teased and
quizzed about the duties of a position he is ignorant of, he
shows an ineptitude that draws blows from his master
before all the company. He prays,

O, Chiefe, call mee to *Hell* againe, and free mee.

He feels inescapably a victim of humanity:

Who,
Comming from *Hell*, could look for such Catechising?
The *Diuell* is an *Asse*. I doe acknowledge it.

The slight fumbling of the *protasis* betokens a more
serious fumbling of the *catastasis* and the *catastrophe* in a
loss of control that led Dryden to call the play one of
Jonson's dotages.[8] Thus he destroys the aesthetic and
moral structure with which he had unified his mature
comedies. Beginning in Act IV, scene 5, the dramatist
presents three related counterturns in order to precipitate
the *catastrophe* for the sub-actions of Wittipol, Pug and
Fitzdottrel. The decline in satiric invention is evident in
the substitution of sentimental resolutions for ironic expectations. In IV. 5 Fitzdottrel orders a deed of feoffment
drawn up to the benefit of the disguised Wittipol, whom

the cheaters count one of their company and to whom the squire has taken a fancy. When Frances (IV. 6) turns to her lover in her misery, he responds, not to desire, but to Manly's appeal that he follow virtue. This amazing twist supplies the *catastasis* of the Wittipol sub-action. He renounces his love in the kind of reversal that has more in common with the conversion of the rake in later sentimental comedy [9] than with Jonsonian dramaturgy. Such a tear-jerking outcome of a lover's amorous siege marks the decline in Jonson's once infallible tact. The *catastrophe* of this sub-action comes in IV. 7 with Wittipol's removal of his disguise, his baffling of Fitzdottrel and his intention to use the feoffment for the benefit of Frances. The disgraced husband summarizes his fall:

A *Cuckold*, and an *Asse*, and my wiues Ward.

That he is not to remain in disgrace is another token of Jonson's failure in this dotage.

The appearance of Ambler (V. 1), Lady Tailbush's gentleman usher, brings the Pug sub-action to its *catastasis*. It shows how from the very beginning of his earthly term the devil confused honest men and thieves; for he had dressed himself (in I. 1), not in the clothes of the cutpurse whose body he possessed, but in those Ambler had laid aside. The latter (V. 2 )claims that the wearer robbed him. V. 3 catches up the Fitzdottrel sub-action, as the husband, dealing with the problem of setting aside the feoffment, follows Meercraft's suggestion and pretends that his wife bewitched him. This provides the *catastasis* for the Fitzdottrel subaction.

Arrested for felony (V. 5), Pug in desperation solemnly identifies himself as a devil and begs his master not to let him go to prison for his theft, promising to help him in

The businesse, that you haue in hand of *witchcraft,*
And your *possession,* as my selfe were in you.

This echoes the motive of the exorcism of a spirit by
which Belfagor enriched Gianmatteo. But Jonson's foolish
dupe angrily rejects the generous offer and thus transforms the situation in Machiavelli of the crafty farmer
outwitting the ingenuous devil into double gullery. He
orders the constable to take the culprit away. Nevertheless, Meercraft appropriates Pug's suggestion that Fitzdottrel feign madness, sneering,

> 'Tis no hard thing t' out doe the *Deuill* in:
> A Boy o' thirteene yeere old made him an *Asse*
> But t' other day.

And so Pug (V. 6) enters his cell in Newgate bemoaning
humanity's superior cunning.

Jonson assimilates the last appearance of his devil, like
the first, to English lore. The roaring Vice Iniquity brings
a message from Satan granting Pug's wish to spend a
month on earth,

> Till the *Session,*
> That thou mayest haue a triumphall egression,

another allusion to the infernal council of *Belfagor.* Pug's
fate, to be drawn "In a cart, to be hang'd", is (as the Vice
naïvely points out) to ride in "the chariot of Triumph."
Pug bitterly denounces his chief for enjoying

> His tyrannous pleasure on me, to confine me
> To the vnlucky carkasse of a *Cutpurse,*
> Wherein I could do nothing.

Satan now appears to upbraid the impudent fiend for ascribing

> thine owne dull damn'd defects vpon
> An innocent case.

Indeed he makes the humiliating charge, after summarizing the defeats of Pug, that the dead cutpurse served hell better by doing greater harm. He reminds him,

> whom hast thou dealt with,
> Woman or man, this day, but haue out-gone thee
> Some way, and most haue prou'd the better fiendes?

This is the satiric implication maintained by Machiavelli throughout his fable. Unwilling to allow the dishonor to "Sticke on our state, as that the *diuell* were hang'd," he orders Iniquity to take Pug on his back; and all disappear in the noise and stench of brimstone.

Following Meercraft's instructions, Fitzdottrel actually feigns (V. 8) the diabolical possession urged by Pug. The devil's final chagrin is to contribute the device to his master without any acknowledgement. But on the news of Pug's noisome flight the squire desists from his pretense, unaccountably a weakness in its lack of motivation save the need (after the example of Plautus in *Casina*) to end the play. He decides "to tell truth,/And shame the *Feind*." Although he stands before all "an *Asse*, in spight of prouidence," Fortune is good enough to leave his wealth and his marriage intact with his imbecilities unpurged. The return of his signed-away land to the stupid husband is a frustration of the gulling of a dupe in another wholly unwarranted sentimental resolution. What Jonson has done is to clear all the obstacles from the path, not of the young lover, but of the satiric butt who may now live happily ever after. Thus the Corvino of the play gets Bonario's reward, a total confusion of the aesthetic and moral unity that marked *Volpone*. Nevertheless, *The Devil Is an Ass* stands as an impressive final tribute to Machiavelli.

# NOTES

Notes to Chapter 1.

[1] Niccolò Machiavelli, *Le Opere*, ed. Antonio Panella, 2 vols., Milan, 1938, I. 964. See also Letter 199, tr. A. H. Gilbert, in *Letters of Machiavelli*, New York, 1961, p. 218.

[2] For the opinion of a successful Florentine playwright of the Sixteenth Century, see Antonfrancesco Grazzini ("Il Lasca"), *Le Rime Burlesche*, Florence, 1882, pp. 24 and 645. Cf. Ireneo Sanesi, *La Commedia*, 2 vols., Milan, 1954, I. 253-69; and Luigi Russo, *Machiavelli*, Bari, 1957, pp. 147-49.

[3] "Il Discorso o Dialogo intorno alla Nostra Lingua," Panella ed., I. 713-27.

[4] Aelius Donatus, *Commentvm Terenti*, ed. Pavlvs Wessner, 3 vols., Leipzig, 1902-08, I. 22-23. The definition is not to be found in the extant works of Cicero, but through Donatus it became a commonplace ascription in the Renaissance.

[5] Machiavelli's "urbanità" in the sense of the Latin "urbanitas" (as Cicero and Ovid had used it) denotes the refined taste of sophisticated inhabitants of a city like Florence. Ovid was a source for the language of the passionate lover Cleandro in Machiavelli's second comedy, *Clizia*.

⁶ "gravità": the controlling sense comes from the Latin "gravitas," importance and hence power or dignity, as in Cicero and Quintilian.

⁷ "ridiculamente."

⁸ Primarily Lodovico Ariosto, his brother Gabriele and his son Virginio. In 1444 Francesco Ariosto had written a play, *Isis*, for the court of Ferrara.

⁹ "una gentil composizione" in the sense of the Latin "compositio," as Donatus used the word (*Commentvm Terenti*, I. 27).

¹⁰ "nodo": Machiavelli carefully takes note of the critical vocabulary of Donatus in his analysis of Terence; the grammarian's phrase for the point made by the Florentine is "nodus fabulae" (*Commentvm Terenti*, I. 38). Since the commentary of Donatus was regularly printed with Renaissance editions of Terence, Machiavelli might easily have found it ready to hand as he opened the volume of plays.

¹¹ "accomodato" from the Latin "accomodatus," prepared or arranged.

¹² Machiavelli's plural "sali" emphasizes his demand that the language of drama possess the expressive richness of living speech. Horace uses "sales" to characterize Plautus (*Ars Poetica*, 1. 271).

¹³ He uses the pronoun "egli" to specify Lodovico.

¹⁴ Panella ed., I. 602-04. Machiavelli's prologues receive some slight consideration in Emilio Goggio's "The Prologue in the *Commedie Erudite* of the Sixteenth Century," *Italica*, XVIII. 328-29 (1941).

¹⁵ "casi": unexpected happenings, from the Latin "casus," a translation of Aristotle's *peripeteia*.

¹⁶ "con onestà grandissima": verisimilitude, an aspect of decorum.

[17] Again Machiavelli uses the Latinized translation of the Aristotelian "peripeteia," "caso."

[18] *La Mandragola,* Panella ed., I. 550-52. A series of bitter stanzas concedes that by turning to this comedy the author has turned from more significant matters, and it defies the malice of all by threatening them in retaliation with his own well-known satiric art.

[19] *Commentvm Terenti,* I. 35-36.

[20] G. B. Giraldi Cinthio, *Discorsi,* Venice, 1554, pp. 214-15.

[21] Sanesi, *La Commedia,* I. 184.

[22] *Terence,* ed. and tr. John Sargeaunt, London and Cambridge [Mass.]: Loeb, 2. vols., 1939, vol. 1, 1. 194. The corresponding passage in Machiavelli's translation is in Panella ed., I. 657.

[23] "Conversations with Drummond," in *Ben Jonson,* ed. Herford and Simpson, 11 vols., Oxford, 1925-52, I. 134.

[24] For Machiavelli's version, see the Panella ed., I. 651-98.

[25] For example, in Vinciguerra of Raffaello Borghini's *L' Amante Furioso,* Venice, 1584. See the present writer's *The Braggart in Renaissance Comedy,* Minneapolis, 1954, pp. 54 and 58-60.

[26] *Commentvm Terenti,* I. 27. For an analysis of the comments of Donatus and their bearing on Terence, see T. W. Baldwin's *Shakespere's Five-Act Structure,* Urbana, 1947, pp. 1-32 and 49-50. His conclusion is that the effective design for a comedy includes three parts.

[27] *Ibid.,* I. 27.

[28] *Ibid.,* I. 27-28.

[29] *Ibid.,* I. 28.

[30] *Ibid.,* I. 19. Terence never followed the practice of Plautus, who narrated at the beginning in a prologue what

the former left to the play to disclose (see W. Beare, *The Roman Stage*, London, 1950, p. 87).

[31] *Commentvm Terenti*. I. 35-36.

[32] *Ibid.*, I. 227.

[33] *Catastasis* is the term applied by J. C. Scaliger to the counterturn that forms the third part in a structure of four parts (*Poetices libri septem*, [Lyons], 1561, pp. 14-15 and 147). For Jonson, see *The Magnetic Lady*, Herford and Simpson ed., VI. 527-29 and 578.

[34] Beare has some good comments on this aspect of the art of Terence (*The Roman Stage*, pp. 97-99).

[35] *Commentvm Terenti*, I. 193: his key phrases are "error fabulae" and "elegans perturbatio." A helpful discussion of these matters occurs in G. E. Duckworth's *The Nature of Roman Comedy*, Princeton, 1952, pp. 141 and 154-59.

[36] *Commentvm Terenti*, I. 94. Cf. Duckworth, *Roman Comedy*, p. 224.

[37] *Commentvm Terenti*, I. 75.

[38] Donatus, although he explains the literal meaning of the text, fails to note this preparation of a search for Chrysis and her money (*ibid.*, I. 117).

[39] *Ibid.*, I. 118 and 257.

[40] *Ibid.*, I. 193.

[41] *Ibid.*, I. 37-38.

[42] *Ibid.*, I. 193 and 227.

[43] So Duckworth says (*Roman Comedy*, p. 155).

[44] In the commentary of Donatus, Crito appears at Act IV, scene five (*Commentvm Terenti*, I. 227). The Renaissance editions print the pertinent words of the grammarian on the same pages as the text of the plays, so that they are more instructive than as notes placed at some

distance from the text. See the editions of Venice, 1490, 1495, 1497 and 1499: in the last two pen and ink drawings of the personages appearing in the speech heads emphasize the division of acts and scenes.

[45] In *La Calandria*, Siena, 1521, in which the *catastasis* comes in the beginning of Act V. See M. T. Herrick, *Italian Comedy in the Renaissance*, Urbana, 1960, pp. 71-74.

[46] A revision of Donatus, suppressing his insistence on "quattuor partes" (*Commentvm Terenti*, I. 27), would put him in this group. A modern member is Baldwin in *Shakespere's Five-Act Structure*, pp. 1-32 and 49-50. He regards as Scaliger's sole contribution to critical analysis the term, *catastasis* (p. 296).

[47] *Poetices*, p. 14. My notes are from the copy in the University of Chicago library, which Simpson regarded as once in the possession of Ben Jonson (Herford and Simpson, XI. 601). For the most illuminating discussion of Scaliger's place in Italian criticism, see Bernard Weinberg's *A History of Literary Criticism in the Italian Renaissance*, 2 vols., Chicago, 1961, II. 743-50.

[48] Scaliger, *Poetices*, p. 147. The passage shows that he found in the *Andria* an illustration of the four-part theory.

[49] *Ibid.*, p. 15.

[50] "Essay of Dramatic Poesy," *Essays*, ed. W. P. Ker, 2 vols., Oxford, 1900, I. 44-45.

[51] See especially *The Magnetic Lady* (1632), Herford and Simpson, VI. 527-29 and 578. Cf. Chapter 8 below, "Jonson on Comedy," pp. 168-71.

[52] For a brief analysis of this aspect of Machiavelli's plays, see the present writer's note on "Italian and English Comedy," *Renaissance Drama*, Supplement VII (1964), pp. 6-8.

Notes to Chapter 2.

[1] For studies of the debt, see A. H. Gilbert, "The Dates of *Clizia* and *Mandragola*," *PMLA*, LXIV. 1231-35 (1949); and Giovanni Tambara, *Intorno alla Clizia*, Rovigo, 1895.

[2] For the text, see *Plautus*, ed. and tr. Paul Nixon, 5 vols., London (Loeb), 1937-38, II. 1-109.

[3] Duckworth, *Roman Comedy*, p. 165.

[4] Panella ed., I. 601-50.

[5] See Chapter 1 above, "*Andria:* the Argument and Structure of Comedy," pp. 20-21.

[6] *Ibid.*, pp. 27-28.

[7] In the translation of *Amores* by Christopher Marlowe, this is "Elegy" 9 of Book I, in *Poems*, ed. L. C. Martin, London, 1931, pp. 164-66. For the Ovidian element in Machiavelli, see Gilbert's tr. of the *Letters*, pp. 63-64.

[8] Sanesi is representative (*La Commedia*, I. 268-69). H. B. Charlton enigmatically preferred the part of Cleandro to that of Euthynicus for its "persistent moral justification" (*Shakespearian Comedy*, New York, 1940, p. 84).

[9] Maria Sticco has some valuable comments on this aspect (*Una Lettura del Machiavelli*, Milan, 1962, pp. 170-71).

[10] *Ibid.*, p. 170.

[11] "Sofronia" and "soffiona" (i.e., "soffione"), I. 616.

[12] This passage is one basis for the view that *La Mandragola* antedated *Clizia*. The situation, however, is not the same: in the former Fra Timoteo does not impregnate Lucrezia. It seems that a climax of the comedy, not yet clear in detail, was being outlined by the author's imagination.

[13] "questa tua madre pigli un granchio" (I. 621): grasped a nettle or made a blunder.

[14] A short street called Isola delle Stinche still exists in Florence in the neighborhood of Santa Croce. For an interesting account of the prison and its victims, including Machiavelli, see M. E. Wolfgang, "A Florentine Prison: Le Carceri delle Stinche," *SR*, VII. 148-66 (1960).

[15] "io non intendo ch' e' paperi menino a bêr l' oche" (I. 621). Evelyn Waugh puts the locution in the mouth of General Ben Ritchie-Hook: "Don't try and teach your grandmother to suck eggs" (*The End of the Battle*, Boston, 1961, p. 288).

[16] "cotto," drunk (I. 624).

[17] "Quia enim filio/nos opportet opitulari unico" (*Casina*, 11. 262-63): because we both ought to help our only son.

[18] *Ibid.*, 11. 331-32.

[19] "Sta' bene con Cristo, e fatti beffe de' santi!" (I. 627).

[20] Plautus merely affirms that hope in the gods is illusory (*Casina*, 11. 348-49). Sticco notes that the Church is part of the atmosphere of *Clizia*, with a pious Sofronia and a pious Nicomaco—before he fell in love (p. 171).

[21] "La messa della fava!" (I. 630): nonsense.

[22] Chapter 25, Panella ed., II. 89-92, especially p. 92 for the comparison of Fortune to a woman and her favor to young men.

[23] He confidently expects "felicità" and "allegrezza" (I. 632-33).

[24] The best-known English example is the dialogue of the lovers in Shakespeare's *Romeo and Juliet*, III. 2. 1-31.

[25] For Captain Fright-All (Spavento) and his page, see *The Braggart*, pp. 105-18.

[26] "satirionne" (I. 633), the herb ragwort, according to John Florio in *A Worlde of Wordes*, London, 1598, *s.v.* Machiavelli gives the word a perfect aphrodisiacal second

meaning. The senile lover who revives exhausted powers for the amorous encounter with a young girl appears in Boccaccio's *Decameron*, II. 10; and in Chaucer's "Merchant's Tale," where January similarly seeks to renew his virility in preparation for his wedding to May.

[27] I. 612 (II. 1 above) and I. 636 (IV. 5 below).

[28] Sofronia's words, "E' mi resta ora ad uccellare un poco el mio vecchio" (I. 636), are close to the Latin:

nunc ego illum nihili decrepitum meum virum veniat

velim, (ut eum ludificem vicissem, postquam hunc delusi alterum)                         (*Casina*, 11. 599-600).

But Machiavelli, in harmony with his reinterpretation, suppresses any farcical allusion to a furtive whoremonger like the one in Plautus.

[29] The corresponding passage in *Casina* is a description by the maid Pardalisca of the tricks already played on the would-be groom Olympio, not Lysidamus (11. 759-79).

[30] These pitchers were marked by a spout or pipe that rose straight from the round middle.

[31] The *canzona* at the end of Act IV is appropriate to the *catastasis* in its ambiguity. Machiavelli later used the same stanza at the end of Act III of *La Mandragola*.

[32] "e' mi faceva bocchi (uh! uh! uh!) e manichetto drieto" (I. 644). This sign of contempt was made by laying the left fist inside the elbow of the right arm raised and bent, with fist clenched. The sodomite climax has escaped some authorities, e.g., Pasquale Villari and J. A. Symonds (Oliver Evans, "Two Misrepresentations of *Clizia*," *PQ*, XXVI. 90-91 [1948]).

[33] "chè vedi ch' io porto loro queste uova" (I. 646) is a proverbial reminder by Sofronia of Nicomaco's sober duty to get all things ready. She also mimics his speech.

Notes to Chapter 3.

[1] Machiavelli refers twice in the Prologue to the "caso" (Panella ed., I. 550 and 552). See Chapter 1 above, pp. 13 and 15.

[2] "Che 'mparò in sul Buezio leggi assai" (I. 550) glances at Boethius (Boezio) and the ox (bue), and assumes that like Nicia, Boethius was a master of jurisprudence.

[3] Cf. M. T. Herrick, "The New Drama of the Sixteenth Century," *JEGPh*, LIV. 567-68 (1955).

[4] Moreover, he strictly observes the unities of time and place; and his single action has a simplicity that contrasts sharply with the complicated plots of the *commedie erudite* of the century (see C. S. Singleton, "Machiavelli and the Spirit of Comedy," *MLN*, LVII. 585-86 (1942); and E. J. Webber, "The Dramatic Unities in the *Mandragola*," *Italica*, XXXIII. 20-21 (1956).

[5] I. 553. See chapter 22 of *The Prince* (Panella ed., II. 84-85).

[6] I. 554. The role of Fortune in human affairs is the topic of chapter 25 of *The Prince* (II. 89-92).

[7] I. 556. See Book III, chapter 6, of *The Discourses on Livy* (II. 368-69).

[8] In his masterpiece Machiavelli exploits the "salt" of colloquial speech which he praised in his criticism (see chapter one above, pp. 12-13). Here the text reads, "io mi spicco mal volentieri da bomba" (I. 557). "Bomba" is at once a child's game like prisoner's base and the place where one lives (cf. Florio, *Worlde of Wordes*, *s.v.* See Charles Speroni, *The Italian Wellerism to the End of the Sixteenth Century*, Berkeley and Los Angeles, 1953).

[9] "a me non venderà egli vesciche!" (I. 561).

[10] "se e' l' ha per male, scingasi!" (I. 562). Cf. Florio,

235

*Worlde of Wordes*, "Scíngere"; and Mario Bonfantini, ed.,
*Opere di Machiavelli*, Milan, 1954, p. 997.

[11] "ho più fede in voi che gli Ungheri nelle spade" (I.
564).

[12] "cacastecchi" (I. 564): *"A shite-stickes, a hard chuffe"*
(Florio, *Worlde of Wordes*, s.v.).

[13] "imparare due hac" (I. 564). Nicia is talking about the
labor, for him, of mastering a few Latin tags (Bonfantini,
p. 1001).

[14] "potta di san Puccio" (I. 566): "Pótta, *A womans cunt
or quaint*" (Florio, *Worlde of Wordes*, s.v.). In Boccaccio's *Decameron*, the rubric for III. 4 is, "Don Felice
insegna a Frate Puccio come egli diverrà beato." The Frate
is just such an eager cuckold as Machiavelli presents in
Nicia.

[15] "Cacasangue!" (I. 567): *"the bloody-flix"* (Florio,
*Worlde of Wordes*, s.v.).

[16] "Da quel tempo in qua ella sta in orecchi come la
lepre" (I. 571).

[17] The fine parasitical euphemism is "farsi amico el frate
presto" (I. 571).

[18] *The Prince*, chapter 26 (II. 92).

[19] "Come disse la botta all' erpice!" (I. 576). Machiavelli
glossed the expression in a letter to Francesco Guicciardini
(Panella ed., I. 959-60): a toad, raked by a harrow, cried,
"Don't bother to come back!"

[20] "che io m' impecciassi gli orecchi come el Danese"
(I. 576). Ogier the Dane, one of the paladins of Charle-
magne, deafened himself like Ulysses by stuffing his ears
with wax. As Ugier, "il gran Danese," he appears throughout Lodovico Ariosto's *Orlando Furioso*.

[21] "m' hanno qui posto, come un zugo, a piuolo" (I.
576), *i.e.*, like a planted seed and thus unable to move.

[22] "noi concludereno questo parentado" (I. 577): Fra Timoteo usese the euphemism "marriage" for the intended seduction.

[23] Cf. Bonfantini, p. 1011.

[24] Shakespeare's Iago uses a similar cynical expression about Desdemona:

And out of her own goodness make the net
That shall enmesh 'em all (*Othello*, II. 3. 352-53).

[25] "errore" (I. 578), used apparently in its theological sense.

[26] "Io sudo per la passione" (I. 578).

[27] See especially *The Prince*, chapter 18 (II. 66); and *The Discourses*, Book I, chapter 9 (II. 131-32).

[28] Bonfantini makes this point (p. 1015).

[29] "Voi vi beccherete un fanciullo maschio" (I. 581), where the verb has the double meaning of "get" and "cuckold."

[30] Significantly, Ligurio says "opinione" (I. 581) in tacit recognition of Lucrezia's wavering belief and the doubts which the priest complacently sneered away.

[31] See "Ille mi par esse deo uidetur" (51) in *Catullus*, ed. C. J. Fordyce, Oxford, 1961, p. 27; and "Pace non trovo e non ho da far guerra" in Petrarch, *Le Rime*, ed. Giosue Carducci and Severino Ferrari, Florence, 1932, "Sonnetti e Canzoni in Vita di Madonna Laura," CXXXIV. Cf. Gilbert in his tr. of the *Letters*, pp. 64-65. In *The New Inn*, Ben Jonson parodies the Catullan raptures in the words of Lady Frampul (Herford and Simpson, VI. 481-82).

[32] "Io so che la Pasquina enterrà in Arezzo" (I. 590), a sexual joke that defies translation. It anticipates the union of the youth they plan to enlist with the cuckold's wife (Bonfantini, p. 1024).

[33] Perhaps a metathesis of "ghigna," sneer, used by the author in the Prologue (I. 552). The allusion may be to some obscene anecdote in which this Monna Ghinga replied when asked if she'd seen something, "Seen it? With these hands?" (Bonfantini, p. 1024).

[34] See *The Prince*, chapter 25 (II. 91).

[35] "ad entrare in santo" (I. 597): the first attendance, by the mother after childbirth, at church for the priest's blessing.

[36] "alla chiesa, dove la mia mercanzia varrà più" (I. 597).

[37] See Chapter 1 above, pp. 11-13.

[38] "iacitura mia" (I. 597).

## Notes to Chapter 4.

[1] Reginald, Cardinal Pole, *Epistolarum et Aliorum ad ipsum Collectio*, ed. A. M. Quirini, 5 vols., Brescia, 1744-57. The *Apologia ad Carolum V. Caesarem de Unitate Ecclesiae* is printed in I. 66-171. See especially pp. 135-45 and 151-52. For the impact of Machiavelli on Pole and on Tudor England, see Felix Raab, *The English Face of Machiavelli*, London-Toronto, 1964, especially pp. 30-32.

[2] A. F. Pollard follows Pole in his description of Henry VIII as Machiavelli's prince in action (*Henry VIII*, London, 1919, p. 440. Cf. Helen Simpson, *Henry VIII*, New York, 1934).

[3] The inevitable question of Pole's credibility is dealt with by G. R. Elton in "The Political Creed of Thomas Cromwell," *Transactions of the Royal Historical Society*, fifth series, VI. 69-92 (1956), especially pp. 70-75.

[4] *The Prince*, Panella ed., II. 66.

[5] *Ibid.*, II. 64-66.

⁶ See Antonio Panella, *Gli Antimachiavellici*, Florence, 1943, p. 23.

⁷ *The Prince*, II. 61-64.

⁸ Cf. Panella, *Antimachiavellici*, p. 24.

⁹ See Edward Meyer, *Machiavelli and the Elizabethan Drama*, Weimar, 1897, pp. 7-14. Gentillet's treatise, *Discours sur les Moyens de bien Gouverner, Contre Nicholas Machiavel*, [Geneva], 1576, was translated into English by Simon Patrick in 1577, but not printed till 1602. For a corrective to Meyer, see Irving Ribner, "The Significance of Gentillet's *Contre-Machiavel*," *MLQ*, X. 153-57 (1949).

¹⁰ *Il Principe*, ed. Bernardo di Giunta, Florence, 1532, iiʳ.

¹¹ *The Prince*, tr. E. [dward] D. [acres], London, 1640, Epistle Dedicatory.

¹² Alberico Gentili, *De Legationibus*, libri tres, London, 1585, pp. 109-10.

The ironic interpretation later attracted other noble minds. In *A Political Treatise* (1677) Spinoza asserts that the ostensible purpose of the ingenious Machiavelli was to show a prince how to establish and maintain his dominion. His real design, however, was to warn a free people against entrusting its welfare to a monarch (Benedictus de Spinoza, *Chief Works*, tr. R. H. M. Elwes, 2 vols., New York, 1951, I. 315). Almost a century afterward Rousseau came to the same conclusion. In feigning to give lessons to rulers, Machiavelli actually gave better ones to the people; for as a servant of the Medici he found himself constrained, under the oppression of his native land, to disguise his love of liberty. Hence *The Prince* is a treatise for believers in a republic (Jean Jacques Rousseau, *Le Contrat Social*, Paris, 1926, pp. 253 and 284).

More recently a modern scholar has eloquently asserted the accuracy of this view (Garrett Mattingly, *Renaissance*

*Diplomacy*, London, 1955, pp. 116 and 165-66; and "Machiavelli's *Prince:* Political Science or Political Satire?" *American Scholar*, XXVII. 482-91 (1958)). The work, Mattingly found, is an embittered pamphlet which is actually the savage satire of a disillusioned idealist. Hence the form it takes is an imitation, almost a parody, of the handbook of advice for princes such as the *De Regno* of St. Thomas Aquinas. He finds the praise of Caesar Borgia not seriously meant, especially since the specific feats ostensibly commended by Machiavelli were contrary to historical fact. He therefore argues that only in a satire can one understand the choice of Borgia as the model prince, for he was actually a blood-stained buffoon whose crimes and follies had been the scandal of Italy. (See also Hans Baron, "Machiavelli: the Republican Citizen and the Author of *The Prince*," *English Historical Review*, LXXVI. 223-24 (1961)).

[13] Meyer (pp. 39-47) saw only the influence of Gentillet. For an instructive study of Machiavelli and English literature, see Mario Praz, *The Flaming Heart*, New York, 1958, pp. 120 ff.

[14] *The Jew of Malta*, ed. H. S. Bennett, London, 1931, Prologue, 11. 14-21.

[15] See the analysis by H. B. Babb in *"Policy* in *The Jew of Malta,"* ELH, XXIV. 85-94 (1957). See also Napoleone Orsini, " 'Policy,' or the Language of Elizabethan Machiavellianism," *Journal of the Warburg and Courtauld Institutes*, IX. 122-34 (1946).

[16] So runs the chapter heading of *The Discourses*, Book III, chapter 17, Panella ed., II. 406-07. Irving Ribner makes the point in "Marlowe and Machiavelli," *Comparative Literature*, VI. 348-56 (1954).

[17] *The Woman Hater*, London, 1607, II. 1 and V. 1.

[18] This has been called a central theme in Chapman's work (M. C. Bradbrook, *The School of Night*, Cambridge, 1936, p. 74).

[19] *Al Fooles*, London, 1605, I. 1.

[20] II. 1.

[21] *The Prince*, chapter 7, II. 28-34.

[22] III. 1.

[23] V. 1.

[24] *The Conspiracie and Tragedie of Byron*, London, 1608, E2$^r$ and F1$^r$.

[25] K2$^v$ and P3$^v$.

[26] *The Revenge of Bussy D'Ambois*, London, 1613, D1$^r$, E2$^r$ and H2$^r$.

[27] Although printed in 1636, the play seems to have been written before 1600. For its significance, see Praz, *The Flaming Heart*, pp. 121 and 128.

[28] *Alphonsus Emperour of Germany*, London, 1654, p. 2.

[29] Meyer cited Gentillet as the source of these materials (*Machiavelli*, pp. 134-37).

[30] *Alphonsus*, pp. 3-5 and 6.

[31] *Ignatius his Conclaue*, London, 1611, especially pp. 30-40. Praz has a good analysis of this work (*The Flaming Heart*, pp. 134-40).

[32] *Ignatius*, p. 38.

[33] P. 40. The analogy of poison echoes Giunta (pp. 78-79 above).

[34] *Apomaxis Calumniarum*, London, 1538, Xii$^v$; and *A Remedy for Sedition*, London, 1536, Bi$^r$ and Eii$^v$.

[35] *Marginalia*, ed. G. C. Moore Smith, Stratford, 1913, pp. 122 and 149.

[36] See T. H. Jameson, "The 'Machiavellianism' of Gabriel Harvey," *PMLA*, LVI. 645-56 (1941).

[37] *The Prince*, chapter 7, II. 31.

[38] *The History of the World*, London, 1614, p. 711.

[39] *Philosophical Works*, 5 vols., London, 1868-79, I. 729.

[40] I. 762.

[41] I. 789.

[42] I. 729-30.

[43] I. 769.

[44] I. 541.

[45] *Satiro-mastix*, London, 1602, H². Dekker asserts that Horace-Jonson holds it as one of his rules that faith is not to be kept with heretics and infidels—a satiric distortion of the counsel on being true to one's word in chapter 18 of *The Prince* (II. 64-66).

Notes to Chapter 5.

[1] Simpson facilitated a study of the historical background by gathering all pertinent quotations from the Roman writers in one place (Herford and Simpson, IX. 597-635 *passim*). He also printed Jonson's notes from the margins of the 1605 Quarto edition of *Sejanus* at IV. 473-85.

See also Ellen Duffy, "Jonson's Debt to Renaissance Scholarship in *Sejanus* and *Catiline*," *MLR*, XLII. 24-30 (1947); Irving Ribner, *The English History Play in the Age of Shakespeare*, Princeton, 1957, pp. 291-94; and for the dramatist's reading of Tacitus, the present writer, "Jonson's Use of Lipsius in *Sejanus*," *MLN*, LXXIII. 247-55 (1958). All scholars are indebted to J. J. Enck for a fresh critical analysis of the play, especially the scheming that lies at the heart of the action (*Jonson and the Comic Truth*, Madison, 1957, pp. 89-109).

[2] For Jonson's use of the moral attitudes of Tacitus and Juvenal in developing the role of a Horatian chorus, see

my note on "Juvenal, Horace and *Sejanus*," *MLN*, LXXV. 545-50 (1960).

³ Herford and Simpson, IX. 599. In a note on *Sejanus*, I. 70-72, Simpson cited *The Discoveries*, VIII. 599. The chief interest of the latter passage he found in the proof that Jonson had read Machiavelli (XI. 248; cf. 249-50). His remarks dispose once and for all of skepticism as to Jonson's knowledge of Italian. This skepticism derives from Drummond's report that Ben understood neither French nor Italian—this in a passage in which he tells how his guest translated a poem by Girolamo Parabosco (Herford and Simpson, I. 134-35; see also the notes on I. 156).

The allusion in *The Discoveries* which is pertinent to *Sejanus*, I. 70-72, is to be found in *The Prince*, chapter 7, Panella ed., II. 31.

⁴ See Ronald Syme, *Tacitus*, 2 vols., Oxford, 1958, II. 752-54. It is sometimes useful to read the citations from Tacitus in the edition Jonson said he consulted, that is C. Cornelii Taciti, *Opera qvae exstant*, ed. Justus Lipsius, Antwerp, 1600. I have seen these in the 1607 and 1627 printings. See also *Juvenal and Persius*, ed. and tr. G. G. Ramsay, Cambridge [Mass.] and London, 1950; Dio Cassius, *Roman History*, ed. and tr. Earnest Cary, London and New York, 9 vols., 1914-27: the narrative of Sejanus comes in vol. 7; and *Suetonius*, ed. and tr. J. C. Rolfe, 2 vols., London and New York, 1924.

⁵ Panella ed., II. 363-64. This theme is echoed by Tiberius in the "Epistle" (*Sejanus*, V. 612-16). The warning of Machiavelli about ingratitude appears in the play, for example, in the contrast drawn by the Emperor between his "loue" (V. 572) and the favorite's ungratefulness at the climax of his charge to the Senate (643-44). On his first appearance, Tiberius had described Sejanus as "our friend"

(I. 534); the latter insists in the interview of Act III that he is "*Caesars* friend" (520), and Tiberius mocks this by his own seeming trust in his "deare Friend" (565). These passages are variations on the theme of a prince's friends in the statement by Machiavelli on conspiracies. (II. 364). In his note on *Sejanus*, I. 637-42 (IX. 618), Simpson quoted from *The Discoveries* Jonson's assertion that princes who neglect their office open the way to a Sejanus and his imperial ambition (VIII. 601). I might add that the source of this statement is Machiavelli's *Discourses*, III, chapter 6, II. 363-64. Thus Jonson in effect actually comments on his own rewriting, many years before, of Tacitus although the passage in *The Discoveries* is ostensibly a reply to *The Prince*.

⁶ See C. W. Mendell, *Tacitus*, New Haven, 1957, p. 100; and Syme, *Tacitus*, I. 420-32. Most contemporary opinion agreed with Jean Bodin's emphatic assertion that Tiberius "became the most detestable tyrant that euer was for crueltie and voluptuous pleasures" and that he dragged out a life tormented and full of fear (*The Six Bookes of a Commonweale*, tr. Richard Knolles, London, 1606, pp. 414, 214). See also W. A. Armstrong, "The Elizabethan Conception of the Tyrant," *RES*, XXII (1946). 174-76.

⁷ Panella ed., II. 136-37. The 1584 edition of *I Discorsi* emphasizes that among the lessons of history expounded by Machiavelli was "a punto conoscere qual differenza sia da vn principe giusto, ad vn Tiranno" ("Lo Stampatore al benigno lettore"). This text was secretly published in London with the imprint of "Palermo" (H. R. Trevor-Roper, *Historical Essays*, London, 1958, p. 62n.).

⁸ *Political Works*, ed. C. H. McIllwain, Cambridge, [Mass.], pp. 57-67, *passim*.

⁹ Panella ed., II. 379-80.

¹⁰ Chapter 18 of *The Prince*, Panella ed., II. 64-65. That Jonson's English contemporaries read the passage this way is evident from Gabriel Harvey's identifying "the Emperour Tiberius" as a "wily, mischeeuous, coouetous cruel and deceytfull fox" (*Marginalia*, p. 143).

¹¹ Chapter 18 of *The Prince*, Panella ed., II. 65-66; and chapter 21, Panella ed., II. 81.

¹² For a discussion of these points, see A. H. Sackton, *Rhetoric as a Dramatic Language in Jonson*, New York, 1948, pp. 72-75; and L. C. Knights, *Drama and Society in the Age of Jonson*, London, 1937, pp. 180-86.

¹³ Praz notes the resemblance with Seneca in *The Flaming Heart*, p. 126; cf. Herford and Simpson, IX. 607-08; Orsini, " 'Policy,' " pp. 122-34.

¹⁴ Book I, chapter 9, Panella ed., II. 131-32.

¹⁵ See my discussion in "Juvenal, Horace and *Sejanus*," pp. 548-50. Silius, denouncing both "The frowne of *Caesar*, proud *Seianus* hatred" (327), describes a Rome ruled by "minion *Seianus*" (233) as a world of "Wolfe-turnd men" (251). To delude the fury of the spineless senate he proudly relies on "his guards within him, against *Fortunes* spight" (322). He exhorts his countrymen, if they are Romans in the old sense, and "Would know to mock *Tiberius* Tyranny, / Looke vpon *Silius* and so learn to die" (338-39). The scene is not only original with Jonson, but in complete violation of Tacitus, who expresses contempt for such Stoic "guards within" and for the ostentatious gesture of suicide (e.g. in *Historiae*, Lipsius ed., p. 391). It provides an interlude of genuine tragic feeling. Arruntius, admiring the "honourable hand" (340) of his friend, declaims a laudatory epitaph that also violates Tacitus: "Farewell Silius, / Be famous euer for thy great example" (342-43). The episode shows how the

245

dramatist brought his "Poëme" into harmony with the notion of Horace as to "a proper *Chorus*" ("To the Readers.").

[16] Chapter 17, Panella ed., II. 62. Here Machiavelli, debating the question whether to be loved or feared is better, cautions the prince that even though feared he may avoid hatred by refraining from seizing the property of his subjects. Warnings of the same tenor occur in Book III, chapter 6, of *The Discourses*, where the prince is advised to guard against inflicting injury on a man's property (Panella ed., II. 360).

[17] Panella ed., II. 363-64. In the passage on Sejanus against Tiberius, Machiavelli notes that the conspirator, blinded by ambition, allowed himself to be tricked and exposed (II. 368). At the end of Act I, Drusus, son of the emperor, denounces the insolence of Sejanus in words that suggest Machiavelli: "I will naile your pride, at breadth, and length, / And cracke those sinnewes, which are yet but stretch'd / With your swolne fortunes rage" (I. 572-74). In chapter 25 of *The Prince*, on Fortune, the author compares this power in the lives of men to the irresistible current of those swollen streams that sweep all before them (Panella ed., II. 89).

[18] Chapter 23, Panella ed., II. 85. Machiavelli repeatedly declares that all that Fortune gives a man is opportunity ("occasione"). The rest is up to the man himself. He cites Romulus, Theseus, and Cyrus as examples of those who became princes through their own ability and not through Fortune. Without the opportunity provided by Fortune, however, the vigor of their spirits would have been lost (Chapter 6, Panella ed., II. 25).

Tacitus, on the other hand, singles out Fortune as the real cause for the reversal of the prosperity of Tiberius; he portrays Sejanus as her tool (*Annals*, IV. I. See also Mendell, *Tacitus*, pp. 131-33). Jonson has substituted Sejanus for the emperor as the overconfident human personage and has radically altered the Tacitan theme.

[19] Cf. Enck, *Jonson*, pp. 107-09; and Sackton, *Rhetoric*, pp. 136-37. Herford summed up traditional interpretations of the play as the tragedy of a fall (Herford and Simpson, II. 21-24).

[20] *The Prince*, chapter 7, Panella ed., II. 31. Cf. n. 3 above.

[21] Chapter 37 of Book I, Panella ed., II. 190. Cf. chapter 22, II. 164; and chapter 23, II. 165.

[22] Dio's brief account (LVIII. 10. 1-2, pp. 210-12) contains "many obscurities" (Syme, I. 255) and presents no clear denunciation of Sejanus. Hence we look in vain for evidence that the favorite plotted to murder the emperor and seize power.

Notes to Chapter 6.

[1] *Volpone* (Herford and Simpson, V. 17-136), IV. 1. 26-27. J. A. Barish shows how completely Jonson integrated the subplot with the aesthetic and moral structure of the play ("The Double Plot in *Volpone*," *MP*, LI. 83-92 (1953)); cf. his study of *Ben Jonson and the Language of Prose Comedy*, Cambridge [Mass.], 1960, p. 143.

[2] Book III, chapter 6 (Panella ed., II. 362, 364-65 and 369). E. B. Partridge calls attention to the traditional association of the fox with Machiavelli (*The Broken Compass*, New York, 1958, pp. 84-85).

[3] *Every Man out of His Humor* (Herford and Simpson, III. 435), Induction, 1. 201.

[4] *The Prince*, chapter 22 (Panella ed., II. 85).

⁵ *The Discourses*, III. 6, on conspiracies (II. 368 and 375-76).

⁶ Machiavelli concludes chapter 25 of *The Prince*, on Fortune, with the advice to be rash rather than cautious in assailing her (II. 92). The ironic interpretation of the treatise sees in this prescription a secret means of ruining the tyrant, a view of some importance in the analysis of *Volpone*. See chapter 4 above, "The Devil's Disciple," pp. 78-86.

⁷ The song with which the sub-parasites shortly afterward entertain Volpone, "Fooles, they are the only nation" (I. 2. 68-81), is of course based on a theme from Erasmus. But there is a lyrical anticipation of it in the canzone at the end of Act II of Machiavelli's *La Mandragola* (Panella ed., I. 569). This proclaims the happiness of the fool untroubled by doubt. J. D. Rea thoroughly studied the influence of Erasmus on *Volpone* in the introduction to his ed. of the play, New Haven, 1919, pp. xxiv-vii.

⁸ This term reiterates a satiric theme announced at the beginning of I. 1 in Volpone's mocking reverence of the golden "saint" in its precious "shrine." He subverts moral values by blackening "angel" and whitewashing "devil," and yet he remains ironically unaware how complete this subversion is made by Mosca's intention. Elsewhere Volpone calls on this "good angel" to rescue him from Lady Politic Would-Be (III. 4. 115), and he welcomes him "to my redemption" when this peculiar salvation comes at last (III. 5. 2). Mosca compares himself more accurately, with devilish pride, to the Satanic serpent, "a subtill snake" in his unmasking soliloquy (III. 1. 6). The master applauds the knavery of the parasite when he sneers that the gulls in their credulity reject the truth "Like a temptation of the diuell" (V. 2. 28). Yet his exclamation over Mosca's

thwarting of the legacy-hunters in the inventory of the magnifico's wealth, "O, my fine diuell!" (V. 3. 46), signifies a deluded admiration. On these points, see J. S. Weld, "Christian Comedy: *Volpone*," *SP*, LI. 172-93 (1954).

[9] Chapter 17 (II. 62).

[10] Chapter 22 (II. 85).

[11] *The Prince*, chapter 18 (II. 66).

[12] See *The Prince*, chapter 18 (II. 66), and *The Discourses*, I. 9 (II. 131-32). Cf. chapter 5 above. "The Tyrant's Arts in *Sejanus*," p. 101.

[13] For a study of the two-fold impact of the language of seduction in Volpone's mouth, that is the rhetorical splendor and the moral import, see Knights, *Drama and Society*, pp. 186-88.

[14] The episode is an ironic application of Machiavelli's advice to take Fortune by storm (*The Prince*, chapter 25, II. 92).

[15] *Ibid.*, chapter 6 (II. 25).

[16] *The Discourses*, III. 6, on conspiracies (II. 374-75). Jonson corrected the extravagant praise of Venice as the ideal commonwealth (for example in Lewis Lewkenor's *Commonwealth and Gouernment of Venice*, London, 1599, pp. 6 and 33) by the realistic analysis of Machiavelli (*Discourses*, I. 49-50, II. 214-18). See my paper on "Lewkenor and *Volpone*," *N & Q*, N.S. IX. 124-30 (1962).

[17] See Enck, *Jonson*, pp. 123-24.

[18] See Chapter 5 above, "The Tyrant's Arts in *Sejanus*," pp. 103-04.

[19] *The Prince*, chapter 18 (II. 66). Book II, chapter 29, of *The Discourses* bears the eye-catching title, "Fortune blinds men's minds when she does not want them to obstruct her designs" (II. 334-37).

[20] *The Discourses*, I. 37 (II. 190); Chapter 5 above, "The Tyrant's Arts in *Sejanus*," p. 109.

[21] The most familiar statement by Machiavelli is chapter 25 of *The Prince* (II. 89-92).

[22] *The Discourses*, III. 17 (II. 406-07).

[23] *Volpone*, The Epistle, p. 20. For the censure of Jonson's catastrophe, see Dryden, "Essay of Dramatic Poesy," Ker ed., I. 73; cf. Herford and Simpson, I. 307 and II. 65-71.

[24] L. C. Knights, *The Importance of Scrutiny*, New York, 1948, pp. 229-31.

[25] Harry Levin, "Jonson's Metempsychosis," *PQ*, XXII. 231-39 (1943).

[26] Ralph Nash, "The Comic Intent of *Volpone*," *SP*, XLIV, 26-40 (1947).

[27] Northrop Frye, *The Anatomy of Criticism*, Princeton, 1957, p. 165.

[28] See Chapter 9 below, "The Design of *Every Man in His Humor* (Q)," p. 185.

[29] On the quality of Volpone's emotion, see Partridge, *Broken Compass*, pp. 78-82 and 99-102. He sees "love" debased to an erotic spectacle on a par with the performance of the sub-parasites. These physical monsters are actually moral innocents appearing at climactic moments to underline the moral monstrosity of their master: just before the fraud upon the legacy-hunters (I. 2), just before the rape of Celia (III. 3) and just before the frustration of the gulls by the feigned death (V. 2 57-63). This contrapuntal effect is a refinement of the denunciation of Tiberius by Arruntius, "He is our monster" (*Sejanus*, Act IV, 11. 373-409).

[30] *La Mandragola*, II. 6 (Panella ed., I. 569). Jonson may have touched Volpone's passion with the absurdity of

Nicomaco's infatuation for a young girl (*Clizia*, IV. 2 Panella ed., I. 632).

[31] *La Mandragola*, IV. 1 (I. 582-83).

[32] *Ibid.*, II. 6 (I. 568).

[33] *Ibid.*, V. 4 (I. 598).

[34] *Clizia*, II. 3 and IV. 1 (I. 614 and 631).

## Notes to Chapter 7.

[1] C. J. Sisson, "Ben Jonson of Gresham College," *TLS*, Sept. 21, 1951, p. 604. G. B. Johnston (*ibid.*, p. 837) guessed that Jonson was referring to a notebook similar to *The Discoveries* in his lament (in 1623) over the loss of "twice-twelve-years stor'd up humanitie" in his "Execration upon Vulcan" (Herford and Simpson, VIII. 207).

[2] In *Every Man out of His Humor* Cordatus voices the author's disclaimer of any intention to identify his stage personages with real people; otherwise you would by "speaking of MACHIAVEL, comprehend all States-men" (Herford and Simpson, III. 495).

[3] See R. S. Walker, "Ben Jonson's *Discoveries*: A New Analysis," *Essays of the English Association*, N.S., V. 32-51 (1952). Cf. his ed. of *Timber or Discoveries*, Syracuse, 1953, pp. 3, 10-11 and 105.

[4] Simpson dealt with this point in the notes to the passage (Herford and Simpson, VIII. 599-600) in which Jonson names Machiavelli. He quoted extensively from *The Prince* to show how closely Jonson followed it (XI. 248-50).

[5] I have consulted the *Princeps*, tr. Sylvester Telius, [Basel?], 1589.

[6] The text of *The Discoveries* is in Herford and Simpson, VIII. 560-649. The quoted passage is on p. 598.

[7] *The Prince*, chapter 9 (Panella ed., II. 40).

[8] On the subject of Latin translations and English versions of *The Prince*, see Hardin Craig, ed., *Machiavelli's "Prince*," Chapel Hill, 1944, pp. xv-xviii. He notes the use made by English translators of John Wolfe's ed. of Machiavelli (London, 1584).

[9] A. C. Swinburne, *A Study of Ben Jonson*, London, 1889, p. 129 (on Bacon) and p. 149 (on satire).

[10] See Chapter 5 above, "The Tyrant's Arts in *Sejanus*," pp. 89-93.

[11] *The Prince*, chapter 9 (Panella ed., II. 40). Jonson's marginal rubric on p. 599 suggests the dilemmatic organization characteristic of Machiavelli: *"ubi lenitas, ubi severitas, plùs polleat in commune bonum callere."*

[12] *The Discourses*, Book III, chapter 21 (Panella ed., II. 414).

[13] Cf. "The Tyrant's Arts," pp. 91-92.

[14] *Sejanus*, 1605 Quarto ed., Act III, 11. 300-05.

[15] See Herford and Simpson, IV. 402.

[16] *Ibid.*, XI. 248-50.

[17] The phrase (apparently a reminiscence of Horace) is an original insertion by Jonson into a long passage taken almost verbatim from Daniel Heinsius (quoted by Simpson at XI. 289).

[18] The most substantial proof of his early acquaintance with Machiavelli is the extensive paraphrase (*Sejanus*, Act III, 11. 637-46) of a passage from the chapter on conspiracies in *The Discourses* (Book III, chapter 6, II. 359-64). Cf. "The Tyrant's Arts," pp. 91-92.

[19] *La Mandragola*, III. 11 (Panella ed., I. 579); *Volpone*, III. 7. 35-36.

[20] The text reads, "Però la migliore fortezza che sia, è non essere odiato dal populo" (II. 80). The litotes is

Machiavelli's characteristic ironic approach to the uninhibited phrase, Jonson's "love of the people."

[21] *The Discourses*, Book I, chapter 10 (II. 136-37); cf. III. 34 (II. 445-46).

[22] See especially chapter 18 (II. 64-66) and chapter 21 (II. 82). In the former passage occurs the image of the lion and the fox that outraged Cardinal Pole (see chapter 4 above, "The Devil's Disciple: Machiavelli, Cardinal Pole and Jonson," pp. 76-77).

[23] Cited by Simpson, XI. 215-16.

[24] Cf. *The Discourses*, III. 35 (II. 448-49), where the author returns to the problems of public servants.

[25] Cf. *The Prince*, II. 31 and especially 83-84.

[26] Cf. Simpson's note at XI. 247 and "The Tyrant's Arts," p. 96.

[27] Machiavelli points to the success of King Ferdinand of Spain as proof of his contention (II. 81).

[28] Herford and Simpson, XI. 250.

[29] Panella ed., II. 137-38. In Book I of *The Discourses*, chapters 11 through 15 expound the central importance of a flourishing religion in the state (II. 137-50). Machiavelli's praise exalts the happiness of a republic; Jonson had only to change the despicable noun.


Notes to Chapter 8.

[1] On these two kinds of statements, usually prologues, see Chapter 1 above, "Machiavelli's *Andria:* the Argument and Structure of Comedy," pp. 12-17 and 20.

[2] *Every Man out of His Humor*, Induction (Herford and Simpson, III. 432).

[3] See Chapter 1 above, pp. 12 and 20-27, for Donatus and

the use of him made by Machiavelli. That the Italian was in the forefront of Jonson's mind in 1599 is clear from the protest against identifying stage persons with real ones: to do thus you would by "speaking of MACHIAVEL, comprehend all States-men" (III. 495).

[4] The appeal to the ideal spectator and the promise of humorous gaiety occur in the Prologue of Machiavelli's *La Mandragola* (Panella ed., I. 551-52). Cf. also the Prologue to *Clizia* (*ibid.*, I. 603-04).

[5] There is, of course, no such passage in Cicero; our knowledge comes from the ascription of Donatus (see p. 227 n. 4). For the statement by Cordatus, see H. L. Snuggs, "The Source of Jonson's Definition of Comedy," *MLN*, LXV. 543-44 (1950): he finds this in Sebastiano Minturno's *De Poeta* (1559). On Machiavelli's use of the mirror of custom concept, see Chapter 1 above, p. 12.

[6] *An Apologie for Poetrie*, London, 1595, F3 and K2[v] - 3[r]. Herford discussed Sidney's effect on Jonson's conception of character (Herford and Simpson, I. 337-38).

[7] So Jonson names it in the original ending of the Quarto ed. (Herford and Simpson, III. 602).

[8] See Chapter 1 above, p. 20.

[9] *Cynthia's Revels*, Prologue (Herford and Simpson, IV. 43).

[10] Herford and Simpson, IV. 317-24; see Chapter 1 above, p. 20.

[11] The immediate source may be Minturno's *De Poeta*: see Simpson's note at IX. 683.

[12] *Volpone*, Dedication (Herford and Simpson, V. 17-20). For a discussion of the catastrophe and the structure of the play, see Chapter 6 above, pp. 129-32.

[13] Herford and Simpson, V. 24. "Salt" was Machiavelli's

term for linguistic pungency ( see Chapter 1 above pp. 13, and 228).

[14] *Epicoene*, Prologue I (Herford and Simpson, V. 163).

[15] *Ibid.*, V. 164.

[16] *The Alchemist*, To the Reader (Herford and Simpson, V. 291).

[17] *Ibid.*, V. 407. To Simpson, this was "the doctrine of truth to type which Jonson held as of the essence of his art" (X. 116). Actually it is by no means so mechanical.

[18] *Every Man in His Humor* (Folio ed.), Prologue (Herford and Simpson, III. 303).

[19] *Bartholomew Fair*, Prologue (Herford and Simpson, VI. 11).

[20] *Timber, or Discoveries* (Herford and Simpson, VIII. 618-19).

[21] For the quotations from Quintilian, see Herford and Simpson, XI. 263. Simpson explained that Jonson was so careful in his use of this author that he occasionally refreshed his memory by looking up citations (XI. 270). Therefore, dragging in Terence here is all the more worthy of notice.

[22] *Ad Horatij de Plauto & Terentio judicium, Dissertatio*, prefixed to his edition of Terence in 1618 (cited by Simpson at XI. 288).

[23] *Discoveries*, VIII. 642. For Jonson's "sharpnesse," Heinsius uses "sales" (XI. 288).

[24] See Chapter 1 above, pp. 12-13.

[25] Herford and Simpson, VIII. 640-41. On Cicero's *De Oratore*, see Simpson's note on XI. 286.

[26] Cf. Simpson, XI. 290.

[27] The Heinsius work on which Jonson relies here is *De Tragoediae Constitutione*, Leyden, 1611, chapter 4 (Herford and Simpson, XI. 291-93).

[28] *The Staple of News*, Intermean after the Second Act (Herford and Simpson, VI. 325).

[29] *Ibid.*, Induction (VI. 281). Simpson noted that this is the first recorded allusion to Jonson's fatness (X. 261).

[30] *The New Inn*, Argument (Herford and Simpson, VI. 400).

[31] *Andria*, Prologue, 11. 1-3.

[32] *The Magnetic Lady*, Chorus (Herford and Simpson, VI. 510). Northrop Frye has a perceptive comment on the critical passages in the play in *A Natural Perspective*, New York, 1965, p. 15.

[33] See Chapter 1 above, pp. 21 and 27.

Notes to Chapter 9.

[1] See Chapter 2 above, "*Clizia:* from Farce to Romantic Comedy," pp. 34-35.

[2] Frye, *Anatomy of Criticism*, p. 168.

[3] Jonson narrows the scene to a single square in Florence, following the practice of Machiavelli in *La Mandragola* in setting the action at an intersection of streets near a church. In this preservation of unity of place, he allows a bustling movement and yet a concentration of effects. Then he simply labels a few doors and windows with the names of places like "a Gentlemans house yonder by Saint *Anthonies*" for Dr. Clement's, or "at the signe of the water-tankerd" for Cob's or at "the *Miter* yonder" for the tavern of III. 6 (*Every Man in His Humor*, Quarto of 1601, Herford and Simpson, III. 195-289, II. 3. 211, III. 3. 59-60, and III. 4. 95, respectively). On the setting, see Praz, *The Flaming Heart*, p. 99; and Harry Levin, *Ben Jonson*, New York, 1938, p. 20.

[4] *Every Man in His Humor*, III. 2. 54. Pisa was a favorite setting in Italian comedy for the father-son conflict.

[5] *Every Man in His Humor*, I. 1. 162. Cf. "old plodding braine" at II. 3. 234; "This hoary headed letcher, this old goate" and "that wicked elder" at V. 1. 47 and 56.

[6] He and his wife Tib alone among the personages have English names. This impatience with local color, appearing later in the misplacement of Venice's Rialto in Florence (*ibid.*, IV. 4. 65), is the kind of impropriety nowhere exhibited in Jonson's other Italian play, *Volpone*.

[7] See Chapter 2 above, p. 37; and Chapter 3, pp. 59 and 61.

[8] *Every Man in His Humor*, V. 3. 387.

[9] *Ibid.*, IV. 4. 65. The name of this famous Venetian bridge was apparently attracted into a play laid in Florence from Jonson's reading by Bobadilla's mention of Venice at IV. 4. 10. See n. 6 above.

[10] E. C. Knowlton studied the reversal from Act IV to Act V and the final assembly in "Ben Jonson's Plots," *MLN*, XLIV. 77-86 (1929). See also W. A. Bacon, "The Magnetic Field: the Structure of Jonson's Comedies," *HLB*, XIX. 121-53 (1956).

[11] See Chapter 8 above, "Jonson on Comedy," p. 170.

[12] See Chapter 6 above, "*Volpone:* the Comedy of Machiavellian Irony," pp. 130-31.

Notes to Chapter 10.

[1] *Epicoene*, or *The Silent Woman* (Herford and Simpson, V. 161-272), Prologue, 11. 2 and 20.

[2] On the unity, see Dryden's famous praise in the "Essay of Dramatic Poesy," ed. Ker, I. 83-88: he centered the action on the settling of Morose's estate on Dauphine. Cf. Herrick, *Comic Theory*, pp. 125-27. Enck, commending the neatness of the structure, declares that the unifying theme of the play involves marriage (*Jonson*, pp. 134-36 and 145-46). On the variety, see F. L. Townsend, *Apologie for Bartholomew Fayre*, New York, 1947, pp. 62-70.

[3] Barish expounds the unfolding of the major themes of the play in this opening scene (*Ben Jonson*, pp. 174-82).

[4] See R. L. Heffner, Jr., "Unifying Symbols in the Comedy of Ben Jonson," *English Stage Comedy*, ed. W. K. Wimsatt, Jr., New York, 1955, pp. 74-97.

[5] Clerimont expresses the Horatian view in the song now recited by the Boy, "Still to be neat, still to be drest." Truewit retorts with an Ovidian defense of "a good dressing" and other facial aids, by which a woman becomes "like a delicate garden." See J. A. Barish, "Ovid, Juvenal and *The Silent Woman*," *PMLA*, LXXI. 213-24 (1956); cf. *Ben Jonson*, p. 148.

[6] On the allusiveness of the name "Epicoene," see Partridge, *The Broken Compass*, pp. 161-63.

[7] See my note on "*Clizia* and *Epicoene*," *PQ*, XIX. 67-69 (1940).

[8] Truewit's arguments against marriage ultimately derive from Juvenal's sixth satire on "The Characters of Women," as Simpson's notes indicate (X. 14-18). They seem to owe a debt also to Pietro Aretino (see O. J. Campbell, "The Relation of *Epicoene* to *Il Marescalco*," *PMLA*, XLVI. 752-62 [1931]; cf. Herrick, *Italian Comedy*, pp. 91-94.) Certainly Ambrogio's denunciation of marriage to the Farrier ("il marescalco") has a dramatic vividness similar to

Truewit's (see especially Act II, scene 5, in *Le Commedie,* ed. E. Camerini, Milan, 1875).

[9] See Chapter 3 above, "*La Mandragola:* the Heroine Emerges," p. 68.

[10] *Ibid.,* p. 70.

[11] See n. 2 above.

[12] *The Alchemist* (Herford and Simpson, V. 273-408), I. 1. 135.

[13] "The Argvment," 1. 1.

[14] *Ibid.,* 1. 11.

[15] IV. 1. 165-66. Enck stresses that the plot exploits the discrepancy between the actual and the impossible (*Jonson,* pp. 152-55).

[16] III. 1. 11-16. See *The Prince,* chapter 18 (Panella ed., II. 66); and *The Discourses,* Book I, chapter 9 (II. 131-32). Cf. Chapter 5 above, p. 101; and Chapter 6, p. 121.

[17] The First Monarchy Men were a group of Puritan millenarians expecting the imminent advent of Jesus to rule the earth.

[18] A different interpretation is advanced by Partridge, who sees in the explosion an objectification of what happens to the plot (*Broken Compass,* pp. 114-16).

[19] Herrick locates the *catastasis* at the moment of Surly's defeat (*Comic Theory,* p. 120).

[20] On the theme of decorum in the epilogue, see Chapter 8 above, pp. 161-62.

[21] *Essays on Elizabethan Drama,* New York, 1932, 1956, p. 75.

[22] For example, Townsend, *Apologie for Bartholomew Fayre,* p. 73; Heffner, "Unifying Symbols," pp. 87-89; and J. E. Robinson, "*Bartholomew Fair:* Comedy of Vapors," *SEL,* I. 65-80 (1961).

[23] Enck, observing that the structure is slight and that

episodes digress at many points, compares the similarity of treatment in *Every Man out of His Humor* (*Jonson,* pp. 191-93).

[24] Barish notes the expansiveness of the plot, contrasting it with the strict action of *Epicoene* (*Ben Jonson,* p. 189).

[25] *Bartholomew Fair* (Herford and Simpson, VI. 11-141), I. 6. 73-75.

[26] On the topic of Adam Overdo's fallibility, see E. A. Horsman in his ed. of *Bartholomew Fair,* London, 1960, pp. xix-xxviii.


Notes to Chapter 11.

[1] Panella ed., I. 701-11. For calculations of Jonson's debt, see Ernst Hollstein, *Das Verhältnis von "The Devil Is an Ass" zu Machiavellis Belfagor,* Halle, 1901; A. Ott, *Die Italienische Novelle im Englischen Drama,* Zurich, 1904, pp. 29-35; and W. S. Johnson in his introduction to the ed. of *The Devil Is an Ass,* New Haven, 1905.

[2] Machiavelli and Jonson both reach back of Renaissance exaltation, as in Marlowe and Milton, to the medieval theme of the Devil's discomfiture (cf. C. S. Lewis, *English Literature in the Sixteenth Century,* Oxford, 1954, p. 51).

[3] For a helpful analysis of *Belfagor,* see Russo, *Machiavelli,* pp. 170-78.

[4] *The Devil Is an Ass* (Herford and Simpson, VI. 161-270), I. 1. 6-7.

[5] On this point, see Herford's notes (I. 143-44 and 169).

[6] This device has an Italian original also, Boccaccio's *Decameron,* 3. 5 (cf. Simpson's note on X. 229).

[7] On the moral inferiority of the Devil among people of

fashion on earth, cf. Partridge, *The Broken Compass*, pp. 67-68.

[8] On the promising conception of the play and its disappointing execution, see Enck, *Jonson*, pp. 210-15.

[9] For the history of this denouement see R. R. Reed, Jr., "Jonson's Pioneering in Sentimental Comedy," *N & Q*, CXCV. 272-73 (1950).

# INDEX

262

263